I WAS THERE

I WAS THERE

DISPATCHES FROM A LIFE IN ROCK AND ROLL

ALAN EDWARDS

London · New York · Sydney · Toronto · New Delhi

First published in Great Britain by Simon & Schuster UK Ltd, 2024

3 5 7 9 10 8 6 4 2

Simon & Schuster UK Ltd
1st Floor
222 Gray's Inn Road
London WC1X 8HB

Simon & Schuster: Celebrating 100 Years of Publishing in 2024

www.simonandschuster.co.uk
www.simonandschuster.com.au
www.simonandschuster.co.in

Simon & Schuster Australia, Sydney
Simon & Schuster India, New Delhi

A CIP catalogue record for this book
is available from the British Library

Hardback ISBN: 978-1-3985-2524-5
Trade Paperback ISBN: 978-1-3985-2526-9
eBook ISBN: 978-1-3985-2525-2

Typeset in Bembo by M Rules
Printed and Bound in the UK using 100% Renewable
Electricity at CPI Group (UK) Ltd

CONTENTS

Part 3

Prologue

Lazarus

'Alan, it's Coco.' The familiar authoritative tones of David Bowie's long-time personal assistant, confidante and right-hand woman, Coco Schwab. 'He'd like you to come and listen to the album.'

I hadn't been very involved in *Blackstar* – there was such huge secrecy around it and the label was handling everything. I knew that David didn't want to do any interviews. Apart from the odd email checking in, he'd been head down in the studio. I looked at my diary, almost completely covered in its usual handwritten scrawl of appointments.

'Sure, I could be there in a couple of weeks,' I said.

'Could you come out . . . sooner?' Thinking David was clearly excited by the album, I agreed to come out as soon as I could.

A few days later, I was walking through Greenwich Village. It was one of those crisp Manhattan mornings, the sky a bright, polished blue. People were out in winter coats, shopping and having brunch; there were tourists on a pilgrimage to one of the centres of American culture. I turned into Electric Lady Studios. I was taken into one of the studios, which was dark and empty, apart from David, who was watching *The Good, the Bad and the Ugly*. He looked tired and thin, but this was in no way unusual. David had spent much of his life unwilling to waste time eating while he was working.

We said hello and watched a little of the film. Then he paused it and looked at me.

'Did you ever meet John Bindon?' he asked. I shook my head. And he was off, telling me about the actor and bodyguard who had links to the London underworld. Bindon was famous for doing 'something' to people's balls to get them to see things his way. David told me about the gangster tactics of the '60s music scene and we traded tales of characters we'd met. Every now and then we'd listen to a song from the album. I could hear it was remarkable, but David didn't need me to tell him what I thought. In the almost forty years we'd worked together, we actually rarely talked about the music. He wasn't someone who was waiting for me to say I liked the way a drum had been recorded. We were more likely to talk about the latest book one of us had given the other.

This time he was in the mood to reminisce and, in between listening to songs, we continued to exchange stories. Some of his I'd heard before, some were new to me. It turned out I'd never told him about the time I played football with Bob Marley, which he enjoyed. There was no business discussed. Coco came in with her new dog. We listened to some more of the album. We went outside. We embraced, said a simple farewell and he walked off. It would be the last time I ever saw him. A few months later, on his sixty-ninth birthday, 8 January 2016, *Blackstar* was released to universal acclaim. He died from cancer two days later.

*

In late 2021, I was publicising a David Bowie pop-up shop. The marketing people wanted to throw a party in store, but I wasn't sure that's what David would have done. My idea was pretty simple. Why don't we get the people who influenced David's career, who knew David, to get together and tell stories about him?

Despite it being a private event, everyone in the room would be able to talk about it on social media, the photos would go out to millions of people and we'd get lots of profile without it looking like we were trying.

We hosted it at the Hotel Café Royal on Regent Street, which was over the road from the site of the shop and was where David held his 'retirement' party in 1973 with the likes of Lou Reed and Mick Jagger. It was scheduled for just before what would have been David's seventy-fifth birthday. It would be the celebration he never got to have.

Bob Geldof spoke about blagging his way backstage at a Bowie concert in Brussels and having the audacity to ask Bowie to sign a Boomtown Rats demo tape. Boy George spoke about the time before he was famous when David was scouting for extras to appear in a music video. George spent an hour in a nightclub trying to catch David's eye, only to be devastated, George recalled with a big laugh, when David remarked that his look reminded him of the singer Klaus Nomi.

Tony Visconti, Bowie's longstanding producer, spoke about talking to him on the phone just before the release of *Blackstar.* It was two and a half weeks before Christmas, and David was happy. 'We're going to lick this thing,' he'd said, referring to his cancer. 'And I'm looking forward to going back into the studio next year.' As Tony recounted Bowie's words, he broke into tears. The whole room stopped and for a minute it felt as if we couldn't carry on. But we did; musicians and photographers and producers and childhood friends continued to share stories and memories with one another.

We told stories that weren't really about the music but what the music and David meant to us all – about the mythology of the man who had made it, who he worked with and how, what he'd been trying to do. We swapped clues about who he was, the multitudes he contained, what he had meant to us at different times.

I had started working with David in 1982, just as he was about to set out on the Serious Moonlight Tour in support of *Let's Dance*. It was the moment that David went from being a very well-known but essentially cult artist to arguably the biggest music star on the planet. He was playing enormous stadiums and had, briefly, made peace with the role of mass-market entertainer. I remember the Australian leg of the tour I joined as one suffused with laughter and happiness. Enormous crowds following us everywhere we went, David happy and healthy and looking like a matinee idol. I eventually spent so much time with him at interviews that I knew exactly the subjects he liked to talk about, and, as importantly, what he didn't like to get into – it was a kind of mind meld. So with David's blessing, one time I stood in for him on the other end of the phone during a radio interview. I didn't put on a voice – perhaps we just sounded similar – but looking back it was incredible that nobody picked up on it.

Of anyone I ever worked with, David was the most curious about how the media operated (perhaps only rivalled by Mick Jagger, but Mick's focus felt different). He never saw it as separate or frivolous, but as part of the process of communicating. He fundamentally understood the natural impulse to try to know the people who made art. Where did it come from? How did they do it? What did it mean? That moment when you hear a song that seems to reach into your life, that so precisely describes something you're feeling, and you suddenly have to know who made it.

David was an expert. Over the years, I received emails from him asking me what the circulation of a niche French music magazine currently was, or whether specific music journalists were still in favour – all mixed in with musings on art and politics. He had a clear vision for how music fitted into the culture and would often come up with what became the central strategy for his publicity. A call from David would be a rundown of a long list of questions about different media in different countries that would require days of research to answer. He was utterly forensic about what was a good use of his time, and his first question was always whether it did anything new or interesting. Money was an afterthought.

He was interested in the people who wrote about music, about their lives and motivations and where they were coming from. His emails were littered with deliciously catty asides about 'a bit of a prune' or 'that most courageous of prats'. His speech was dotted with these kinds of constructions too, like a maiden aunt from the '50s. He was a nostalgic futurist, amongst his many contradictions, who loved travelling on the *QE2*, who passionately supported the national teams, who was determined that Scotland should remain in the union and who retained his British passport and didn't take up American citizenship. As an Englishman abroad, he had lived in self-imposed exile and had seemed to become ever more English over the years. He liked to go to the English teahouse, espoused the sturdiness of Clarks brogues, admired the stitching on classic Paul Smith suits, and had numerous BBC programmes sent over from our office.*

But he was also eternally curious about the intersection of culture and technology, and its potential to have us connect in new ways. I have been accused of being a Luddite, but he pushed me to get an email address as soon as it was possible. In an interview in 1999, he tried to impress upon an underwhelmed and clearly sceptical Jeremy Paxman that the internet was going to radically transform culture. He understood how this new type of communication and community would change everything. (Ever the consummate professional, David had also bought several books about fishing to read in preparation, in case Paxman, famously a keen angler, wanted to discuss that.)

Throughout the Hotel Café Royal event, I kept thinking back to that day in Greenwich Village: David watching the Sergio Leone epic, a film he would have first seen in the cinema as a nineteen-year-old, the year he changed his name to David Bowie, a string of failed singles behind him and imagining what the future might hold. I realised that encounter had been David's way of saying goodbye, of making a story just for me.

When the event was over, I walked around Soho, along the same London streets I'd fallen into all those years before in

---

* It wasn't just David. I saw it in LA with rockers holed up in pretend English pubs with the blinds down, drinking pints of bitter and playing darts. After years of chasing chicks and riding Harleys along Sunset, deep down they just wanted to be home, but they didn't know where home was or how to get there anymore.

1975 when I started working in the music industry, a clueless, tousled-haired twenty-year-old just back from the trail in India and Afghanistan. I thought of how the twenty-year-old me wouldn't recognise this version of Soho, with all its sharp edges sanded away. Of how punk had become part of the official marketing of London to tourists, the spit used to polish its brand. Of how he'd react if he knew how many of the bands in his record collection I'd ended up working with – Bowie, the Stones, the Who – and all the ones he hadn't heard of yet.

I thought of how I'd explain the Spice Girls to him and suspected he'd recognise something in their energy that was appealing (though I didn't think he'd be able to get his head around Westlife). He'd definitely have understood Beckham and his right foot. He'd also have understood my impulse to keep on moving: out of PR and into management and even briefly a record label; out of music and into other mediums and industries – fashion, sport and politics – always following where I thought the interesting story was.

Above all, I thought of how I'd tell him how wonderful it had been to work with the artists I had, playing a small part in them telling their stories. Stories that mattered to millions of people around the world, which became part of the fabric of their lives.

I thought of how lucky I was that I could say: I was there.

Part 1

1

My Generation

'Right, I'm off for a cheese roll and a pint of mild,' said Keith, pulling his jacket around him and calling over his shoulder: 'If Bill phones, tell him I've asked Pete and I'm waiting to hear. If Keith Moon phones, tell him I'm at lunch and I'll call him back as soon as possible. Anyone else, say I'm on tour with the Who.' With that he was gone.

I had spent the morning following Keith Altham around as he fired a dizzying list of names at me. A fair few I recognised, but with lots of them I just had to nod and make a note to ask someone later. He'd introduced me to our downstairs neighbour, the high-profile PR Tony Brainsby, who represented stars like Paul McCartney, Thin Lizzy and Be Bop Deluxe. In our cramped office in Pimlico, there was me, Keith and, two days a week, a delightful French woman called Claudine who did the books. But today wasn't one of Claudine's days. As Keith had held forth, he'd interspersed his stream of consciousness with his commandments for working in music publicity.

'One: always return calls,' he said, counting on his thumb. 'Two: do what you say you're going to do,' he counted on his index finger. 'And the most important thing of all. Three: if the company, me, is buying the drinks, it's halves; if the client is buying, it's pints.'

I still couldn't get over how quickly everything had happened.

Only a few weeks previously I'd been at Bingley Hall in Staffordshire to review a Who gig for *Sounds*, and had found myself talking to the legendary publicist Keith Altham, who represented about twenty of the biggest bands in the world at that time, including the Rolling Stones, the Who and the Beach Boys. It had famously been his idea for Jimi Hendrix to set fire to his guitar at Monterey Pop, the first-ever major rock festival, in 1967. I introduced myself to him in the bar after the gig and he leaned over to me to ask what I thought of the show. For a moment, I toyed with flattery, but I decided to be honest.

'Nowhere near one of their best for me. The acoustics in there are appalling, so I'm sure that's the problem.' He stared at me carefully and for a second I was worried I'd gone too far.

'Would you like a job?' he asked.

The honest answer to that was no. Or, more honestly, I didn't know.

I certainly needed money. I was twenty years old and, after a brief stint driving around London collecting laundry from hotels, I had somehow landed myself two jobs at *Sounds* – the day job was selling advertising out of an office building on Holloway Road and drinking at the local pub, the Lord Nelson, which doubled as our staff canteen.*

The Nelson was a dive: fights breaking out, glasses flying,

* Though I didn't know it then, I was to spend my life dealing with dirty laundry of a different sort, often involving the same hotels.

windows getting smashed. Bored-looking strippers, who were really just housewives looking for some extra cash, languishing at the bar. But I loved it because it had a jukebox. I'd spend the morning fantasising about hearing new singles, usually by Bowie or Alice Cooper, and then lunchtime was a game of wits to get them played. If you didn't arrive with your coins at the ready, you were in for another sorry blast of the Dubliners' 'Irish Rover'.

The editor of *Sounds* was an encouraging chap called Alf Martin, and it was he who had given me the go-ahead to try my hand at gig reviews. It was a win-win, as I would have gone to see most of the concerts anyway. Although the industry was dominated by big, megastar acts like the Who, the Stones and the Eagles, there was a burgeoning pub rock scene: outfits with funny names like Ducks Deluxe, Bees Make Honey, Kilburn and the High Roads, and Dr Feelgood. Few other journalists wanted to go to the back of beyond on a weeknight to write about them, so I got my opportunity. Any venue, any time, I was there – and that was useful to the paper. As well as rock, I'd developed a taste for soul music. At that time, you could see major US acts, like the Thymes and the Delfonics, playing places like Baileys nightclub in Watford. This was partly because nightclubs had looser licensing laws than other gig venues and as a result were able to pay performers more. There was also an element of racism in respect of the mainstream venues not wanting 'Black' music. These acts just weren't considered important in the way rock bands were.

I was paid £5 per review for *Sounds*, but the money would take months to come through. Even with the day job, I was having to supplement my earnings by taking albums from the office's review cupboard and selling them on. Fortunately, there always seemed to be an album launch to attend where I could fill up with grub, before departing with a logo-emblazoned T-shirt of whichever band was unknowingly paying for the bash. Dining and wardrobe expenses taken care of, I was just about managing to scrape by – but it was a skin-of-my-teeth existence. I was, though, being given endless free drinks and seeing as many bands as I physically could. I went to the Reading Festival with my sister Mary to hand out copies of *Sounds*, for which I was paid in booze, and we ended up just sleeping on the grass.

I was living in a single room by Archway tube station. It was pretty basic, with a shared toilet on the landing, occasional hot water and an old stove in the corner, which had been advertised as a kitchen. The landlady left cold toast outside the door in the mornings, so that she could claim to be running a B&B as opposed to a doss house. All this meant that when I met Keith, I was ready to listen to his offer.

'I can start you on £25,' said Keith, almost apologetically, though it sounded like a fortune to me. I figured I could work for a couple of months, sort my finances out, and then go back to journalism. So we shook hands on it and that's how I found myself standing in a poky office in Pimlico, still not entirely sure what I was supposed to be doing.

At that point, music PR wasn't really a job. There were probably about half a dozen people doing entertainment PR in the whole of the UK. 'Public relations' was still very much an American idea – and a relatively new one at that. It had come out of Hollywood and the need to try to control the coverage of stars like Ingrid Bergman and Rock Hudson by the influential LA columnists. This American invention had travelled to the UK, and unsurprisingly had found its way into the music industry. There were plenty of brilliant operators – like Andrew Loog-Oldham, manager of the Rolling Stones, who was in effect a publicist – who picked up on this new-fangled phenomenon.

Working at *Sounds* I had developed an acute awareness of what most journalists thought of PRs. There was one character called Keith Goodwin who was especially unpopular. He was always pushing for extra publicity for his clients, even though many of them sounded dreadful. Every journalist in the office seemed to have stuck a Post-it note on their colleagues' desk phones that read: 'If Keith Goodwin calls, I'm out!' They weren't seen as 'music people' – more like guns for hire driven by cash and acting for dodgy managers or crooked record companies. They would lure you in with free drinks and then pressure you to review some godawful album. They were part of the establishment. And I very much saw myself as not part of the establishment.

As far back as I could remember, I'd known I was adopted. My adoptive parents, Elizabeth and Harrington Edwards, had been honest with me as soon as I asked. I looked so different to them, it was obvious. I had very dark, curly hair, large eyes and long eyelashes – not classically British. People would ask me, 'Where do you come from?'

'England,' I'd reply.

'But where do you *really* come from?'

My adoptive parents were decent, loving people: he a solicitor who had been raised in Shanghai and she a former primary school teacher who had worked in Hamburg after the war. We lived in a nice suburban street in Worthing, Sussex, the sort of place where people used to stand up and salute the national anthem when the television had finished for the night. They made a loving and welcoming home for me and my brother Tony and sister Mary, who were also adopted.

But I grew up drawn to the idea that I came from somewhere else, imagining who my birth parents were. And this meant I was obsessed with getting away and doing something. I just wasn't sure what. I used to fantasise about a life of travel and even considered joining the merchant navy at one point.

One of my strongest memories is from when I was nine, staying up late with my dad to watch a flickering black-and-white transmission from the US of the Cassius Clay fight with Sonny Liston in 1964. I couldn't remember a time I didn't want to see other places and other ways of living. But I also went to watch Brighton & Hove Albion's every home game. My father would drive us through Worthing, then Lancing, before slowing for a wooden toll bridge where you had to queue up. I would become more and more excited the closer we got to the Goldstone Ground. We would hand over our money at the turnstiles and I'd stand on a wooden box so I could see over the fence that separated the pitch from spectators. At half-time I'd have a cup of Bovril and a packet of Smiths crisps, with the little blue bag of salt in it. It was the highlight of the week, and I was only allowed to attend under the proviso that I did my times tables in the car on the way.

My father was one of those men who showed he cared with what he did, rather than what he said. He was badly ill with heart attacks and nervous breakdowns, and my mother resigned herself to me being a hopeless case, concentrating instead on trying to keep my sister Mary on the straight and narrow.

I left education at sixteen with three O-Levels, determined to see the world, my knuckles still scabbed from where the Catholic brothers who ran my school would hit you with rulers. The school had an open-air swimming pool which used to ice over in the winter, but that didn't stop the swimming lessons. One day I hesitated before taking the plunge and one of the brothers just picked me up and threw me in through the broken ice. Even scarier were the rumours about Brother Athanasius, who would call you to his room, lock the door behind you and draw diagrams of the devil and the evils of masturbation. I left the school as the proud holder of the record for the number of canings administered in a single term: fourteen to be precise. Towards the end, it had been decided I was so unteachable and disruptive that I was made to stand outside certain lessons in the corridor on my own for whole terms at a time.

But I'd made friends with some older kids, including a guy called Ian Grant who went to a school a few miles away and had started promoting local bands in the area. Later, he used to organise 'meeps'. These were underground happenings in the dead of night. Meeps were a way of trying to make sure the police didn't know what was going on. They used to cost a pound to get into, and the admission ticket would be a piece of blotting paper – not the sort of blotting paper you had at school, though. This stuff was laced with acid and you had to take it on arrival. Often the meeps were held at a place called Cissbury Ring, one of the oldest Iron Age settlements in England. As dusk fell, the powerful sound system blasted out hardcore West Coast psychedelia like Jefferson Airplane, the Doors and Canned Heat, interspersed with the best stuff from the British underground. It had an early Glastonbury feel to it. By midnight, there'd be two or three hundred people tripping out among the trees, illuminated only by a crackling fire which threw all kinds of spooky shadows, adding to the vivid hallucinations everyone was experiencing. Around 3 or 4am there was the promise of live music; often a band like the Pink Fairies or Hawkwind came down after a gig elsewhere to play for free. They'd travel down in a truck, get power from a generator and just set up and play. Hawkwind's anthemic 'Hurry on Sundown' really was the best way of seeing in a Sunday morning – definitely more exciting than church. As the day got going, the festival would wind down and the 'freaks' disappeared back into the hills and normality. Every now and again, the police would raid, charging through the woods, truncheons swinging. No better way to get a bad trip going.

Music had always been a part of my life. I'd started listening to Radio Luxembourg with the DJs Tony Prince, Kid Jensen and Emperor Rosko. I hid a little transistor radio under my pillow so I could listen to music as I fell asleep.

When I was twelve, Radio 1 had launched to big fanfare and Tony Blackburn was its best-known face. Sometimes I'd get a lift into school with some of the older boys and the dial was always locked on the station. There were ten of us packed into a Mini listening to the Love Affair, Mungo Jerry, Marvin Gaye ... A few years later, we would meet up at each others' homes and listen to the new Stones or Who album, rolling joints and discussing every aspect of the songs, the lyrics, the production and the artwork. Then we'd turn the record over and listen to it again. There was also a second-hand record shop in Worthing called Trading Post run by a guy called Martin, and he used to turn me onto records that I hadn't heard, like the first album by Soft Machine.

There was a lot of acid around. I remember dropping a tab one day when my mother came to pick me up for a dentist appointment I'd completely forgotten about. I sat there while the dentist stuck things in my mouth. It could have gone either way. I was staring out the window at the sky, which had gone pink and orange, and the colours were swirling. I never had a problem with dentists after that.

When I left school, I also moved out of my parents' house; I think they had essentially given up on me by this point. My first court appearance had been at fourteen years old when I'd masterminded the theft of some instruments from the school music room. The plan was that my friends would sell them at a local music shop. Of course, they were all arrested, and the police traced the plan back to me. I was fined £5 and featured in the local paper.

My second court appearance came shortly after. I had started working in a factory that made music speakers. My job was to drill holes into wooden boxes, four holes in each, box after box, for eight hours. The only way to get through this was to smoke a few joints and do the shift completely stoned. One of the guys I lived with was a hash dealer, so getting hold of the stuff wasn't a problem. Unfortunately, another of the blokes on the assembly line wasn't paying attention one day, almost certainly in a haze of hash smoke, and lost a couple of fingers in the machine.

One morning, we were all in the flat, and the door suddenly flew off its hinges – it was a raid. The police rushed in and found half an ounce of hash belonging to my friend and we were all arrested. But the worst was yet to come. By coincidence, my father had decided he'd better check in on me and had chosen that morning to pay me a visit. As he walked up the garden path to our front door, he saw me being marched out in a pair of handcuffs. Although it wasn't my hash they had found, the police told me that my friends had all pointed the finger my way and I fell for it. That time I was fined £35.

The next ignominy for my long-suffering parents was having to collect me from hospital after a bad trip when I dropped acid on the South Downs and ended up running across both lanes of a motorway before collapsing. The first thing I remember after that is waking up in hospital, my parents by my bedside. My stomach had been pumped and the plastic tubes were harsh in my throat. My father just looked at me and shook his head. Over the next few months, I dropped a few more tabs just to make sure I didn't have any lasting paranoia. I didn't, but the novelty had worn off too. After that I never touched it again.

Around this time, I was reading *IT – International Times* – and feeling very revolutionary. One night, half a dozen of us left the pub and turned over a police car in the street, actually tipping it over somehow. I didn't get arrested, but there was a picture of me in the local paper being dragged away by my hair by the constabulary. My look at the time was jeans, army surplus jackets and greatcoats.

Throughout all this was music. I used to go down to the record shop in Worthing town centre where Ian Grant worked and listen to new albums that I couldn't afford to buy. I realised that the cubicles were also used to store dope. Ian was conducting 'quid deals' as well as selling discs, so it worked out very well. I regularly travelled to London with older friends, too, gravitating towards Notting Hill, which was then a mix of mainly Caribbean immigrants and hippies. There you could buy a lump of good Lebanese or Moroccan hash and meet fellow-minded souls. Sometimes it got messy. I remember one time taking some Mandrax and seeing the legendary MC5 kicking out the jams at a pub on the Fulham Palace Road.

We had a great flow of bands playing locally – big names, but also underground groups from London like the Edgar Broughton Band and Mott the Hoople, who would often drive the 50 miles down to the south coast to play a set. Still wearing school uniform, I managed to squeeze in at the back to see the Who play Worthing Town Hall. They were so loud and powerful, with such great songs.

I saw David Bowie on the tour he debuted Ziggy Stardust when I was sixteen. There were only a couple of hundred people in the audience. At one point, David sat on Mick Ronson's shoulders while the guitarist walked around the sparse crowd. I'd never seen anything like it.

One night in the pub, someone started talking about the 'hippie trail' and that sounded like my sort of thing. Maybe they would be my tribe? So, after a few months spent labouring on a building site, which mainly involved drinking pints of Guinness and standing at the bottom of a ladder and catching breeze blocks, I saved up enough money to set off. I started the trip with a friend called Rod Cohen, but he turned back at Dubrovnik and made the week's journey back to Blighty. I couldn't countenance returning with my tail between my legs, so I decided to keep going, alone, though travelling by yourself really wasn't recommended. I ended up passing through Iran, Afghanistan and into Pakistan, eating huge, pungent lumps of hash and walking about in a daze. At one point in Afghanistan, bandits with what looked like nineteenth-century muskets got on the bus I was riding. They went up and down, relieving the passengers of money and valuables. Fortunately, they took one look at me and decided I didn't have anything worth stealing, but when the bus got going again, the bandits stayed on. One of them sat down behind me and wedged the musket under my seat for safe keeping. I looked down and noticed that the muzzle had poked through a gap in the slatted wooden seating and was resting between my legs. I decided that I'd better not move an inch and prayed that the bumpy road wouldn't cause the gun to go off.

I went up into the foothills of the Himalayas to see Everest, thinking maybe I'd eventually make my way to Lhasa. A line of twenty or so Buddhist monks appeared out of the mist one day. They smiled serenely as they walked past, coming down from the Tibetan plateau and disappearing just as quickly. One evening, I left the hostel to get some food and felt a squelching underfoot. I thought it was mud. I looked down at my sandals and realised I was walking on a carpet of frogs. Other times, as I looked out from the roof of the world, I had to burn leaches off my arms. They fell on the forest path succulent and full of blood.

I had embarked upon the hippie trail because I aspired to the hippie lifestyle and what I believed it represented. I had thought that hippies might be the family I had always been looking for. But the supposed hippies I had met from time to time were snobby and facile. They weren't my people. Sitting in Kathmandu, I banged my beer bottle on the table in frustration. Once again, I had an acute sense of not belonging.

When the monsoon arrived, the street outside my hotel was reduced to a torrent of mud and flood water. It was at this time that my immune system let me down – I caught both dysentery and typhoid in quick succession. After a few days in a toilet that was effectively a pit, I realised there was actually a good chance I would die and wrote to my father to wire me money. As I waited for the money to arrive, I spent the weeks reading books and eating rice and dhal donated by kind-hearted strangers.

I arrived back at the front door of my parents' house, seven months after I'd set out. I still had typhoid – apparently it would be the first recorded case on the south coast of England for about fifteen years. I'd lost more than two and a half stone, had long straggly hair and my skin was the colour of chestnuts. My father barely recognised me when he opened the door.

'Oh hello,' he said. 'What have you been up to?'

Standing in Keith's office, I was woken from my reverie by a knock at the door, swiftly followed by someone wearing a massive fur coat, monocle and top hat, and carrying a cane.

'Hello, my man. Can you tell me where I can find Keith?' he asked. Of course, I immediately recognised Keith Moon, the legendary drummer from the Who.

'Ummm, he's just having lunch at the moment, but he'll call you as soon as . . .'

Moon strode over to Keith's desk and flipped it, sending papers and coffee mugs flying and causing absolute chaos. He walked back, tapped my desk with the cane and said sweetly, 'Do tell Keith I called, won't you?'

I stood in the mess of papers and cold coffee. I didn't know what to do. I could try to turn the desk over, but there was no way I'd ever be able to get things back as they were. Would it be better or worse to leave it? There was a good chance I wasn't even going to last a day in music PR. If I was honest, my journalistic career hadn't yet caught fire and consisted of forgetting to turn on the recorder when I'd interviewed Alvin Lee and not noticing that the guest keyboardist for the Average White Band was Elton John, who was arguably the most famous performer on the planet at that point. Luckily nobody knew who I was, so I escaped the embarrassment that Richard Williams once suffered at the *Melody Maker* when he reviewed a test pressing of John Lennon and Yoko Ono's *Wedding Album*, each side of which consisted of a test signal and nothing else. Richard assumed that this was a new Yoko-inspired piece of high art and gave the blank record a glowing review. John and Yoko sent Williams a telegram afterwards saying they both felt 'this is the first time the critic has outdone the artist'.

And it wasn't like I had many other avenues to explore. So far, apart from *Sounds* and driving the laundry van, my career had mainly consisted of successfully getting to London. There had been a spell working in advertising when I first moved from Worthing – I'd always been really interested in art and the visual side of things, so I'd decided that might be the career for me. Propaganda, pitch, why something went on the cover of a magazine, why a poster was effective. I couldn't articulate why it appealed to me, though; there wasn't anyone around me giving me any guidance or training. I didn't know anyone who had anything to do with art. It wasn't my parents' background, and none of my friends were involved in that field or even aspired to it. But I was strongly drawn to it.

For some reason, my initial attempt at getting into advertising by taking drawings I'd done of the Velvet Underground to the local building society and asking for work in their art department had failed, but through a guy who ran a local recording studio, I heard about a job in London.

I was excited to work at an advertising agency. A vacancy had arisen at a company called John Chesney & Associates. It all seemed very glamorous. My mum even came to London and bought me a nice new suit and paid for a posh haircut somewhere in Knightsbridge. I was ready to go. When I got to the agency, I found was it was based in one of those big old houses on the Gloucester Road, and there were people running around with bits of artwork; executives looking and acting self-important, pointing at designs and meeting clients; and lots of self-consciously cool women in super-trendy clothes. It was a small agency, and I was going to be right in the middle of it.

Disappointingly, I spent the next twelve months learning almost nothing other than the stops on the Underground map as I travelled around on various errands. Instead of the principles of design and copy writing, I got to know the different tube lines like the back of my hand – and all the bus routes as well. On the plus side, I got to visit the HQs of a few newspapers. I also started making up for a lost education by reading piles of paperbacks: George Orwell, Graham Greene, Hermann Hesse, V. S. Naipaul, anything I could lay my hands on. At some points, I had so little to do that I could get through a book in a day. I probably learned more than I realised during that year, although almost none of it at the agency itself, which was a shame. Nobody ever really gave me the time of day. I met endless receptionists and assistants at other advertising agencies around town who talked down to me – they only had eyes for the senior execs or the stars coming in for photo shoots. I had decided then that the straight world wasn't for me. But now I wasn't sure if the world of music PR was for me either. Or perhaps I wasn't for the world of music PR.

Staring at the overturned desk, I was still pondering the least worst move when Keith Altham came back into the office. I saw him look at me and look at the desk. Then he shrugged as he took his coat off and hung it up.

'Moon's been in, has he?'

2

High and Mighty

'Right, my dear boy. Thinking cap time,' said Keith late one Friday afternoon, as he opened his desk drawer and began rolling an especially large joint. It had become a habit of ours that, if there was a problem to solve, he would smoke a joint and I would act as his sounding board.

'We have been tasked by our friends at Bronze Records with creating, and I quote, "the ultimate press conference" to announce *High and Mighty* by Uriah Heep.' He took a deep drag.

I blew air out of my cheeks. Uriah Heep were a heavy rock group who had formed in 1969, played big venues and had a deservedly massive fanbase for their amazing live performances. But with their long hair, denim flares, large crucifixes and mystical energy, they were in no way the sort of band who were critical darlings. An attention-grabbing press conference was one way of trying to get alternative coverage for the band safely away from the album reviews. On the plus side, the boys were always up for a laugh and knew the importance of good publicity.

'Any ideas from our friends at Bronze?' I asked.

Keith shook his head, exhaled and offered me the joint. I declined.

'Just that it needs to be ultimate with a capital U and no expense is to be spared.'* I sat back with my hands behind my head. Capital U indeed.

My first months with Keith had flown by in a daze. There was so much to try to get up to speed with: journalists, editors and records execs, their rivalries and relationships. All of it had to be learned so that we could try to make sure the press were saying good things about our clients. There were no rules because no one had come up with them yet, so everything seemed up for grabs – you lived or died by your wits, your confidence and a dollop of good luck. I spent my days running around London, buying hundreds of halves and being bought hundreds of pints, then scoffing a Wimpy on the way home to soak it up. Cliff Busby, who ran United Artist Records and EMI, wasn't a classic music industry type. He was from a different era and turned up for work every day immaculately attired in a suit and tie. If you went to see him in his office, he would usually produce a bottle of scotch, especially at the end of the day, so we all knew that was the best time to schedule as many meetings with him as possible.

I'd nearly fallen at the first hurdle (well, second if you counted Moon and the desk) when, in my first week, Keith asked me to take some important journalists to see the Who at the

* This wasn't an unusual occurrence for the bigger bands. As was to become clear a few years later, the result of no expense being spared was that the band would often have these costs deducted from their royalties. This made it almost impossible to earn out their advance and they were effectively handcuffed to the label.

Empire Pool in Wembley. I had never organised a press trip and Keith wasn't one for detailed instructions. I was simply given a list of writers to call – respected, powerful critics, including people like Judith Simons from the *Daily Express*, and David Wigg and Bill Hagarty of the *Mirror*. People whose opinions really mattered.

One by one, I called and asked them to meet me at Oxford Circus tube station that evening at 6pm. After all, that's how I would have gone to a concert with my friends. It never occurred to me that you wouldn't dream of taking a journalist to a gig unless there was a limo laid on with champagne on tap. And so it was that about fifteen of the country's top music critics congregated at Oxford Circus station, followed me down the escalator and got on the tube to Wembley. At that time of evening, it was packed. They were clearly annoyed.

As we got off the train at Wembley Park, I realised that I would need to pull something impressive out the bag. I suggested to the media that perhaps they would like an exclusive interview with the Who. At the time, they were one of the biggest rock groups in the world. I took the journalists backstage and knocked tentatively on the band's dressing room door. Eventually it opened. 'Hello. I'm Alan Edwards from Keith Altham's office, and I've brought some media along to meet . . .' Before I could finish, someone out of sight yelled 'Fuck off!' and the door slammed shut.

Conscious of fifteen pairs of eyes boring into my back, there was nothing else for it but to try again. I braced myself and knocked. As the door opened, I saw Keith Moon fly halfway across the room having been punched by another member of the band, but not before shouting for me to 'fuck off' again.

My embarrassment was so great that most of the journalists took pity on me.

At the behest of the Who, I had been working on the campaign to secure the release of George Davis, who had been accused of an armed robbery of the London Electricity Board offices in 1974. I spent hours putting endless press releases protesting Mr Davis' innocence into envelopes and posting them to Fleet Street journalists. It never occurred to me that it might be otherwise. Keith, and the Who's manager Bill Curbishley, told me that it had all been a mix-up, and Roger Daltrey wore a T-shirt on stage saying that George wasn't guilty. That was good enough for me. The 'Free George Davis' and 'George Davis is Innocent OK' slogans appeared all over London.*

As well as the disastrous press trip, Keith Altham and I also eventually managed to get over the fact that our downstairs neighbour and landlord, Tony Brainsby, didn't like me because I'd slept with his secretary at the end of the first week. He only knew because he'd called her about something and I'd answered the phone.

Keith forgave me. More than that, he clearly sensed my need for a father figure, so he took me under his wing and taught me everything he knew. As befits the man who advised Jimi to set fire to his guitar at Monterey, he always said he thought that at

---

* The public support for the campaign to free Davis eventually led to his release in 1976. It was the first time in the UK that a convicted felon had had his sentence overturned as a result of public pressure. Unfortunately, Davis was jailed for another robbery in 1978, which rather spoiled the whiter-than-white campaign. That said, Davis saw his conviction for the 1974 robbery quashed in 2011 after a judge decided the evidence had been unreliable, so the Who were right all along.

its best, PR is hidden in plain sight. And he was always thinking about what would give the press the best chance of covering something, about what would deliver the biggest impact. How to be big and bold. And he saw part of my education as understanding journalists. So he took me down to 'the street'.

Fleet Street was like nothing else I'd ever seen. Men with beer guts bumbled around the editorial offices wearing those iconic green-tinted visors to protect their eyesight and shouting 'Hold the front page!' Underneath the offices were the printing presses. Hundreds of workers toiled down there on the assembly line, covered in oil, weaving in and out of massive machines. The presses clanked loudly and the papers would slide down the conveyor belt at speed, where they were intercepted and checked. It was like something from another age and utterly thrilling. The journalists were smokers and hard drinkers, and had very little time for Keith's long-haired, baby-faced apprentice. But gradually I learnt the ropes.

I had been obsessed with newspapers as a child, mainly for the football coverage. I would pore over the different stories and had a feel for the differences in how a tabloid like the *Mirror* would describe a game compared to a broadsheet like *The Times*. It was the same game and their reporters saw the exact same thing, but the emphasis was completely different, the vocabulary and the angle. They were telling different sorts of stories for different sorts of reader and I found it fascinating. I had always wanted to know how it worked. Now I was finding out.

Upstairs, photographic prints would be rolled up inside a canister and shot across the newsroom in a pipe, easily the length of a football pitch. The pipes were steam-powered and you would see the picture go up the tube – whoosh! – before dropping down on the picture editor's desk. It was a significant part of my training. Photographs were studied carefully in editorial meetings before a decision was reached. The image had to be of the right quality for use in such an 'important title' as whichever one they were working on at the time. If the star didn't look good and it wasn't a sharp shot, then the story wouldn't make the paper and the PR's hard work would have just been a waste of time and money. I learned to think how a story I pitched would work in that environment, to see the headline and the image as one, the angle that would work for each different paper, for each different audience.

Early on, Keith was doing publicity for Slik, a teen group fronted by Midge Ure, who would later go on to huge success in various bands, including Visage and Ultravox. The tour was selling badly and Keith wanted to provide a reason for cancellation that didn't draw attention to the fact Slik were being overshadowed by their rivals, the Bay City Rollers. The big idea was to stage a car crash. To make the story really convincing for the music papers, the PR maestro rigged up a photo with Midge, complete with a broken arm, standing in front of the wrecked car looking sorry for himself. It was widely used and, unbelievably, not one of the papers picked up on the fact that Midge had seemingly received immediate medical attention at the scene of the crash, and was standing there, bandaged up, in front of smouldering wreckage looking quite chipper.

'It doesn't matter, my boy,' said Keith, smiling when I pointed this out. 'It's a good story. That's all that matters.'

As I sat there mulling over Uriah Heep, a bolt of inspiration hit.

'Keith?'

'Yes, Alan.'

'Stay with me here. But the album is called *High and Mighty*?'

'Indeed it is.'

'How about if we do the press conference somewhere high . . .' I caught his eye. 'And mighty.'

He looked at me with an eyebrow raised. I dug around in the chaos of papers on my desk. Flicking through a magazine, I found the article about Piz Gloria, a flashy revolving restaurant perched at 2,970m on top of the Schilthorn, a summit in the Swiss Alps. The restaurant had recently been used in the Bond movie *On Her Majesty's Secret Service*, which gave it an especially glamorous patina. Keith's eyes lit up.

'So we book out the entirety of the restaurant and fly the press there?' He held out the picture of the restaurant at arm's length, his eyes shining. 'Now that's a story.'

And so we set things in motion. Keith was always very patient with me. He once invited me down to play for his local football team – Epsom Rovers. Also in the team was Derek Green, later head of A&M Records. I remember dutifully getting out of bed one Saturday morning for the game after a late night. I needed a bit more than a half-time orange for this one. I ran around covering every single inch of grass during the first half, to little or no effect and, predictably, I ran out of steam during the second half and had to be substituted. The pre-match amphetamine had clearly run its course. That was my first and last appearance for Keith Altham FC and I stopped bragging about my prowess on the pitch.

Another time, I received a call at the office asking where the boss was. I replied, following the instruction I'd been given, saying he was away on tour with the Who. The caller turned out to be one of the touring crew who'd just read that the Who weren't touring for the rest of the year and was wondering what was going on.

One day, a couple of months in, Keith was suffering chest pains and was rushed to hospital with a suspected heart attack. I sat at my desk alone, somewhat daunted. One of the first calls was from Marc Bolan, the lead singer of the rock band T Rex. Bolan was constantly changing up his image. One minute he was a mod with button-down shirts and bum-freezer jacket, the next he was in a beautifully tailored satin suit. He was always sharply turned out. Having come of age in London's Swinging Sixties music scene, Marc turned to books for style inspiration; one character he was fascinated by was Beau Brummell, a fashion icon from the nineteenth century famed for his suits. Marc's black curls, made-up eyes and startling androgyny – teamed with a Brummell-inflected wardrobe – coalesced into a look that proved hugely influential. He was a star, not a celebrity.

'Hi man, where's Keith?'

I told him the bad news.

'Wow man, that's really uncool, really a drag, man. Really bad. I'll come over in a minute!'

I put the phone down and thought nothing more of it. The next call came from Justin Hayward, lead singer of the Moody Blues. When I explained the situation, he was obviously concerned.

'That's terrible news,' he said. 'But what am I going to do about the album? It's out next week!' Clearly, without Keith around, I was going to have my work cut out.

Twenty minutes later, the doorbell rang. I went to answer it and there stood Marc Bolan in all his glory – heels and the rest. 'Hi, man,' he said. 'How can I help?' Despite the fact he was a massive star, he spent the rest of the day answering the phones. And it turned out Keith had just smoked a particularly strong joint.

I would go on to look after Marc's day-to-day PR duties. By that point, he was in thrall to his appetites. I once arranged a press conference which he turned up to in a Rolls-Royce (it later transpired that he was friends with a chauffeur who had agreed to drive him around for the day). I had been given strict instructions he wasn't to drink, so had a beady eye out for any bottles. However, I was somewhat reassured when he arrived complaining of a cold and swigging cough medicine. As the day went on, his claims became ever more grandiose and outlandish. By late afternoon, he had sold more singles than Elvis Presley and the Beatles combined. I couldn't work out what was going on. At one stage, he went to stand up, pulled on some curtains for support and brought them crashing down, rail and all. It was then that Keith came in to check how things were going only to find Marc thrashing around under the curtains, quite obviously the worse for wear.

'I thought I said no booze,' he hissed.

'Keith, scout's honour, I've been watching him like a hawk. All he's had is cough medicine.'

Keith went and got Marc's cough medicine, gave it a sniff and reported it was neat vodka. These kinds of shenanigans aside, Marc was once described by Elton John as 'the perfect pop star' and his death in a car crash in 1977 would rob us of one of the greats.

When I was first working for Keith, I would always, without fail, be in the office before him. He couldn't understand it. He started coming in earlier and earlier, sometimes 7am, but I was already at my desk. Being a junior publicist wasn't exactly an overpaid job. So, to save money, and unbeknown to Keith, I used to stay overnight in the office. I had a sleeping bag secreted under my desk. At the end of the working day, I'd go to a gig and then come back later to sleep on the sofa.

In the morning, I would have one ear cocked for the sound of the door latch and the fumbling around of keys. Our office was on the top floor, which gave me just enough time to roll up the sleeping bag, hide it away and be sitting earnestly at my desk. Keith thought I was the keenest employee he'd ever had. I wrote my mother short, urgent letters, apologising for not being able to get back to visit because things were so frantic at work.

One evening, Keith had left for the day and I was by myself. Our downstairs neighbour, Tony Brainsby, wandered in and pulled up a seat. He didn't say much; he just produced a little bag, started making neat white lines on the table and asked me if I'd like some. I paused for a minute, unsure, but gingerly accepted as it seemed like the sociable thing to do. Plus, I reasoned, it was a good way to build bridges with him after the incident with his secretary. Perhaps he was considering offering me a job?

I watched as Tony carved out a line of what I assumed was coke. Once we were finished, he decided he was done with this brief encounter and mumbled something about rushing off to see Wings.

Alone in the office, I suddenly felt like I'd been hit around the head with a hammer. It slowly dawned on me that it can't have been cocaine that Tony had given me – he had so many little bags of powder on him, he must have accidentally given me the heroin. Panic gripped me. I knew that even in my incapacitated state, I had to stay awake or I would probably die. I staggered to the bathroom, turned on the cold water and stuck my head under it until I could no longer feel my face. I was drifting in and out of lucidity, so I paced around in an attempt to stay alert.

Over the next few hours, I holed up in the office, waiting for the effects to wear off. I never told anyone the story. It was a terrifying experience and I worried it could be damaging if it got out – I certainly didn't want the police or Keith involved.

Keith was still leaning on me for help with the grunt work on the Who, his most demanding client, but more and more he was giving me responsibility, asking me what I thought. And, gradually, I was working out which journalists I got on with, the ones I could call up and be honest with. And there was something about me that seemed to convince people I wasn't part of the establishment. Whether it was the fact I looked so young and scruffy, or that I'd spent so many hundreds of hours listening to music and going to gigs, they could tell I wasn't faking it. But I also wondered if they responded to something deeper and more fundamental: they could tell I was a kid looking for somewhere to belong.

Over the coming months, plans started to firm up for the *High and Mighty* launch. In the end, a mob of about fifty media from both the music press and national papers, including the *Daily Mail, Melody Maker, NME* and the *Daily Express*, were assembled by us at Gatwick early one morning for the flight over to Switzerland. It was a chartered plane and each journalist was given a set of headphones so they could listen to the album on the way out. Whether many of them actually did so is doubtful. The beer cans piled up quickly at the back of the plane.

By the time we arrived at the airport in Switzerland, it was clear that some had been enjoying the refreshments more than others. Uriah Heep's drummer Lee Kerslake was one of the casualties. Walking through the airport, he caught sight of a 'bear'. The bear was in fact a man in a costume, a local mascot that had been sent to welcome us. Already in an emotional state, Lee somehow ended up wrestling the bear to the ground. The press watched on in bewilderment as man and bear rolled around on the airport floor.

Once peace had been restored, we were ferried into limousines and whisked off in the direction of the Alps, with no shortage of booze in the cars. We got to the foot of the mountain and were bundled into ski lifts. Soon we were perched above the clouds. Quite a few of the journalists were already a bit wobbly, only partly due to the altitude. We all headed into lunch, which was more like a banquet: course after course arrived over several hours and yet more alcohol flowed. This, combined with the fact the restaurant was revolving, meant that by the end of the meal people were dropping like flies. It had certainly all become too much for Radio 1 DJ Alan Freeman, who passed out into a bowl of soup and was sitting there as the room went round and round, face down in his minestrone.

Keith and I attempted to keep some sort of order, but we realised the trip was on the edge of going wrong. On top of everything else, some of the band were slowly losing interest in the most important bit: the photocall. The main point of this trip was to get images of the band in front of the stunning snowy backdrop to communicate the 'high and mighty' idea.

Somehow, Keith and I managed to get Uriah Heep to stand together in a line outside on the restaurant's viewing platform.

However, the photographers were hardly able to take any pictures before the band started pushing and shoving each other, causing Keith and I considerable anxiety given their proximity to the edge of the platform, with a sheer drop below. The photographers thought it was hilarious.

Resigned to the launch being a write-off, we shepherded the assorted media down the mountain. In some cases, in scenes reminiscent of Rorke's Drift, they were carried down. By the time we arrived back at Gatwick at about six in the evening, it was evident we had an unholy mess on our hands: a horde of media banjaxed on booze, a band at each other's throats, an almighty bill for the whole trip – and, worst of all, we would barely get any publicity out of it because the combination of alcohol and blurred limbs meant there were pretty much no usable shots.

'Ah well,' said Keith, putting his coat on. 'You can lead a horse to water and all that. To the pub.'

3

We Vibrate

'This is called "Did You No Wrong"'.

Some distorted chords. Nodding towards something that felt vaguely familiar, that chugging blues-rock riff, but so much louder and so much more aggressive. Then Johnny, the little, thin lead singer with the spiked-up hair, started singing and it came with such a sneer. It was 1976 at the Nashville Rooms in West Kensington. There can't have been more than thirty of us packed into the run-down space, only a small contingent of whom were punks; everyone else was just a music fan like me. The group had an odd name – the Sex Pistols – but I'd heard they were the future. It was immediately clear that they were ripping up the rule book. It was like they had barely listened to any music from the past, because their songs seemed to have none of the same old reference points. They didn't seem to care about playing their instruments either. The whole thing was about the terrifying and intensely exciting atmosphere they conjured up. As they headed into a song called 'No Fun', I felt a shiver going up my spine. Something about it felt like two fingers up to all I'd wanted to get away from: that post-war dinginess, men in hats and overcoats, saluting the national anthem. Something about it felt like a gang.

I was still loving working with Keith, but his orbit was full of rock superstars, people like the Moody Blues, Eric Burdon and Alvin Lee. Most of them were whizzing around in limousines, drinking champagne and living the high life.

These rock-star lifestyles were so far removed from my situation. By this point, I was living in a bedsit with an art teacher above a launderette in Maida Vale called 123 Cleaners. I recall having a bath one wintry Sunday afternoon before going to see Dr Feelgood play at Dingwalls, and a window-pane being missing. It was blowing a blizzard outside and soon snow started swirling in, although luckily it melted on contact with the water. Undeterred, I dried off, took a line of speed and headed out into the frosty evening. Dudes in denim from California singing about hotels didn't resonate with me, not yet anyway – I craved something I could relate to. I had wanted a tribe for years. I thought I'd find mine on the hippie trail, but had come away disillusioned. Here were these bands who hated the hippies and everything they stood for. Suddenly everything fell into place.

I had noticed something else. Apart from the thrilling music, punk also generated headlines. At that Sex Pistols gig in 1976, the audience were getting whipped into a frenzy thanks to a wild man in a gabardine coat running around the pub like a whirling dervish, bumping into people. He was spilling their drinks, deliberately jostling people and causing chaos. Within minutes there was a melee by the stage. However, it soon became apparent this was all premeditated. I noticed a photographer step in and, under the madman's guidance, start snapping away. This puppet master turned out to be Malcolm McLaren, the band's manager. Within a week, the photos had made their way onto the cover of *NME*: 'Riot at Sex Pistols gig!' Punk rock. Now that was a story. What McLaren had realised is something that has now become a cliché: all publicity is good publicity.

The following morning, I said to Keith, 'We have got to take on the Sex Pistols as clients!' He agreed to a lunch meeting with Malcolm McLaren, and I picked up the phone to get the wheels in motion. Fortunately for us, Malcolm was a big fan of the Who and readily agreed to see us.

In those days, the most impressive place you could go for lunch was the swanky San Lorenzo in Beauchamp Place in Knightsbridge. It was the kind of restaurant where Elizabeth Burton and Richard Taylor would be having a drink with Rod Stewart. The height of luxury – authentic Italian food and a roof that fully retracted in summer.

In his nasal drawl, Malcolm spoke of big ideas. Of the establishment and the people. How they were tired of being told what to do. How punk was the sound of that feeling, the noise of the generation gap opening up as a chasm. Lunch lingered on, and soon three hours had passed by. I was transfixed.

But while I was getting swept away by it all, Keith – the most accomplished music PR of his age – was thinking about the money. He wasn't prepared to budge from our standard fee, but Malcolm didn't have any budget. Nada. That meant that Keith was never going to take the Pistols on.

Initially, I was disappointed, but when I reflected on the big picture, I realised that rock and roll had had a close escape. I came to see quickly that it wouldn't have worked for the Pistols to be launched in the traditional way with some pics in pop magazines, a mention in the *Mirror* or *Express* and lunches for members of the band with selected influential journalists. They would have just been another promising rock band and punk would never have happened.

I bumped into Malcolm from time to time after that, but his and the group's rise was so meteoric our lunch was ancient history and long forgotten. About a year later, I would see Malcolm in full flow and realise he never really needed a PR. It was at a gig at the tiny old church called the Paradiso in Amsterdam, and the Pistols were public enemy number one by then, causing uproar and creating headlines everywhere they went. They had especially upset the big wigs at EMI, their very conservative record company, so much so that the senior acts like Cliff Richard and Queen were demanding that the group be dropped forthwith.

Eventually, EMI, under pressure from shareholders, would be forced to throw the group off the label. It was a massive news story. Nothing like this had ever happened before in music. The national newspapers had a field day.

I was handling publicity for two 'punk' groups – the Vibrators and Johnny Thunders and the Heartbreakers – who were both supporting the Pistols. The Vibrators had sprung to fame with the imaginatively titled 'We Vibrate' before bouncing back into obscurity. Johnny Thunders and the Heartbreakers distinguished themselves by making some great music but taking a lot of drugs along the way. Their theme song was called 'Chinese Rocks' and was a bit of a clue.

Standing outside the Paradiso, I was freezing cold waiting for the Pistols to arrive. As they were headlining, the show couldn't start without them. News about them being dropped by their record company was filtering out. In those pre-social media days, it was all about word of mouth; someone had spoken to someone on a call who had heard a rumour that the Sex Pistols had been dumped. It seemed inconceivable but at the same time thrilling.

At Heathrow Airport, the group had been ambushed by the media. All hell broke loose and there was lots of spitting and swearing, which provided fantastic copy for the papers. Some of those images are still used today, featuring the Pistols spraying beer at the cameras as they walked by.

The journalists had given chase and hastily bought tickets to Amsterdam. In those days, newspaper reporters were very much from central casting – raincoats, trilby hats, fags hanging out of their mouths, pen and notebook in hand. It was the first week in January and news was thin on the ground. This was a godsend. The editors had told them to get stories on the Pistols whatever it took.

Inside the gig itself, there were probably only about thirty or forty people: hardcore punk fans and a PR or two if you counted Malcolm. The gig was incredible – Johnny Thunders and the Heartbreakers brought a special, unpredictable New York vibe. Thunders had been in the New York Dolls and Malcolm had managed them, so they knew each other.

The Pistols were electric. Johnny Rotten was mesmerising as he did his Richard III routine – back hunched, eyes glaring madly, fixed on the audience. The band opened with 'Anarchy in the UK' and by the time they reached 'God Save the Queen' midway through the set, the place was going wild. It was an unforgettable performance and the band were superb. Glen Matlock on bass, Steve Jones on power chords, Paul Cook keeping the rhythm tight and Rotten at his incredible best.

Outside the hall were all the 'straights', mainly the media

who, of course, weren't allowed into the gig. Malcolm knew that the less you gave the pack, the more they wanted. The journos were getting increasingly hysterical, demanding quotes and interviews. Malcolm had to say something, of course, and there was going to be a lot of it.

It was bitterly cold and the nearby canal had frozen over – the perfect location for an atmospheric press conference. Malcolm stood on the canal, with hordes of journalists hanging on his every word as he went on an inspired rant about the 'injustices done to his boys'. He explained that they were just 'bored and misunderstood teenagers'. As he had in his lunch with Keith and me, he peppered the speech, for that is what it was, with great soundbites and slogans, phrases that seemed ready-made to feature in articles. Again, he positioned them as representative of huge shifts in the tectonic plates of art and culture. To listen to him, this wasn't a dispute between a record label and a band – this was a battle between the establishment and an entire new generation.

The journalists were lapping up this priceless copy. Someone had a torch and was pointing it at Malcolm. At times, all you could see was a silhouette of this figure, shaking his fist in the air. It was like the flickering black and white images of Lenin addressing the crowds during the Russian Revolution.

One of Malcolm's tactics was to book venues for the group that were entirely out of context – for instance, somewhere bourgeois like the Talk of the Town. The Talk of the Town was an entertainment institution. Established in 1958, it had played host to Eartha Kitt, Shirley Bassey, Alma Cogan and even Judy Garland. Despite a vaguely cool start, it had ended up being the ultimate middle-of-the-road venue. In their advertising, they offered dinner, dancing, revues and cabaret, and by the mid-'70s, it was about as old-fashioned as it got. However, the venue's name still resonated and that was what caught Malcolm's attention. He loved upsetting people; chaos and anarchy were a genuine philosophy for him. It worked brilliantly for someone trying to promote a new group that needed to get noticed. At that time, the Sex Pistols were playing any venue they could get, from the Marquee in Wardour Street to Central Saint Martins, and even the exotically named El Paradiso strip club. Malcolm had to get them in front of a bigger public. He understood that publicity was the way and, luckily for him, we weren't his publicists; he had a million ideas a minute all by himself.

The owners of the Talk of the Town weren't even aware they'd booked a soon-to-be notorious and outrageous punk band. They thought this was just another act looking for a break. Of course, when they did find out they'd been duped into nearly promoting a group that sang about anarchy and the Queen's being a fascist regime, they freaked out and cancelled. An uproar followed, which was exactly what the agent provocateur Malcolm had planned. He couldn't have cared less about the gig; the publicity was priceless and it was just another stepping stone on the Pistols' road to fame. There was no shortage of lurid stories bubbling under about the Pistols when, out of nowhere, they exploded onto the front pages, not thanks to some splashy, PR-organised launch, but because they swore on TV.

They were booked on *Today*, a regional Thames Television show hosted by Bill Grundy, as a last-minute replacement for Queen – Freddie Mercury having pulled out because of toothache. When Steve Jones, dared by host Grundy to 'say something outrageous', replied 'You dirty fucker, what a fucking rotter', everyone froze. The word 'fuck' simply didn't make an appearance on TV in 1976 – and the fact it came out of the mouth of a belligerent punk further fuelled the flames. Viewers were horrified, outraged! One lorry driver was reportedly so incensed that he kicked in the screen of his new TV. Rotten's less than sympathetic response was, 'Haven't they ever heard of the off button?'

Frustratingly, as rock history was being made, I was in Zürich to see a singer called John Miles. The next morning, my flight was delayed; there was snow on the runway. While I waited, news came that the Anarchy tour had been cancelled after just one gig. It felt like the storming of the gates at St Petersburg. There I was with the ultimate boring-old-fart music while the revolution was happening. I knew instinctively that this was a moment rock historians would pore over in the future. I kept all the cuttings.

We might not have lured the Sex Pistols onto our roster, but there were plenty of new punk bands springing up. It was beginning to feel like a wave that would envelop everything. The British music PR industry was relatively small and, since I was the only publicist to feel an affinity with punk, I started scooping up bands. Thanks to what I had learned from Keith, I was able to furnish these grassroots outfits with the kind of top-flight PR normally reserved for bigger acts.

Sometimes, the roots of my relationship with a new client went back further than was at first apparent. It was like that with Generation X. I first came across singer Billy Idol long before the Bromley Contingent had even been thought of. Back then, I knew him as a boy at my school called William Broad. He was a bit of a goody-goody. In fact, it was said he was a member of the school folk club, where he used to play 'Froggy Went A-Courting'. William later changed his surname and became a fearsomely lip-snarling punk. I, in turn, became publicist for the group he joined. One day, Billy and Tony James, the band's bassist, came into our office and said they were looking for a name. We threw around a few ideas and then they went to the bookshop next door. There they picked up a copy of the seminal '60s book about British youth culture, *Generation X* by Charles Hamblett and Jane Deverson.

We had no money, but lots of energy and ideas, and we were always looking for ways to get in the music papers. The general strategy was to make the group look as big and successful as possible. One day, I suggested we should all go to Heathrow, take a photographer and pretend we'd returned from an all-conquering tour of the United States. The band certainly looked the part: Billy with his shock of sculpted blond hair and matinee-idol good looks, Tony all boyish enthusiasm and curly black mop. In those pre-security days, it was much easier to walk around the terminal. We went in and out several times while the photographer captured the band, pushing their way through imaginary crowd saying, 'No pictures please!'

We got the Piccadilly Line back into town. I went to my office and quickly crafted a story about how the band had just come back to the UK from sell-out dates on the East Coast. In my PR imagination, they were on the verge of playing Shea Stadium. In that era, there was no way of really checking these stories, short of calling up journalists on the other side of the Atlantic. You couldn't google it. In a way, nobody really cared. It was a great story and the band looked good. I was so excited when I picked up a copy of *Sounds* the following week on the way into work and read the headline 'Generation X Takes US by Storm'. I felt very much like a mini-Andrew Loog Oldham setting up pictures of the Stones pissing against petrol pumps.

Although I was young, I was comfortable picking up the phone to editors and I had developed good contacts among the news reporters. They were often from backgrounds similar to mine and we would bond over drinking and football. Now I was calling them about these bands who were part of the same movement as the Sex Pistols. There was nothing bigger than the national press back then, but mostly they didn't cover 'music stories'. Punk was the moment that changed that. The aggression and outrageousness of the punk scene generated proper news – riots, fights, public outrage – and I worked my contacts to try to get as much coverage for my clients as possible. It was the Malcolm McLaren approach all over. As the punk scene went mainstream, my clout grew with it. Suddenly I was 'the punk PR'. I realised I had a business opportunity in front of me and I dived in.

I was living with a wonderful girl called Hilary, who would come to see gigs with me, and we'd go and have a curried egg for dinner on the King's Road afterwards. But one day, she asked me to go with her to the dentist and I couldn't because I had to see a hot new band. She finished things, saying, 'You're so obsessed with your job. Your life is like a bus, Alan. You have to be either on the bus or off it. So I'm getting off it.'*

---

* A few years later, she would write and record a song inspired by our relationship called 'How Come You're So Dumb', produced by Queen's Roger Taylor, which I would release on a short-lived record label imprint. I'm sure a therapist would have something to say about that.

But the bus kept going. Keith was extremely supportive of me and let me run my own smaller company, New Wave Publicity, while simultaneously working for his organisation. However, the writing was on the wall (in the form of all the newspaper cuttings I was amassing) and soon I was itching to go solo. Through Tony James of Generation X, I met a jovial character called Andy Czezowski. He was to become my landlord and set me up in the home of my new PR company, Modern Publicity, which was formed with £150 and four clients out of 29 St James St, Covent Garden, a stop on my old laundry collection beat.

One early client was Motörhead, which in many ways didn't make logical sense, but Lemmy was probably the most authentically punk of anyone I ever represented. I had always marvelled at his basslines whenever I'd seen Hawkwind live because he played his instrument like a lead guitar.

Near the start of our working relationship, Lemmy was up on a routine cannabis possession case at Marylebone Magistrates Court and we decided to use it to get some press. We built a massive fake joint ready for him to pose with afterwards for the waiting paparazzi. It was a bit juvenile, but it worked in terms of column inches. The courts got their couple of hundred quid fine, the police were seen to be not too lenient, the newspapers had an amusing picture and Motörhead sold some more albums.

I felt at the centre of the world in our little office. Soho was next door and was where a lot of gigs happened. I loved the cast of out-of-work actors, geezers with sawn-off shotguns, bent coppers, teenagers looking for action, talent scouts and hard-drinking artists that we were surrounded by. In those days, it seemed excitingly exotic with all the French prostitutes, sailors, punters, Italian coffee shops, markets, unlicensed clubs, Maltese pimps, Chinese restaurants, and clip joints where Albanian men with broken noses would charge unsuspecting tourists £50 for bottles of 'champagne'.

I stood in the tiny office and felt like I'd come home.

4

Strangled

'Look at this, ja,' said the Hell's Angel in the balaclava, as he placed the barrel of the revolver against my head.

I froze. The Angel had clearly had some rather obvious plastic surgery and I was close enough to see the skin pulled tight over his skull.

'Gut, ja? It is .22 calibre. Powerful for such a little gun.'

'Oh ja, ja,' I said, hoping he didn't notice I was trembling.

It was November 1977 and I had taken Bob Hart from the *Sun* to see the Stranglers perform at the Paradiso in Amsterdam. The Stranglers were my first big, solo account and I was extremely committed to them. Afterwards, we accompanied the band to a Hell's Angels joint. Like the Stones, the band had made a connection with the Angels, who would occasionally provide security at their gigs. We had been on edge as soon as we arrived at the club – there was a guy at the top of the building using a machine gun for target practice on the nearby windows. Then we walked inside and saw one of his comrades riding a Harley Davidson through the bar. I felt very self-conscious, nervous of saying the wrong thing – it seemed like anything could happen.

I had spent those early months out on my own feeling

permanently pulled in multiple directions. I had started seeing a striking woman called Valerie, who I'd first met back when I began working with Keith. She had been a waitress alongside someone called Susan, who was just about to see the Sex Pistols gig that would inspire her to form her own band: Siouxsie and the Banshees. Valerie had Ghanaian heritage and used to have this huge afro, and I was drawn to her natural magnetism and lust for life. I would often see her around town and we gravitated towards each other. Though she could give me a run for my money in terms of capacity for going out, she had recently complained that I was never really there. The conversation hadn't improved when the columnist John Blake turned up and we headed off to see a gig. The band weren't great, but there were enough people I knew for it to be fun. If I wasn't listening to music, or talking to someone about music, I was reading the papers to see what they were saying about our bands, other people's bands, trying to work out who was coming next. Punk was like a cultural big bang and all sorts of bands were hurtling out of its centre. Some were barely there for a couple of months before they imploded. Everyone wanted to know where this energy was going next.

I spent my days trying to convince them it was going into the bands I worked with. You'd make ten calls and only one would land. Then you'd call everyone up and say, 'It's a real shame you're not featuring them as the *Express* are going very big on it.' I was constantly trying to create angles by putting clients in different situations. I knew that if you could get both fashion and music press going for something, for instance, you were going to increase coverage manyfold. So it was that I approached the then most famous football manager in England, Brian Clough, with a new singer I was presenting called Philip Rambow, inviting him to a gig. I had no idea whether or not Rambow was a football fan, but I knew the value of a pic with Brian Clough. Even having had a response from him might give me a few inches in a column somewhere. Clough actually wrote to me personally saying that it was 'impossible to make definite plans with the state of our fixture list at the moment'. He went on to wish Philip the best for 'a successful tour'.

Covent Garden at this time was just a ramshackle fruit market – disused boxes everywhere, long shadows and cobblestones – but it was already changing. A young crowd was moving in: proper entrepreneurs taking advantage of the low or non-existent rents. Paul Smith had just opened his first shop nearby and would stand behind the counter serving customers. Our building, which was partly being used as a squat, was split across four floors, accessed by an old wooden staircase. My office was just one small room, which I painted white and kitted out with brown-gloss filing cabinets – not that there was much to file. A single light hung from the ceiling, no lampshade, and, more often than not, no bulb either. My desk was bare except for an ashtray – I was up to forty Marlboros a day at this point. I'd arrive every morning to find the phone already ringing. Punk was news and I wanted my newest signing to be seen as at the heart of that.

I had been introduced to the Guildford Stranglers by my old friend from my schooldays, Ian Grant, who was now working in partnership with Derek Savage and Dai Davies, who had been Bowie's publicist. They were part of an agency called Albion, who had a monopoly on most of the live music pubs in London, like the Nashville Rooms, the Red Cow and the Hope and

Anchor. They could pretty much break an act via that circuit, so when they started managing the Guildford Stranglers, the band began to appear everywhere. Ian got me involved as the band's publicist and Dai signed a cheque off for £25. Somebody suggested that they drop Guildford from their name, and I had my first real client: the Stranglers.

From the beginning, they didn't fit anywhere neatly. The lead singer, Hugh Cornwell, was more of a hippy academic. One time, when he was staying at my flat, along with my brother Tony, I came back to find a note from Hugh saying that he'd gone to 'seek the great beast'. He wrote brilliant songs that referenced poems by Shelley and the predictions of Nostradamus, as well as the underbelly of London life. There was an urgency and a force that connected them to punk, but their musical palette felt broader. They were all so different: drummer Jet Black, a former ice cream salesman who resembled a pub landlord; keyboardist Dave Greenfield, quiet as a dormouse and an obsessive doer of crosswords; Jean-Jacques Burnel, the handsome biker who played extraordinarily powerful bass; and Hugh, with his old overcoats that made him resemble a schoolteacher, which of course he had been in a previous life.

My job was to get them publicity and, to do that, I set about making them punkier. I came up with the idea of a fanzine called *Strangled*, which featured stories about the band but also other up-and-coming acts like the Jam. I interviewed people like Paul Weller, although the questions were pretty basic. I even interviewed John Cale, formerly of the Velvet Underground. Everything was going brilliantly, with John tall and resplendent in a white suit and sunglasses, every inch the musical icon – until, annoyed by a fly, he smashed the drinks and my recorder off the pub table and stormed away. I was relentless about getting the band noticed. By this point we were working with Buzzcocks too, who were starting to get serious attention. But they were based up in Manchester, so I saw them much less frequently, popping up every now and then to sit in their horrifically untidy flat.

Every week I called up news editors like Derek Johnson at the *NME* with exclusives about the Stranglers having been booked into a club in Middlesbrough or a university in the Midlands. The band had done nearly three hundred gigs by the time they released their debut album *Rattus Norvegicus* in April 1977.

They were tough, and they had to be, as brawls would often break out at the concerts. When they got a break supporting Patti Smith at the Hammersmith Odeon, they rocked up in Jet's old ice cream van, which unfortunately broke down on the roundabout in heavy traffic after the performance. I jumped on every incident like that and developed an angle so that they became omnipresent in the music press. When there was a punch-up or they got banned from a venue, I'd hype it up for all it was worth. Apart from getting column inches, it was placing them right in the middle of punk. They were the real bad boys in some ways. One night, over a few beers at my flat, Hugh confided his anxiety that 'two policemen would turn up at a gig and the next day in the papers it's two vanloads, Alan'. But I assured him that two policemen isn't a story. Two vanloads – now that's a story.

But it did become a bit of a self-fulfilling prophecy. The crowds had clearly started reading about what Stranglers crowds did, so they did it more. Bottles and punches would be thrown. It became part of what people expected. Only a few weeks previously, Jean-Jacques had waded into the crowd and knocked someone out for spitting on the bassist of the reggae band Steel Pulse, then called the entire crowd 'wankers'.

Eventually, even the management began to worry about their reputation. So, it was suggested that we take a couple of friendly journalists out to see that the Stranglers were actually just another touring group.

And that's when the Hell's Angel put a gun to my head. He was muttering and I couldn't hear exactly, but I'm pretty sure he said something that sounded like 'Russian roulette'. Then he pulled the trigger with an audible click.

It all happened in slow motion and somehow I didn't freak out. Maybe there wasn't time.

'Bet it wasn't loaded!' I muttered as the Angel sidled off.

At that moment, the photographer walked in. 'Hey!' he said. 'There's a bloke in the back in a balaclava shooting bottles off the wall with a revolver.'

One afternoon, I went to see Cliff Busby, the head of EMI with the whisky – at 5pm, of course – to discuss the Stranglers. Following our meeting, totally inebriated, he drove home from the EMI office in Manchester Square. He bumped into several cars along Baker Street, before turning onto Marylebone Road and heading for his house in the stockbroker belt. A few hours later, the police knocked on his door.

'Sir, have you been drinking and driving?'

Cliff vehemently denied it.

'So how can you explain this?' the police officer asked, as he produced Cliff's registration plate, which had been left attached to another car just up the road from EMI.

Soon afterwards, Cliff signed off on a spectacular press trip to Iceland with the Stranglers. Accompanied by a dozen or so journalists, we flew out to Reykjavik to meet the 'men in black', as the band were known, who were already out there finishing their album *Black and White.* Their arrival in Iceland had caused a local media frenzy and the week provided endless photo opportunities for the group. Alluding to the title of the album, the idea was that all the images would show them in black clothes against white backgrounds: posing by geysers, riding snowmobiles . . . There was even a set-up involving horse riding, although only keyboard player Dave Greenfield was game for that one. A copious amount of drinking was done by all, including the locals who came to the shows; the booze culture in Iceland was so extreme there would be people lying in the streets unconscious.

The trip was to be rounded off with a gig in Reykjavik. The band performed to a sell-out crowd of more than four thousand, but this being a Stranglers concert, things got out of control. Someone decided to open a side door and let in a throng of ticketless fans. The audience doubled in size and the ensuing scenes were wild. Despite the best efforts of police, the locals were soon clambering onstage.

On the last day of the tour, a journalist called Peter from the *Evening News* challenged Jean-Jacques to a drinking competition before heading to the airport. 'Could you drink a whole bottle of vodka?' the writer asked cockily. Big mistake. By the time the bus arrived to collect them for the airport, the writer was so inebriated he had to be carried on. He didn't fare any better at the terminal when, now almost catatonic, the airline wouldn't let him board the plane. Without so much as a backwards glance, the band simply ditched him in the airport lounge and flew to

London. He was left to sober up and catch the next flight out, which wasn't for a few days. Early the next week, Ian Grant said he saw him and that he was sleeping under Brighton Pier.

The following month, the band played Glasgow Apollo, which was considered the best rock venue in Europe for atmosphere and excitement. The first floor had the nickname the 'bouncy balcony' as it moved so much when the fans jumped up and down; it was said to have been fitted with springs beneath it for this very purpose. The Stranglers' fans wanted to get on the stage, but the venue's security were having none of it. So, in an act of extreme provocation, the band asked the spotlight to be put on the guards and encouraged the crowd to break through. Soon there were thirty or forty people up there, jumping about, spitting and throwing beer everywhere. The guards were outnumbered so they couldn't do anything, but afterwards they were furious. They went backstage and gave the band a piece of their mind – and they weren't met with any resistance as even the Stranglers didn't want a fight with that lot.

Our PR strategy did start to become a problem. Along with other punk bands, the Stranglers were banned by the Greater London Council from performing anywhere in the capital. People had been getting more and more worried about promoting them, and there were even concerns that they wouldn't be granted visas to perform in the US.

In the autumn of 1978, the band returned to live performance in London with a massive outdoor show at Battersea Park. Determined to stick it to the authorities, they took to the stage with strippers and with one of their followers, the Finchley Boys, holding a whip.

The winter of that year would subsequently become known

as the Winter of Discontent, characterised as it was by widespread strikes and bitterly cold weather. When the electricity was cut off, we had no choice but to start burning the office furniture to try to keep warm. After months of travelling around the country with bands full of angry young men, Britain had begun to feel like a very dark, angsty place.

Luckily, I had started working with a band who would broaden my horizons forever.

5

Parallel Lines

'Yeah?' said the intense skinny guy who opened the door, gazing unperturbedly at the leather jacket-clad twenty-something before him. We were backstage at Dingwalls in Camden Town, where I had just watched, transfixed, as his angular guitar work had formed the spine of an utterly enthralling set of new-wave rock, played to a half-empty room.

'Oh, hello. I wondered if you need a PR?' I blurted out.

He turned back to the room.

'Hey, Debbie?' he shouted. 'This kid wants to do our PR. What do you think?'

The almost ridiculously beautiful singer came to the door wearing a towel and looked me up and down.

'Yeah. OK.'

I didn't know at the time, but that impulsiveness was typical of Blondie – and Debbie Harry especially. The whole band were a hoot: Clem Burke, an incredibly talented drummer whose hero was Keith Moon; Frank Infante, quiet but friendly; Nigel Harrison, the English chap; Jimmy Destri, the sweet keyboardist; and Chris Stein, the intellectual and the drive behind the band, affable but fiercely intelligent. Debbie was the most lovely, special, eccentric person you could wish to meet. Always warm and generous – and of course, at that point, every schoolboy's fantasy. Much later, when I found out that Debbie had been adopted too, it made me feel an even stronger bond with her. Every now and then, she'd take pity on me and ask me if I'd had a hot meal that day. The band became something of a surrogate family to me. And I couldn't help but admire how irreverent they were about the industry.

Shortly after I started working with them in 1978, Blondie were on a German tour for their album *Parallel Lines*, and we had to go for dinner in Hamburg with the regional office of their label Chrysalis. There used to be a longstanding ritual where record labels' local offices would take their bands for a celebratory post-gig dinner when they came to town. The whole process was painfully dull, with the execs making feeble attempts at conversation, claiming credit for the group's success and mumbling about half-baked plans for the future.

Bored to tears halfway through the meal, Debbie, Chris and Clem made an executive decision to bail – and I followed suit. We all pretended we were off to the toilets, and then escaped via a first-floor window at the back of the restaurant. Out in the street, Debbie announced she wanted to do some sightseeing. Specifically, she wanted to experience the underbelly of Hamburg, the notorious Reeperbahn.

The Reeperbahn – Ropemakers' Walk – was home to Hamburg's famous red-light district and Debbie, who had herself been a Playboy bunny, wanted to see the sex workers. We headed for St Pauli where the action was. First we walked into a small alley behind a wooden gate with a sign saying: No Minors. I looked behind the barrier and was greeted with a most astonishing sight – the brightly lit alley was thronged with strolling men. At first sight, the neat three-storey houses on both sides of the alley looked like any others except that they were all brightly lit as if for Christmas. When you strolled along the alley, you found that the bottom floors had been elegantly furnished and decorated to resemble small parlours or drawing rooms, and in each showcase, sitting in comfortable chairs or reclining on chaises-longues, were scantily clad women.

We ventured down into the subterranean gloom of what seemed like an underground car park. Once our eyes became accustomed to the dim lighting, there appeared seemingly hundreds of ladies of the night patiently waiting for clients. Prostitution was legal and this was a purpose-built facility. There were bedrooms for the completion of the transaction lining the walls of the massive space. The women soon clocked us and realised that we weren't there on 'business'. They hated being gawped at and treated like a tourist attraction. Step-by-step, a number of them started moving towards us. We weren't bothered at first, too distracted by our own fascination at this surreal encounter. However, it soon became evident, as shiny leather boots shuffled towards us threateningly from all directions, that we really were not welcome. We slowly retreated backwards from the advancing horde of prostitutes, who by now were literally snarling and hissing and spitting.

We found our way outside and fled into the night. It felt like interesting things always happened when Blondie were about. And I was desperate for interesting things.

Although I had been making a name for myself in music, and developing a lucrative niche as the PR for all sort of bands looking to ride the wave of punk, it was fundamentally culture and ideas that I was interested in, and I found Blondie's eclecticism irresistible. Through them I started to expand my horizons beyond the strict confines of the British record business. Blondie were part of a New York creative scene that had all risen up together and was firing on all cylinders: the likes of Jean-Michel Basquiat, the actor Joe D'Alessandro, the photographer Stephen Meisel – all of them knew each other and created a melting pot of music, art, poetry and design, sharing inspirations and influences. Blondie was therefore as much a part of the art scene as the music world; Andy Warhol painted Debbie and called her his favourite pop star. If he could have anyone else's face other than his own, he told Debbie, it would be hers.

Looking back on it, my PR strategy for Blondie was remarkably simple. I had two main aims, with the overriding one being to ensure a state of perpetual coverage. It must have worked because, after a year, such was the visibility of Blondie in the UK that many people began to assume that the band were British. This approach flew in the face of the perceived comms wisdom of the time, which was to save all the interviews for when the band arrived in the country. I thought this stop-start approach was outmoded. By this time, relatively affordable transatlantic flights had arrived, courtesy of the English entrepreneur Freddie Laker and his Laker Airways, and young bands and journalists had started bouncing with ease between London and New York. It brought the cultures of the United States and Britain clashing together like never before. I felt we could use this and do something different. Of course, it helped that Blondie had Debbie Harry as a lead singer.

I had set myself the target of securing all four covers of the biggest-selling music titles in a single week: *NME*, *Melody*

Maker, *Sounds* and *Record Mirror*. I don't think that there had been an instance of all four featuring the same artist simultaneously. Imagine the impact on the newsstands, though. All music PRs fantasised about pulling it off.

Getting the four covers would take considerable planning. It meant numerous conversations with journalists, editors and, of course, the members of Blondie and their management. My first task was to get the writers on board. This was the culmination of months of painstaking conversations and bringing journalists along to gigs to see how the audience was responding to the band, so they knew it wasn't just an overenthusiastic PR spinning them. Then there would be discussions with editors to convince them that Blondie were transitioning from cool punk act into major global superstars. This wasn't always easy as the men in charge were often unapproachable and it might mean ambushing them in the pub at lunchtime to bend their ear. Then there were the logistics of ensuring the group's availability, especially Debbie and Chris, who were key to interviews. If they weren't in London, there was always the phone, but photographs were a much trickier problem. The band liked working with a couple of photographers – Chris Gabrin and Brian Aris – and felt comfortable with them. Gabrin was working with artists like Elvis Costello and wasn't on the staff of a paper at the time, so a certain amount of persuasion, usually of the picture editor, needed to be done. Also, we were looking for four different images so they couldn't just be knocked off in the same session. In some instances. the paper insisted on using their own photographer.

Then came the hardest thing of all: making the interviews themselves work. This would involve agreeing an angle with the writers and ensuring that the band were well briefed and knew the quotes they were going to give to each publication. I always try to be transparent with the media and sometimes you have to temper that with a bit of discretion. I didn't at any point lie about other people getting access to the band and no publication was promised an outright exclusive. That would be suicide for me in terms of my long-term relationships with the publications as they wouldn't deal with me after that. But everyone had to feel reassured and comfortable that they were getting an exclusive slant on things.

Inch by inch, I pulled all this together, mostly in my head and scribbled in diaries. It's funny to look back at all these scribblings about different journalists and various other details. Even the timing of when I made a call was relevant. This was the last part of the challenge: to somehow coordinate things. Everything had to run like clockwork as, if an interview was late or a picture didn't work out, the plan could have fallen apart. I kept on it hour by hour and prayed that nothing unforeseen went wrong, such as a printers' strike or a cancelled flight for Debbie. *Sounds*, *Record Mirror*, *Melody Maker* and *NME* all hit the newsstands around Wednesday/Thursday, so Monday was the absolute cut-off, although really things needed to be in place going into the weekend. Come Monday, I was sure that I'd done everything I could. My Blondie media blitz was now in the lap of the gods.

Hanging around the newsagents watching one title after another appear, my excitement built until finally, on Thursday, I knew we'd got the full set. Bingo! There was no opening of champagne in celebration. I took it as just being part of the job and didn't really think about the broader significance of getting the band on all four titles. I was more concerned that some of the editors might not be happy, but everyone was pleased with their particular story. Blondie were chuffed, but they were so rock and roll they didn't overanalyse it any more than I did. Within hours it was on to the next challenge for me, maybe getting an obscure band playing at St George's Hall in Bradford reviewed in next week's *NME*.

Suddenly, as well as cheese rolls in Soho and endless trips in vans to British market towns, I had meetings in New York and even Los Angeles in my diary. I got into the habit of sending my mum a postcard every time I went on a trip. Wherever I was, whatever I was doing, the first thing I'd do was make sure I found a postcard.

One evening, while hanging out at Chris and Debbie's apartment in New York after taking the *Evening Standard* journalist John Blake to review one of their gigs, I was handed a joint. I took a few puffs, presuming it was cannabis. I wasn't keen on drugs when on duty, but I thought it would be impolite to decline. What I didn't know was that somebody at the party had laced it with heroin 'for a laugh'. I fell over like a cartoon character, landed face first on the floor and promptly threw up. The last thing I remember was seeing the faces of Debbie and John Blake peering over me. When I came to, I saw a boot next to my face. It turned out to be that of Shep Gordon, the legendary music manager they were working with. He was less than impressed by the unprofessional state the UK PR was in. I was dragged to my feet and Debbie hung me over the balcony to be sick. I opened my eyes again and a blurry New York took shape in front of me. I suppose it's something to have thrown up twenty storeys above Manhattan, loosely clutched by a sweetly concerned Debbie Harry.

Despite this infelicitous meeting, Shep would later take me under his wing. He used to try to drill his three rules of success into me.

'Alan, I've got some good advice for you if you want to work in this business.'

'What's that, Shep?'

'Don't forget the money.'

'OK,' I'd reply.

'Another piece of advice, Alan.'

'What's that, Shep?'

'Just don't forget the money.'

'OK, Shep.'

'One last piece of advice, Alan.'

'What's that, Shep?'

'Never forget the money.'

While riding the Blondie carousel, my job was, of course, to ensure that they were a constant source of interest to the UK media. I was in LA one time with Nina Myskow of the *Sun*. She was doing a spread on Blondie and the launch of their new album, and I was trying to help her get an interview nailed down. We chased the band around LA as they did various store openings and signing sessions. Blondie were having the time of their lives and sitting down with a journalist wasn't really at the top of their list of priorities. We were always on the verge of getting the interview. Then they'd suggest it would be better to talk in San Diego, a few hundred miles away. So, we hired a car and drove down there, but predictably the chat didn't happen. Late that night, Nina and I drove back to LA. On the way the car ran out of petrol . . . on a level crossing. With no way to contact anyone for help, we just left it there and walked away.

We found that we were in a deserted stockyard somewhere in southern California and it felt dangerous. Luckily, we found a taxi. The missing car was charged to the record company and presumably someone was sent out to retrieve it.

Shep had hired Fiorucci for the launch party, which was the hottest store in LA at the time. Blondie liked to arrive in style, so they commissioned a Sherman tank, which was driven down the street with the band perched on top of it and into the store. It made for some outrageous photographs.

I'm not sure that the interview ever happened, but Nina was very smart and would have pulled some cuts and added whatever quotes she'd managed to grab. Either way, a big feature appeared in the *Sun* a few weeks later. The band knew how to have a good time. And sometimes my job was to stall the journalists until Chris and Debbie were ready to talk to them.

I would watch Blondie go from outsiders playing to a handful of people to arguably the most famous band in the world. But they never lost their restlessness. They were spontaneous and experimental – you could see it in how their music roamed across reggae, disco and rap, and how they were interested in performance art. My regular flights to Manhattan meant I was at home even less than I had been before. I would sit on the bed with my suitcase packed, barely able to face leaving, before saying goodbye to Valerie and heading out into the night. But I felt like I had to. To me, it felt obvious that the energy that I had been attracted to in punk had left the centre and was rippling out, away from the increasingly formulaic idea of punk itself. And I was determined to follow it wherever it went.

6

Stir It Up

'Do you want to join in?'

I blinked, wondering if I'd misheard or misunderstood.

'Here? With *him*?'

We had been stood under a purple jacaranda tree watching the football match for a while, as the easily recognisable figure of Bob Marley passed the ball expertly about. Did I want to play football with Bob Marley?

'Yes please,' I said.

It was 1979 and I was twenty-four. If you'd told seventeen-year-old me that one day someone would ask me that question, I'd probably have had to sit down. When *Catch a Fire* had come out in 1973, I'd listened to it so much I wore out the grooves in the record. I was in my flat in Worthing then, dreaming of travelling to London. He sang so powerfully of dislocation and not belonging.

A couple of years later, I had been in the Lyceum Theatre off the Strand to watch Marley play his iconic show, only a couple of months before I'd spoken to Keith Altham at that fateful Who gig.

The critic from *The Times*, reviewing the Lyceum show,

had remarked on a 'curious odour in the air' that he couldn't identify, and the *NME* journalist had his pocket picked. It was a warm day, as I remember, and this was the hottest ticket for ages. People were spilling out into surrounding streets, many looking to find a way in. I was so lucky to have one ticket – I think it was just one because I don't remember being with anyone else. I was offered a lot of money for it, but I held on tight. The atmosphere was crackling; you could feel the excitement as you pushed your way into the packed crowd. This was more of a celebration, a statement, as opposed to just being a concert. Reggae had arrived. Multiculturalism was the reality and, most significantly, King Bob was being crowned that night.

Bob was incredibly animated from the get-go. He realised the significance of the night and understood what a truly watershed moment for his dream of world domination this was. After a particularly up-tempo version of 'Burnin' and Lootin'', he and the Wailers segued smoothly into 'No Woman, No Cry'. Sensing the moment, he stretched the performance to seven minutes.

That night it felt like everybody knew every word of every song and was determined to sing along. At times, the two thousand-strong crowd almost drowned out the band, sharing the backing vocals. A recording of 'No Woman, No Cry' made that night would become Marley's next single and the breakout song for him and the Wailers. There was apparently some debate over whether to feature the audience so prominently in the mix, but Island Records boss Chris Blackwell, having noted the crowd's rapturous reaction, insisted on it.* Maybe he

---

* I still tell people I sang backing vocals on a Bob Marley album, which isn't technically a lie.

understood the incredible subliminal marketing possibilities. The audience participation caught the mood of the moment, the sense of community and importance of the message: the fight against racism and injustice, the end of the empire, the coming together of the tribes. Somehow, having the crowd and the singer as one said it all. It was as if there was a bigger genie in this bottle than anyone realised.

The following year, 1976, I had seen Marley at rain-soaked Ninian Park in Cardiff on 19 June. It was at the misleadingly titled West Coast Rock Festival and the headliner Steve Stills had dropped out. I was still working for Keith at this point and my job was to persuade a coachload of journalists to make the journey one Saturday morning on very uncertain promises, mainly free booze. On arrival, it was apparent that only about four thousand people had turned up. The rain was incessant. Going to the box office, staff were still writing 'Bob Marley and the Wailers' on the tickets in biro. I was thrilled to be seeing Bob play again, but not many people in this more traditional rock crowd seemed to realise who he was.

By the summer of 1977, punk was at its zenith. Marley's music somehow chimed perfectly with the sense of alienation that punks were feeling. Here was a genuine rebel leader. London was having a real punk and reggae moment, but the National Front was beginning to rise as well. There were plenty of people who weren't happy about the conversation between Black and white musical cultures.

I had been aware of the musical divide ever since I had started reviewing bands for *Sounds* and *Record Mirror*. I naturally wanted to write about Black bands. That was unusual because if you were a rock journalist you typically stuck to white artists like

Tom Petty or the Stones, but I would often be out and about reviewing Kool & the Gang or Cameo. This was the era when I was told with a straight face by an editor that a reason not to feature a Black artist was that photos of Black people didn't print properly on the paper they used. Marley was smashing through those old divisions and he wasn't afraid to release a single called 'Punky Reggae Party', which included callouts to the Clash, the Damned and the Jam.

But, to be honest, even if I hadn't been so into reggae, it was now January 1979, London was freezing and someone was offering to pay for me to go to Jamaica. My arm didn't need much twisting.

By early 1979, punk was becoming less interesting. The genre had changed the media landscape, with national newspapers making more space for music stories and a number of big magazines such as *i-D* and *The Face* about to emerge from the punk milieu. But the good bands had become mainstream arena acts, the less good ones had fallen by the wayside, and suddenly it was no longer a small, crazy, exciting scene. It had been absorbed into the record business as yet another mainstream musical style. That had bolstered my standing in the industry, but blunted the revolutionary element of the music that had originally grabbed me. I was on the lookout for another adventure.

Although I had been working with punk bands, my musical tastes were diverse. When I was first buying music seriously, I couldn't afford the price of individual albums, so I started buying *Motown Chartbusters*, brilliant compilations that featured the best of the Temptations, the Supremes and Stevie Wonder. I also started picking up the Trojan Records *Tighten Up* albums, partly because of the sexy covers showing sultry-looking girls in bikinis, but mainly because of great reggae tracks like 'Return of the Django', 'Long Shot Kick De Bucket' and 'Skinhead Moonstomp'. Although I'd 'gone heavy' at fourteen and begun listening to bands like Led Zeppelin and the Stones, I never fell out of love with reggae.

Now, I was being tasked by Island Records with taking a group of journalists out to Jamaica to talk to Jacob Miller, the charismatic lead singer of reggae band Inner Circle. The band had moved to Island in 1978 and released the album *Everything Is Great* without it having much impact. Even though reggae was rebel music and was still on the margins like punk had been a few years before, Inner Circle weren't considered cool. My suspicion was that label MD Richard Griffiths thought I might be able to bring some of my punk ethos and credibility to the party. The link between reggae and cool had been broken and it was my job to investigate. First thing was to meet this Jacob Miller and the mysterious Inner Circle organisation.

Barry Cain from *Record Mirror* and Hugh Fielder from *Sounds* had signed up and, after a ten-hour British Airways flight, we walked out of Norman Manley International into a welcoming blast of heat. Piled into a taxi, we threaded our way through the outskirts of Kingston. Despite the late hour, music was blaring, and the streets were still packed. The car stopped and started every couple of feet because of people walking in the road. The air was thick with bass. It was technicolour to London's black-and-white. It was perfect.

When we arrived at the sumptuous Jamaica Pegasus Hotel, we were surprised to see it was surrounded by police and armed guards. We swiftly learned that the two main political parties, the Jamaica Labour Party (JLP) and the People's National Party

(PNP), were quite literally fighting an election. It was another front in the Cold War: the JLP was reportedly armed by the CIA because the PNP, under the dynamic Prime Minister Michael Manley, was getting cosy with Castro's Cuba. Gangs and guns and shootouts were fast becoming the reality of life on Kingston's streets.

After posting my mum a postcard telling her 'Jamaica is hot' and settling into our room to spend a little time relaxing, I was given the nod later that evening that we would be meeting Inner Circle. The journalists and I were anticipating some cool Rastafarian types, especially since the pictures we'd seen of Jacob in the press had shown him with heavy dreadlocks. It came as a surprise, then, when someone told us the band were in fact already here and pointed in the direction of the hotel pool. There we found five guys in white suits with diamond rings and gold watches performing to guests. The vibe was more Barry White than Haile Selassie. They looked like the hotel band. This couldn't be Inner Circle, surely?

Unfortunately, it was, and that pretty much scuppered my PR plans. I had been instructed by Richard Griffiths to position Inner Circle as a cool, conscious Rasta-type act. Clearly, that wasn't going to be possible with a cover band playing standards for the tourists.

I let the press get on with their interviews and hoped for the best. At the end of the day, the PR is often just the messenger and if the client hasn't sorted the message, there's not much you're able to do. At that point you can either keep trying to convince the journalist not to believe the evidence of their own eyes and ears, and thereby lose all credibility, or you can let it go and see where the flow takes you. I chose the latter. My relationships with journalists would last a lot longer than my relationship with Inner Circle, I concluded.

After their gig that evening, Inner Circle joined us for a drink at the hotel. Barry Cain asked if they were aware of the National Front or any of the racial conflict in London. This unexpectedly provoked Jacob, who launched into a rant. 'Black and white shouldn't live together!' he shouted. His explosion caught us off-guard. This kind of Black separatism wasn't exactly in harmony with the peace-and-love Rasta image that we were expecting to promote. It was the final nail in what could have been a beautiful PR strategy.

The next day Barry, Hugh and I made a pilgrimage to a famous record shop in Trenchtown, the notoriously tough district of Kingston. It was like a war zone. Apart from our group and a few Americans, whom we suspected were probably CIA agents, there weren't any foreigners in downtown Kingston, and the locals were wary. As we approached the door, we were threatened by some local men who started pushing and shoving us and asking what our business was.

It was no joking matter on the capital's streets. The rival parties were arming gangs and urban warfare was actively being encouraged; it's been estimated that there were nearly a thousand killings in that period. We were feeling the heat, and I don't mean the 86 degrees outside.

We were being escorted around Kingston by Chris Blackwell's right-hand woman, Suzette Newman. When the locals noticed her, suddenly everyone became very polite, invited us in and were only too keen to play us their latest tracks. After all, music was one of the only ways that you were going to get out of the ghetto. Historically, Jamaican producers would buy a song for around $100 and, no matter how big a hit it became, the musician who wrote it wouldn't see another dime. Blackwell, however, did everything by the book and paid musicians properly. Suddenly, successful artists would be getting a cheque for $100,000. No wonder we were shown to the front of the queue and played the latest 12-inch dub plates.

On the last day of the trip, we received an unexpected surprise when the record company casually asked if we'd like to go to Bob Marley's house. Obviously, there was only one answer. Suzette said we would just 'go over to 56 Hope Road' and walk in. I asked if he would be expecting us. She said that Bob's house operated under an 'open door' policy. She wasn't kidding; when we arrived, there wasn't any door at all. We just entered.

The house was empty, but we could hear voices floating in from somewhere nearby on the warm breeze. We spotted Bob straight away at the centre of a game of football – he was so quick on the ball, fast and skilful. He could beat a man, but he was very much a team player, always looking for the pass that would help the cause. They were all good players, and the ball was moving fast.

After the game, we were invited into the house to listen to Bob talk about Rastafarianism. He sat there wearing denim and Adidas trainers. He wasn't physically tall, but it still felt as though he was the king, and we were the visiting dignitaries. He strummed an acoustic guitar gently the whole time and had an almost spiritual presence. At several points, the ganja smoke in the room became so thick that we could no longer see him.

*

Back in London, I had begun to dip my toe into music management with the Damned and Generation X. My reasoning was that a career focused solely on publicity came with the risk that, if you weren't careful and things took a wrong turn, you'd end up just distributing tickets to journalists and cutting out reviews from the papers. In the case of Generation X, my role as manager lasted only a single weekend: on the Friday I was supposed to organise a van to take their equipment to a gig on the Sunday. When it failed to turn up, they had another manager by the Monday.

My old friend Ian Grant and I had formed a company together, Grant Edwards. It was a fantastic partnership: Ian was the 'guy on the road', the one more likely to deal with confrontations, give the band a telling off or square up to a promoter. I, on the other hand, was focused on the band's image and dealing with the record company. Our business styles complemented each other perfectly and we quickly became inseparable. What's more, I loved the atmosphere of rehearsal rooms, seeing new bands and watching how they developed. I wanted to be part of the action and go on the journey with them.

One journey I hadn't quite been expecting was with Motörhead on their *Bomber* album tour, for which they decided to cart an actual Lancaster bomber around with them. Given that it was only about twenty-five years after the Second World War, this was pretty outrageous, though nobody said anything – not even on the German dates. They played at an incredible volume, so much so that the wall at the back of the venue in Berlin partially collapsed.

I joined them for the flight out to France – not in the bomber, I hasten to add, but on Gerry Bron's private plane, which sounds impressive but was actually a rickety old propeller job with about ten seats and not much else. I had a photographer and journalist with me. Bron, who owned the label Motörhead were signed to, insisted on flying the plane himself. It was his hobby. Nobody had much choice other than to go along with it. However, copious amounts of beer had been consumed before take-off so nobody really cared. Once we were airborne, more and more cans appeared and we continued drinking out of plastic cups. We were all having a high old time.

One thing nobody had explained to us was that the plane didn't have a toilet. By then, everyone had consumed four or five pints and was desperate for a leak. There was nothing for it but to urinate in the plastic cups we had drunk the beer out of. This worked for a while, until we hit turbulence somewhere across the Channel. At that point cups started flying around, spilling their contents everywhere.

We arrived somewhere in southern France and literally fell out of the plane. The band and media decided a drink was called for, so we went to find a bar in the tiny airport terminal. A few drinks later, the high jinks started up again. Somebody jumped off the first floor of the building and someone else managed to climb the flagpole where the *Tricolour* proudly flew. What the officials made of these leather-clad, long-haired lunatics looking like extras from a biker movie is anybody's guess. One thing's for sure: nobody asked us for passports.

By this time, Grant Edwards had moved into an office in Winchester Walk, right in the middle of what is now Borough Market but what then was pretty much a wasteland. The office was a disused fruit warehouse and very inexpensive to rent. Because of the fruit market, there were strange licensing laws.

The workers used to clock off at about seven in the morning, having loaded all the crates of apples, pears and plums that had arrived from around the country. They needed a drink at the end of their shift and a couple of pubs right opposite us opened at around 6am. It was proper Cockney and suited us fine. No one got in the way.

The office was so big that we'd even have bands rehearsing downstairs and nobody complained about the noise. It was where we had rehearsals for the concert organised for the Stranglers' singer, Hugh Cornwell, who'd been put in prison early in 1980 for possession of heroin.*

These days pass in a blur: one minute I'm planning a trip up to Birmingham Odeon to see a new band I'm looking after support Black Sabbath, next I'm talking to an Irish promoter about how sales are looking for some gigs over there, all the time conscious that I'm due on the 10:20 train from Euston to Manchester Piccadilly the next morning with my mates Tony Parsons and Barry Cain to see Buzzcocks. Back in London, I rush along Oxford Street to Chrysalis to discuss an impending Blondie visit. They also want to know who I'm taking out to see Pere Ubu at a bar in Cleveland – writers aren't exactly biting my hand off for that one. Then I pop around the corner to see

* It was around this time I was offered the publishing rights for a band called U2 for £4,000. I couldn't raise the money and went to see my bank manager, Mr Graham, at the NatWest at 319 Archway Road. When I asked him for a loan to secure the song rights for a rock group, he looked at me like I was mad. He was a kindly enough man, but in this instance he peered down his spectacles at me and said no. I moved on quickly enough, but what I should have done was find another way of raising the money, even if it meant robbing his bank.

Cliff Busby at EMI to discuss the new Stranglers album. I briefly consider grabbing a sandwich over the road, but then realise I'm supposed to be going up to John Henry's rehearsal room in north London to watch another of our new bands.

Sheila Rock wants to know if she's got a photo pass for a gig at the Roundhouse at the weekend. I go the extra mile, as I've got a secret crush. Harry Docherty, the affable *Melody Maker* writer, has left a message asking for tickets for the show, as has Mike Mills from *What's On*. *Ring, ring* – someone wants some gossip for a column. I can't think of anything much, so I tell them that Billy Idol has a quiff now. That will surely earn Generation X a plug.

I last saw Bob Marley on 7 June 1980, in what turned out to be his final UK appearance – and also the curtain call for the Crystal Palace Garden Party. The Crystal Palace Bowl was a quaint left-over from the Festival of Empire in 1911. Quite fitting, I suppose, that a son of the empire should be bringing the curtain down on an event at a venue built to celebrate it. The crowd were in party mode and some people fell in the lake in front of the stage.

Less than a year later, news broke of Marley's death. Nobody had known Bob had a tumour but I thought back to his appearance at his last show, how frail and vulnerable he'd been; his solo, acoustic rendition of 'Redemption Song' was particularly poignant. Apparently, an injury to a big toe picked up playing football had become cancerous and spread. The next day, one of the journalists from that memorable trip to Jamaica called me concerned that he had tackled Bob too hard during the game at Hope Road and that it could have been the cause of the injury. I reassured him it wasn't. That night, as Valerie headed out for the evening, I sat and played Bob's albums, as if hearing the songs for the first time.

I often think about the songs he had yet to write, the things he would never accomplish. I had already experienced many moments of professional pride by this point in my life and would go on to have many more. But nothing has ever got close to getting a thumbs-up from Bob Marley for playing a good pass to him.

7

(I Can't Get No) Satisfaction

'Oh, all right,' Mick Jagger said. 'You can have your fucking job back then.' He sashayed off as only he could. I was extremely relieved that I had been unsacked. I was *pretty* sure I had been, anyway.

It had only taken three days of walking around as if I hadn't obviously been sacked in front of lots of people. I'd turned up after the show in Vienna to a deserted airfield near the city. It was about midnight and, as usual, everyone had their cases and baggage in hand as we climbed the stairs to find our allocated seats. However, when I got to mine, I'd discovered someone else sitting in it. There were a few smirks, and general avoidance of eye contact, but nobody said a word. I sensed quickly that this was Mick's idea of telling me that I was surplus to requirements. Goodnight Vienna indeed. I had been embarrassed and, of course, I was hurt, but there wasn't much I could do about it because the plane was about to leave. I found myself back on the runway. It was like the final scene in *Casablanca*: I stood there holding a cheap suitcase as the airliner thundered off into the sky. Tears welled; I just wanted to get back to the UK. The one thing that they hadn't thought of was to confiscate my all-access pass, which remained safely around my neck during the whole miserable episode. I knew that if I turned up at a gig, the security would let me backstage. I'd seen my chance to brazen things out and got an overnight train to Cologne in Germany, the venue for the next two concerts. I had arrived at the Müngersdorfer Stadion and walked around all day, cheerfully acting as if nothing had happened, fulfilling as many of my duties as was practical. Everyone was too embarrassed to say anything. I did the same thing again the next day, carrying on as if oblivious to the fact I'd been fired. After a third day of this charade, Mick walked over to me . . .

It had all begun towards the end of the previous year when I'd picked up the phone in our office in Winchester Walk.

''Allo, this is 'Arvey,' growled the voice at the other end. 'Would you be interested in taking on the PR for the Stones?'

There was only one 'Arvey: Harvey Goldsmith, the legendary promoter who practically invented stadium rock in the UK. And, of course, there was only one Stones.

My head told me they were about as far away from the energy of punk and reggae as you could get. Had the band become too stale? Five years previously, in 1976, I had been a huge Stones fan and had gone to see them play at Earl's Court. Like many, though, I had been disappointed by that gig. They were sloppy and lacklustre on stage, the sound wasn't great and Keith Richards didn't seem able to remember all the lyrics. Their less-than-stellar performance had even later been credited with helping to inspire the wave of punk bands that I went on to be involved with.

At a practical level, Ian and I were really trying to build the musician management side of the business. No one we were looking after had really broken through yet and it took a lot of work to keep this going alongside the PR. Bands needed such nurturing early on. Was now really the time to be taking on a hugely demanding new client?

But my heart told me: it was the Rolling fucking Stones. My answer, obviously, was yes.

And as for any reservations that I might have had about where the group were musically right now, I reminded myself that a publicist is a bit like a garage mechanic: it's our job to fix the engine, regardless of whether it belongs to a Mini or a Merc.

About a week later, I was summoned to a meeting with Mick Jagger in New York. The Stones' team bought me an economy-class British Airways flight and the interview took place in Mick's rooms at the Dakota Building in Manhattan, outside of which John Lennon had been shot the year before. The room was really big – much bigger, in fact, than many of the clubs that the bands I'd been looking after played – and had very high ceilings. It reminded me of a school room, which turned out to be apt. Mick asked me to sit down and then fired off a volley of questions. He wanted to know about the UK music press and nationals, what their circulations were and who owned them. Next, he started quizzing me on the European media. In those days, a UK PR's purview never really went beyond Dover. 'What's the circulation of *Libération*? How big is the reach of *El País*? Which papers come under the Axel Springer group?' The only foreign titles I dealt with regularly were Japanese rock magazines, German pop publications such as *Bravo* and the odd grumpy music writer from *Rock & Folk* in France. Fortunately, however, I had a decent sense of the wider continental press from looking after punk acts.

The grilling lasted at least forty-five minutes. I swiftly realised that Mick wasn't so much interested in the actual figures; he just wanted to test my knowledge and see how well I performed under pressure. It was also his way of making something clear to me: he was an international superstar and if I wanted the job, I'd have to think globally.

At the end of the meeting, he gave me no indication of how I had done, but it turned out I must have passed the test. I was hired soon after to manage the media operation for the Stones' European tour in June and July of 1982. Or, at least, I thought I'd been hired.

It fast became apparent that Keith Richards had other ideas. I heard from him a few weeks later, when I was sitting in my office at nine in the evening. The phone rang and an unmistakable, gruff voice said, 'Listen 'ere, Sonny Boy Jim. If you want to work with the Rolling Stones, you'll come and meet me now. I run the Stones, not that fucking poof Mick Jagger.' He told me that if I wanted the job, I had to meet him at a rehearsal studio in Shepperton, a village outside London, at midnight.

I was confused, as I thought that I already *had* the job. I knew where Mick was having dinner – at a swish Italian restaurant on Cheyne Walk in Chelsea – so I thought I'd get clarification. I slipped in quietly and told the singer what had happened. He looked at me imperiously, said, 'Well you'd better go then, hadn't you?' and carried on eating. I didn't have a cab account, so it was the last tube to Ealing Broadway and a bus to Shepperton.

On arrival, I was shown into a tiny room with a broken window, a rusty sink and no chairs. I stood there for hours – the sound of music playing in the distance – until chinks of light appeared under the door and dawn broke. At about half-seven in the morning, Keith burst into the room, firing a succession of questions at me about blues and reggae – both things, luckily, I knew a lot about. He was very intense yet strangely relaxed and all he wanted to talk about was music. I guess he was just sizing me up and teaching me a bit of a lesson. The conversation lasted about fifteen minutes and then he simply departed. It was becoming clear that Mick was the business mind and Keith was the music brain, and they had both tested my wits and willing in their own ways.

I would come to realise that hiring a relatively young publicist from the punk scene was smart PR on the part of the Stones themselves. Any band or brand, no matter how successful, needs to have its image constantly refreshed and, in the music world in particular, made to look bang up to date. I think Mick liked the idea of me, a scruffy kid in a football shirt, running around the world with the Stones.

A few days later, the band's business manager, Prince Rupert Loewenstein, invited me to his oak-panelled office in St James's and offered me a glass of sherry. 'The chaps seem to quite like you,' he said. 'They wondered if you'd be their PR. How does £150 a week sound?' It sounded like more money a week than I was making from the rest of the bands I was working with put together. Valerie and her two wonderful daughters, Bryony and Lola, had recently moved into my flat in Archway Road, so this would make a massive difference to our household finances. I went back to the office and sat at my desk, feeling like I wanted to tell someone but not sure who. The phone rang.

'Alan, it's your mum. I'm afraid your father has died.'

At the funeral, as I stood arm in arm with my mother in

the windswept south-coast cemetery, unable to cry, one of my distant male relatives came up and looked me up and down.

'Hello Alan. How's it going in London then?'

'I'm working with the Rolling Stones,' I whispered.

Towards the end of that year, 1981, as I accompanied the R&B singer Teddy Pendergrass across north-west America, the papers were full of the Rolling Stones' US tour. Touring with Teddy really brought home to me just how segregated the country still was in practice, even if it wasn't in law. I had become familiar with many of the US venues by now from trips with bands I was working with. But the theatre Teddy was appearing at would be in a run-down district where only Black performers were allowed to play, the audience would be Black and everyone working on the show would be Black. Teddy's manager, Shep Gordon – before I met him through my work with Blondie – had agreed to work with me after I wrote him a letter when I heard Teddy singing on the radio in the back of a taxi one night on the way home from a punk gig. He had come up from a tough background in Philadelphia and had been playing what they call the Chitlin' Circuit, which consisted of exclusively Black venues and Black promoters. Shep was determined to take Teddy out of that scene and break him out to a bigger, wider and, controversially, a whiter audience. Shep wanted him to be the Black Elvis.

I followed the Stones tour closely in the press; it was rumoured to be earning them the unheard-of sum of $1 million a night. The next step was to replicate and develop the formula for Europe, where the band hadn't toured for six years. Mick and the promoter Bill Graham planned a thirty-two-date tour of the continent, beginning with four theatre or club shows in Scotland and London, then going on to twenty-eight stadium, park and festival gigs, before finishing up in Roundhay Park, Leeds, on 25 July, the day before Mick's thirty-ninth birthday. The group also managed to release the live album *Still Life (American Concert 1981)* in time for the European leg. These guys were no slouches.

Back in the UK, Teddy sold out five nights at Hammersmith Odeon in February 1982 and songs such as 'Love TKO' were really beginning to catch on. He was a big deal, but the PR was heavy going. I kept approaching newspapers full of energy and enthusiasm with great stories and pictures of Teddy. Every time I handed the pictures over, the editors would make up fantastic excuses for why they couldn't use them. Again, I'd hear about how a Black face doesn't print properly on white newspaper or some other technical bullshit about how the newsprint would come off. I saw through it quickly and realised that it was obviously because Teddy was Black that they didn't want to use him. In my own life, I was witnessing first-hand the fortunes that the Stones were making mining the deep seam of US Black musical tradition, but this in no way seemed to translate to the same level of media interest in what was perceived as Black music. I couldn't help but think of Bryony and Lola at home, of the stories the industry I was part of told about who was important and who wasn't.

I was determined in my own small way to break this down and make a change, and I think we could have done so with Teddy. Then everything came crashing down in seconds when Teddy lost control of his Rolls-Royce one March night outside Philadelphia and was critically injured. I went to see him in the hospital, and he'd lost the use of his legs. The day I was there, a paparazzi from *National Enquirer* or somewhere like that smuggled himself into the ward disguised as a doctor and whipped out a camera. They had no trouble with the ink printing those photographs.

There was no time to stop and process this terrifically sad news, though, as the UK media launch for the Stones tour had to be carefully staged in April at a very cool underground club in Soho called Le Beat Route. All the characters from the Fleet Street papers were there, such as the legendary *Daily Express* reporter Judith Simons. Judith was affectionately known as 'Fag Ash Lil' because she always had a cigarette hanging out of her mouth. She was married to a Polish count and lived at the top of Kilburn High Road. She invited me around for tea and cakes one day and was lovely in her own eccentric fashion. There were also old-guard reporters and senior editors there whom I hadn't yet met – and I was surprised when Mick introduced *me* to them. I was having a masterclass in PR. A photo of thirty-eight-year-old Mick looking happy appeared right on the front page of the *Sun* the next day with a caption saying: 'We are going to rock Europe!' Alongside was a small update from the Falklands War. One key bit of PR spin we wanted to feed the newspapers was the oldest ticket-selling trick in the book: the suggestion that this tour might be the last time. With the death of John Lennon and the split of Led Zeppelin, both in December 1980, the Stones and the Who were the only big '60s acts still going.

Business-wise, Mick was way, way ahead of his time. The Stones were doing deals with The Man before anyone else and broke new commercial ground by setting up tour sponsors, including cassette tape manufacturer TDK. For the 1981 American tour, Mick sold exclusive advertising rights on all tickets to the fragrance firm Jovan Musk for a million dollars. Initially this mainstream product seemed at odds with the Rolling Stones' bad-boy image, but corporate rock tour sponsorships would fast become an industry norm.

The Stones built arguably the best rock and roll brand of all time. Mick certainly thought so and loved having the promoter announce, 'Ladies and gentlemen, the greatest rock and roll band in the world!' before they hit the stage every night.

And his name opened doors. I remember once going with Mick to see media baron Robert Maxwell when he had just bought the *Daily Mirror.* We squashed into the lift at the paper's building in Holborn alongside some astonished messengers and junior journalists, and went up to the boardroom where Maxwell was.

'Hello Mick. I have always loved the Beatles. Great band.'

Mick looked at him as if it was a joke, but he wasn't quite so sure.

Then, for some reason, Maxwell started detailing his Second World War exploits; according to him he had won the whole thing single-handedly. He ordered his pop writer 'Robert Blake' up to join us. The journalist's name was actually John Blake, but Mick was amused at the error. Maxwell then rang up Our Price Records and demanded that they send over 150 copies of Mick's album for a competition.

While we waited for the records to arrive, Maxwell continued showing off, picking up the phone saying 'Get me the Queen now' and slamming the receiver down. For someone used to spending a lot of their time trying to convince relatively junior music writers to cover an act by buying them a cheese roll and a pint of mild, this felt like a very strange new world indeed.

And then, in May 1982, we were off on tour. The Stones were travelling on their own 747 jet, an unimaginable luxury compared with the cramped tour buses I was accustomed to. The plane, complete with glamorous hostesses, was more like an ocean-going cruise liner, as opulent as you could imagine – white leather seats and endless fine food and drink. One time, the tour manager couldn't wake Keith up in a hotel room to fly to the next country, so roadies carried the bed, with Keith sleeping in it, out of the hotel, loaded it onto the plane and then hauled it off when the plane touched down again. Keith woke up in another hotel room in another country without even having stirred. Of course, there were none of the normal constraints in terms of when or where the plane departed, or tedious things like customs checks. And there was no question of being late for the flight either, because you had a police escort with lights flashing and sirens blaring all the way to the airport.

Soon I was getting to grips with the more workaday reality of life on the road with the Stones, which basically consisted of running up and down hotel corridors checking whether members of the band were ready for interviews, while at the same time trying to placate frustrated journalists waiting downstairs who were worried that their interviews weren't going to materialise. I barely had time to scrawl a message on a postcard to my mother before I was running off again. Now I understood why Mick had to keep so fit; the tour was about stamina as much as anything.

Mick knew that media coverage would be key to selling out so many big shows. He decided to do 'spontaneous' press conferences across the continent – ten of them in two days. So, like a US president, he would fly to Munich in the morning, Düsseldorf at lunchtime, Paris in the afternoon – and I, of course, went with him. At each stop, he wanted dossiers on journalists and asked me to brief him on the local scene, the football teams and, interestingly, the politicians. He figured out all the local angles in advance and practised how he was going to work them. I even had to visit the local record stores to make sure the album was stocked and prominently displayed. After each press event, he wanted to know which 'messages' were not coming across well enough. He was very strategic and this kind of marketing jargon suited him. It was the same with the concerts. Mick was interested in which songs the journalists particularly liked and he would scour the resulting coverage for comment. He was nothing if not methodical. He seemed to combine the role of lead singer and manager.

As we went from city to city, I spent most of my time managing logistics, making sure that the journalist from Australian *Playboy* was supplied with endless bowls of tiny garlic olives and a beer or two while the minutes ticked by and Mick became two and a half hours late for the interview.

One of the prerequisites of front-line PR is to always appear to be reassuringly in control of the situation whilst being as flexible as possible in case things don't go to plan and you need to readjust. It's never the client's fault, but always the fault of some unexpected business call or as yet diagnosed illness. The artist is dying to sit down with the journalist, but maybe just not this minute. I spent my time convincing journalists that theirs had been the cleverest or the funniest or the most relaxed interview that Mick or Keith had done that day. The key was to make them feel as if they had a moment of authentic connection, as that would mean a better article. Mick and Keith, in their own very different ways, knew how to give good copy.

The Stones had learned a lot about publicity from their original manager, Andrew Loog Oldham. The Beatles were nice guys in suits, so the Stones went the other way. Anti-heroes were popular all the way through the '60s, and not just in music – take Michael Caine's downbeat spy Harry Palmer, making eggs and bacon for a 'bird' in bed before slouching off to the office, which was a response to the cleaner-cut James Bond. Loog Oldham had duly dreamed up the picture of the Stones urinating against petrol pumps and leaked it to the *Daily Mirror*. Mick, Keith and bassist Bill Wyman were all fined £5, but the publicity was worth thousands.

Mick was a very smart, natural salesman. He understood that you had to turn the PR tap on when you had a product to sell, and off in between so you didn't saturate the market. His approach was always strategic. If he had a tour coming up, he'd know it was time to be visible and to be seen getting ready for the shows; images of Mick jogging would pop up in the *Daily Mirror* and newspapers would suddenly be welcome at the rehearsals. I learned lessons from Mick that would stay with me forever: how to prepare properly for interviews, how to imagine the subsequent story and how to, as much as possible, dictate its outcome. He was a mentor for me as much as my first boss, Keith Altham, had been.

The only member of the band who wasn't the slightest bit interested in publicity was drummer Charlie Watts, who seemed to be in a world of his own. I only ever managed to get him to do one press interview, and that was with the *Daily*

Telegraph, talking about upcoming Test matches with their cricket correspondent.

The band's professionalism and my legwork helped ensure the tour was well received. But never mind the '19th Nervous Breakdown', I started to worry if the intense pressure might give me my first. The band members wanted a report under their door each morning, including reviews of the previous night and the schedule of media to be done that day. This meant I had to run to the local railway station around midnight and find early editions of the newspapers, then rush back to the hotel, ignoring all the distractions, and sit behind the reception desk translating the reviews into English with the help of the staff, who I had pre-emptively 'charmed' with handfuls of free tickets. I then dressed the collection of papers with some fanzine-style cover – maybe some '50s US crime magazine artwork or communist propaganda I'd picked up in Chinatown – to create a newsletter, photocopied it and distributed it. That meant going around thirty or forty rooms and sliding it under everyone's door. Sometimes the hotels were very posh and the sight of a scruffy young kid running up and down the corridors caused alarm. That happened at the Kempinski on Kurfürstendamm – the West Berlin equivalent of Piccadilly – where the manager was informed about this weird behaviour and a slightly bewildered receptionist was sent up to investigate. I tried to explain that I was distributing press and '*das was gut*', but it was only when I mentioned the name Rolling Stones it was all cleared up. Anything they wanted was *gut*, seeing as they had taken so many rooms.

Some mornings, I found myself running alongside Mick on his morning jog, reading him the previous day's press clippings.

Days were long and hard, with calls back to the office in London to catch up on what was happening with our other clients on both the PR and management sides. Working for the Stones was exciting, yes, but very intense. I was absolutely exhausted.

Although I liked to think I got on with the band, I wasn't their friend. The world of the Stones was full of intrigue and politics; it was a bit like a medieval royal court with everyone jostling for influence and favour. Everyone was older than me and nobody was particularly friendly. The fact that I had been handpicked by Mick and Keith meant I wasn't exactly welcomed with open arms by some of the other characters in the Stones machine; the jealousies and rivalries were evident. I felt very lonely a lot of the time. My relationship with Mick was businesslike. Working with someone like him is always a bit *Upstairs, Downstairs*, so, naturally, he didn't include me in his social circle. He was charming and generally good company, but he didn't suffer fools. And that worked for me. All I really cared about was making their records successful or helping to sell out a tour. For the Stones themselves, however, the evenings were packed with lavish parties. In those days, the record companies competed to throw the biggest bash, whether it was an album launch at Penn Station in New York or hiring out an entire club.

Mick and Keith were going through a period of open warfare about their prospective solo careers and were barely on speaking terms. To Keith, the band was everything. However, he felt like Mick was more interested in recording his own albums and that a conspiracy was afoot to use the band as a platform for his own records. Rumours that Stones promoter Bill Graham was going to be Mick's main man made Keith incandescent. By the time I got caught in the crossfire, they were conducting much of their dialogue through the front pages of the *Sun* and the *Daily Mirror.* Needless to say, highly public 'off-the-record' comments weren't the best form of communication for repairing their relationship. Much of my time was spent undertaking crisis management, responding to Mick's outbursts, feeding them back to Keith and vice versa. I found myself empathising with Keith, partly because of our mutual love of reggae, but mainly because of his swaggeringly authentic style. Keith was always warm and generous with his time, and I really enjoyed talking to him about music. He was so authoritative and without doubt the heartbeat of the group. His manager, Jane Rose, was tough but always kind and straightforward in her dealings with me. She always had Keith's interests at heart and I liked her.

Mick's posse was led by a tall and very striking African-American woman called Alvenia Bridges, who had once been Jimi Hendrix's girlfriend. Keith used to do battle with her on a regular basis because she epitomised everything about Mick's seemingly flash and glamorous world that he didn't like. Arguments often got nasty. In one dramatic incident in a dressing room in Milan, Keith flew into a fury and called her a Black bitch, warning her not to get in the middle of him and Mick.

While moments like that were very serious, I now realise that the broader power struggle between Mick and Keith was really just a way for them to amuse themselves. It was like they were playing ping-pong with various personnel on the tour to see what would happen. I definitely started to feel like a pawn in the game and soon became aware of just how expendable I was.

After many of the gigs, we would fly back to Nice, which was the hub for the whole tour. This made sense to the Stones, as they had all decamped to France in the '70s and knew it well.

Bill 'Je Suis Un Rock Star' Wyman had a house in the South of France, and of course *Exile On Main Street*, the Stones' tenth studio album, had been recorded just down the road. The Côte d'Azur made for a rather splendid base. After all, who wanted to wake up in rainy old Düsseldorf?

A couple of weeks after I was sacked and unsacked, I was back in London. I hadn't realised how much stress I had been under until I got home and had what I can only describe as a kind of nervous breakdown. I needed some 'Emotional Rescue' myself. The Stones tour had been punishing – they were the biggest band in the world, playing huge stadiums before that was commonplace, so the pressure on me had been enormous, in addition to all the other bands I was PR-ing with the help of a handful of people in my office. I alone was representing the Stones throughout Europe, across thousands of print titles, TV channels and radio stations, with journalists from all the different countries bludgeoning me constantly with requests. I was having to try to make the right decisions about outlets that I had very little knowledge of without any easy reference points; I just had to figure everything out as I went. On top of that, while the members of the band could be lovely, fascinating, talented people as individuals, the politics and power struggles within the group were relentless. It seemed to bring out every bit of paranoia and competitiveness in them.

I would get a weird feeling that would come and go in waves: everything would seem a bit disjointed, colours seemed strange, sounds seemed too loud. I knew how bad it had got when I was at an event in Chelsea and started feeling ill. I got a cab back and thought I was about to have a heart attack – I felt like I couldn't breathe. Arriving home, I lay on the floor for hours thinking that I was going to die. It really frightened me because I had no forewarning it was going to happen.

Back then, people didn't talk about mental health, especially when it concerned men who were supposed to be keeping it together and running things. Who knows what would have happened if I'd gone to pieces. The vultures would have surely swooped. They managed that well enough when I was of sound mind and body. I had no idea what the problem was, which was half the problem. I found a book on stress and meditation, which helped me find ways to cope with these panic attacks – breathing exercises, clearing my mind – but I was keeping it all to myself. I was running a company, I had come all this way in the industry and if I said I was taking three months off for stress there would be no business when I got back. I knew that I'd have to find a way to get through this.

I went to a doctor who gave me some pills called Ativan. They helped to an extent, but I was concerned I'd become dependent on them. I cut down my intake, but I always kept one in my wallet just in case a panic attack hit me, which occasionally it did. Finally, I was put in touch with another doctor, who turned out to be my saviour. She was an older Spanish woman called Dr Gomez and was very no-nonsense in a motherly way, always telling me to 'pull myself together'. Strangely, her approach worked; I think I just needed a mother for few hours here and there. Talking it through with her gave me a great deal of inner strength and really helped me. But I would still get scared about the panic attacks happening – scared of having to make an excuse and find somewhere to be on my own for a quarter of an hour while I got it under control – which made me very withdrawn and uncomfortable socialising, which is not ideal for a PR. Every time I was invited to an event, I would dread it and get out of there as soon as possible.

Although I was in turmoil on the inside, on the outside I looked fine – in fact I looked more than fine because I was running and playing football so much to help me cope. That meant nobody knew there was anything wrong and nobody acted as sympathetically as they might if they had known what I was going through. How would a total collapse have impacted my family? In situations like this, you begin to understand how people slip through the cracks when they get mental health issues and end up on the street. It could happen.

It took me months to get over the worst of it. I ratcheted up the exercise, quit smoking, stopped drinking coffee and mastered my breathing exercises. I kept at least one of those pills in my wallet for years afterwards and while the attacks did revisit me now and again, by then I knew how to cope. I never uttered the phrase 'nervous breakdown' to anybody, though, because then people would say I wasn't cut out for this game. I tried to develop a recovery regime, or at least a way of managing my stress levels. One thing I taught myself to do was make a long-term plan and then cut it down into daily portions using a desk diary. This way things didn't look so potentially overwhelming. I'd look at what I'd set myself for the day ahead and stick to that as much as possible.

Above all, I promised myself that I wouldn't take such demanding work on. A week later, I got a call that would change my life for ever.

8

Let's Dance

'I'm sorry, sir. I understand, I really do,' said the stony-faced Perth Airport official. 'But without a visa I'm afraid there's nothing we can do. You'll have to take the next flight back to London.' I was starting to panic by this point. It had been a succession of mistakes over the previous thirty hours and ten thousand miles, as various people, in various countries, including Oman and Singapore, had told me I did, then didn't, need a visa to enter Australia – only for me now to be told in no uncertain terms that I *really* did. Out of desperation, I leant forwards, my career flashing before my eyes, my relationship with my most important ever client over before it could begin.

'But . . . David Bowie is waiting for me.' The official's eyes widened.

'*The* David Bowie?'

I nodded.

'Let's get you on your way then, darl.'

I checked into my hotel several hours later and decided I really needed a drink. As I was standing at the bar, I felt a tap on the shoulder and turned round to find a bemused and red-faced barfly.

'Well, it seems *you're* not a Sheila,' he slurred before he slalomed off in disappointment.

It was November 1983 and I was finally, belatedly, on tour with David Bowie. I was feeling especially fraught because I was originally supposed to join a few weeks earlier for the Asian leg of the tour. About two weeks before I was due to take off, I began to have misgivings about going on the tour at all. I was still burnt out from the Stones tour and trying to recover without anyone knowing there was anything to recover from. I was under pressure at the office – the Stones were becoming more demanding of my time – and I wasn't as prepared as I'd like to have been. I began to wonder whether it really was sensible to jet off to South-East Asia for months on end. On top of that, Valerie, who had become such an important part of my life, was pregnant and we were looking for a new house.

A few days before I was due to leave, it all came to a head in a long, rambling meeting with my partners, and they expressed concerns about me disappearing indefinitely on the Bowie tour. We had just moved to a new office in Notting Hill, which had increased our costs. They were of the opinion that it was more important that I concentrated on the Stones, and on the management front, we had a band called Big Country who were taking off Stateside.

It wasn't going to be easy to pull out of a David Bowie tour having already committed to it. But over two days of long conversations with Wayne Forte, David's agent, which included plenty of awkward silences, that's where we got to. It felt like my relationship with David Bowie was dead in the water.

David and I had first met in 1982 at the Carlton Tower in Knightsbridge, when I had lunch with him and his personal assistant Coco Schwab to discuss becoming formally involved. I'd heard that he'd been 'checking me out' for a few years, but this was our first proper meeting.

A couple of weeks later, we had a highly structured series of meetings over the course of a few days, including a long discussion at David's office on Fifth Avenue in New York. At one point, I was with him in the Power Station studio on West 53rd St while he happened to be recording 'Let's Dance' with Nile Rodgers (the studio's work experience kid was a very nice guy with the memorable name Jon Bon Jovi).

David was forensic in his questioning, although at all times incredibly charming and friendly. He was very interested in the people I knew and wanted to understand how close the relationships were, especially those from the punk world. He wanted to know all about the new generation of writers like the brilliant Tony Parsons from the *NME* and my friend Dylan Jones, who was then running *i-D*. He wanted to know about my strategies for generating positive coverage for clients.

It was clear that he wasn't one of those 'stay in lane' types of artists who just want a publicist to follow orders. Those clients end up with glorified PAs, not PRs. He was much cleverer than that and wanted to get right inside my head. He absorbed ideas from everyone around him and was almost sponge-like in that respect. Sometimes he has been portrayed as being very insular and even self-absorbed, but really he was the opposite. Once he had acquired every available bit of knowledge and advice he needed, he'd then decide on a strategy. He was a right magpie and relationships could be intense if not necessarily long-lasting. David was very clear, but at the same time flexible, and he was both pragmatic and decisive. He could also be ruthless when the situation required, but he was the quintessential gentleman. I got the job and was quickly hurled straight into the fray with a press conference at Claridge's.

Claridge's was about as swish as it got in those days. It had history, of course – Churchill stayed there during the war – but it was somehow still cool and contemporary. It was very classy, and perfect for David. This was in the days when press conferences were no-expense-spared affairs and journalists expected lavish treatment. There were mounds of food – piles of smoked salmon – and the waiters were omnipresent in black tie, hovering around the journalists.

With a conference of this size and importance, you spend weeks, even months, planning it – working out where TV people plug their leads in, where journalists stand, what kind of press pack they will get. On the day itself, you lose all sense of time; everything passes in a blur. The key is in the preparation and planning. As long as you've thought it out in advance, you're just playing your role and are generally there to keep the star happy.

I was the young kid on the block. The rival PR Bernard Docherty was also in the room as he was working with EMI. I'd come in to work on the tour and was becoming David's 'person', so there had been a little bit of tension about who the point man was for an event that would be about the tour *and* the album.

About seventy-five assembled journalists of one sort or another had been invited and they came from Europe as well as the UK. It was very much like a film star's press conference; you wouldn't have been surprised to see Elizabeth Taylor or David Niven walk out in front of the assembled throng.

David was absolutely brimming with confidence and good

vibes, looking every inch the star in a beautifully cut light grey suit and open-necked shirt, with blond hair and a suntan to die for. When he came downstairs, I had all the photographers lined up; there was quite a mob of them and we did a photo-call just before he entered the main room. In the room itself, the questions were fairly straightforward. There were piles of microphones and cassette recorders on the table in front of him. In those days, most journalists had a tape recorder, but they weren't infallible and the batteries had a tendency to run out. The older writers were still using pens and notepads.

David was obviously excited to be there, although he was coy when asked about the many millions he'd been paid by EMI for his new record deal. Prior to that he'd been at RCA, who had released the seminal albums *Low* and *Heroes*. But the relationship had run out of steam at the end. Even though both are still influential albums to this day, they didn't exactly smash the charts. In any case, David was thrilled to be with his new EMI family.

This conference wasn't just about launching his brilliant new album, *Let's Dance*, and the tour to support it, Serious Moonlight. David was also announcing he'd just completed the film *Merry Christmas, Mr. Lawrence*. He seemed as much a movie star as he was a rock star at that moment.

When you've got an artist at the top of their game and relaxed, then it's going to be a great day – and it was. It seemed to go by so fast. By the time David left Claridge's, we'd been there a few hours. Like all great stars, he knew when to leave the stage and didn't hang around.

My phone was ringing a lot and, coming off the back of the Stones, I was getting calls from friends I didn't even know I had, but it was David who was generating the real interest. There had been a phenomenal response to the single 'Let's Dance' around the world. And almost every venue he was booked to play was reporting huge demand for tickets. At some venues, demand outstripped supply by as much as five times and there were plans to try to bump him up to ever bigger and bigger venues. As with the Stones, this wasn't about convincing people they were interested in an act they'd never heard of; it was about people already desperate for a piece of something. Your job was to find the absolute best places to communicate one particular aspect of that phenomenon to the right audience. But while the Stones were a known quantity by the time I worked with them, David's new album and tour marked the moment that a beloved but fundamentally cult artist hit the mainstream.

There were constant meetings to attend at EMI in Manchester Square and calls with Coco and the management team in New York. There were also lots of conversations with Bill Zysblat, who so brilliantly took care of the financial side of things, and David's agent, Wayne Forte. They were the producers of the Serious Moonlight tour, which quite quickly everyone could see was going to take David to another level. Although very busy and still fragile from the end of the Stones tour, I told myself I would be working for one person so there wouldn't be the same complexity of issues and politics. Also, it was a long way away, which I think somehow suited me then. In fact, it couldn't be further away: Australia.

As the Bowie tour rumbled around the States in a highly organised if uneventful fashion, I was working long into the night trying to clear the decks. I spoke occasionally to tour photographer Denis O'Regan and there didn't seem to be much happening. He reported that he had chanced across David and Mick Jagger's ex-wife Bianca in a conversation, but not much else. I figured I hadn't missed much.

I attempted to collect information from the Japanese and Australian promoters, Mr Udo and Paul Dainty respectively. This proved surprisingly difficult, given the tricky time differences, and the fact that details were not terribly forthcoming from either party. I also had the added distraction of Mick Jagger's presence in London. Then I was off to Paris for the week to supervise Keith Richards' interviews. And it was starting to look like Big Country were on the brink of something in the US and that Ian and I needed to get out there soon.

This all culminated in me telling Wayne Forte that I now wouldn't be able to join for the first Asian leg. I sat there waiting for the phone call from Bowie or Coco, expecting them to either freak out at my unprofessionalism or try to cajole me into doing the tour after all. The call never came. A conversation with David personally would have embarrassed me to such a degree that I probably would have ended up boarding that Japan Airlines flight anyway. Apparently, Forte didn't even tell them about the problem until a day before they set off, and then they were so annoyed and let down that they thought it best not to call.

After this ordeal, the stress of thinking I might not get into Australia was the worst possible preparation for actually joining the tour. The next morning, after popping to the hotel shop and getting my mother a postcard of the beach, I spent the whole day reacquainting myself with the tour itinerary and preparing for the following day's press conference. With all the drama of the journey, I'd had virtually no time to prepare and subsequently had to compile lists of all the media attending and anticipate their questions in a real hurry. After lunch, I went out to the airport to meet the tour party. They had just flown in from Osaka but seemed cheerful despite the long trip. Coco had already called me and thankfully no mention was made of me blowing out the Japan tour at such short notice.

It seemed as though everyone else had forgotten it, too. Here I was with David in Australia, and everything was normal. A publicity meeting was scheduled for 7pm in his room to discuss the forthcoming press conference.

'Hello Alan, welcome. Have you invited the New Zealand press to the event? You should also know I am *extremely* keen to talk about what the *Sun* has reported I said about Aboriginal rights, or really the lack of them. I think there's plenty more to say, don't you?'

David was smoking heavily as usual and punctuated points with a jab of his cigarette. About the event, I waffled. Holding a press conference in Perth was akin to opening a US tour in, say, Alaska. It wasn't easy to get the sort of media turnout that a star of David Bowie's standing would normally expect.

David was at his best when he had something he felt truly engaged with. Off the back of videos for 'Let's Dance' and 'China Girl', he had done an interview with *Rolling Stone* where he'd likened parts of Australia to South Africa and decried the treatment of indigenous Australians. I got the impression that he was positively spoiling for a fight and the mention of journalist John Blake – who had recently written something suggestive about the 'Let's Dance' video that David objected to – still rankled. Between asking me questions, he called promoter Paul Dainty to see if there was any way a portable metronome could be produced to simulate the tempo and length of his songs, so he could use it on the beach to prepare before the concerts; musicians have a tendency to speed up songs live and David wanted to guard against that.

Just like Mick, when doing interviews David prepared like a consummate professional. He didn't hide from the press or rely on anodyne soundbites. He would pepper me with probing questions: Why are we doing this? Couldn't we secure that publication? What is the reach of such and such a radio station? How big is a newspaper's circulation? The questions were unpredictable, but you needed to be prepared. Still, it brought out the best in me and was much better than working with someone sloppy who didn't really care what they were doing. In that environment, you were far more likely to switch off and make mistakes.

David loved reading and it followed that he really bonded with writers. He had many friends in that area and developed new friendships with writers all the time: Hanif Kureishi, Tony Parsons, Jérôme Soligny . . . The list was endless. Part of my job was to keep all those lines of communication open. This was high-end PR and I was in my element. Still, there was plenty of nuts-and-bolts stuff to do and I kept up a steady flow of stories about sell-outs and interesting stars attending the shows Down Under to the global press.

By nature, David was an optimist and totally positive – and so it was with the media. He exuded enthusiasm and energy, and only the most contrary or mean-spirited writer wouldn't be swept along by it. He was also so prescient that writers tended to look at him correctly as something of a guru. His thoughts on any number of subjects were pondered over and analysed. He was certainly the teacher I'd never had.

When an interview did go wrong, or a cover fell through, he'd assess the situation quickly and move on. He wasn't one for recriminations or long sulky periods of introspection. As a PR, I knew when I'd messed up, sometimes because of factors beyond my control, such as when an editor decides to put someone else on a magazine cover. I, too, kept going. It was another illustration of David knowing how to get the best out of people. He understood the obvious fact that you wanted your publicist of all people to be imbued with self-confidence and positivity, not hesitant and afraid of making a mistake. This was one of the many things that went into making him great as opposed to merely good. It's simple stuff in some ways, but you'd be amazed how few artists get that and how many fall for the myth that they have total control, which of course they don't.

The Perth conference itself was almost dull. Half a dozen TV crew and forty or so journalists asked predictable questions about the nature of touring – deeply thoughtful enquiries like, 'What is the name of the tour?' It only gained life when David made a statement against nuclear weapons and the stupidity of the arms race. I was pleased because at least he was putting his powerful platform to good use – and, of course, guaranteeing a few column inches, which was probably what the old master had in mind. I made copious notes, ready to feed nuggets back to London. Afterwards, there were a couple of short radio interviews, one of which started to go wrong when the interviewer asked David if it was true that he changed his name from David Jones to avoid being confused with one of the Monkees. David gave a perfunctory yes and a toothy smile, to which the interviewer asked, 'Which one?' David was temporarily thrown and began to look irritated. He said something about the lack of time and how disappointed he was not to be able to continue talking, and made it clear the interview was over.

After the shows, there would often be one of Paul Dainty's disco parties. These were lively affairs attended by everyone on the tour and a dozen or so inevitably blonde models. David seemed to enjoy these soirees and took the opportunity to relax a bit, putting enormous amounts of energy into chatting with everyone. Even as he held court, he disappeared regularly downstairs to a suite with one of the agents, fuelling rumours. One wag called it the 'serious nosebleed' tour. For a couple of the parties, Duran Duran, who were also touring in Australia, were present. At the Melbourne afterparty, the champagne glasses clinked and the blondes made increasingly desperate glances in David's direction. I was talking to a good-looking girl in a short white dress when David came over. I introduced the two of them and David commented that the dress she was wearing was really 'dirty'. The *Vogue* model, aghast, replied, 'Jesus, I only washed it this morning!' She also expressed surprise that Mr Bowie would wear slippers at such an important do. She wasn't joking.

In Adelaide, the show ended up taking place in the pouring rain with Bowie wearing a raincoat and, Rex Harrison style, jokingly inserting lines such as 'Rain, rain go away, come again some other day' in a posh Pommie voice. This was perfect for local titles like the *Australian*, the *Age* and the *Sydney Morning Herald*, not to mention our old mates the *Sun* and the *Daily Mirror* back in Blighty. Denis O'Regan cooked up a couple of images to wire back and I let my imagination run wild, as the amounts of rain and the numbers in the crowd increased with every retelling.

My relationship with David had grown more relaxed. Shortly after he met with state premier John Bannon in Adelaide, he said to me out of the blue, 'It's a shame you didn't come to Japan with us.' He often joshed about my supposed liking of the 'low' side of life. I wasn't sure if he was referring to the album. Somehow, I was developing a real 'walk on the wild side' reputation. It was just that I was inexorably drawn to the edgier, more exciting parts of the towns we visited. I didn't usually go out much anyway, given my limited budget, even if the per diems were reasonable.

In Melbourne, David said he wanted to pop in to the taping of the final episode of *The Don Lane Show* as a surprise guest. When he appeared, the studio audience went so wild they had to be shushed so the interview could happen. David was utterly charming, said he was a big fan of the show and even managed to smile sweetly when he reminded Don he hadn't worn outlandish costumes for going on a decade now.

At a poolside party hosted by Molly Meldrum, presenter of the hugely popular music show *Countdown*, an array of Australian music biz people rubbed shoulders with David's entourage. The food was served by good-looking young men in togas, and everything was Roman-themed. I think the orgy was later. It was fun although, embarrassingly, we all had to watch *Countdown* when it came on the enormous TV screen at 6pm.

One day, lounging around the hotel pool in Melbourne, David kept cracking up in hysterics. He was listening to a tape of comedian Barry Diamond that I'd given him. He asked if he could borrow it – I made plans to buy another at the next possible opportunity.

I think we were all happy enough to leave Melbourne,

although the thought of scorching temperatures in Brisbane was on everyone's mind. We needn't have bothered with all the sun cream. The bad weather that had plagued the tour continued to roll in. No sunshine and low temperatures was quite an event in this part of the world in late November.

I finally felt I had fully decompressed from touring with the hugely difficult and strong personalities that were the Stones. More than that, this tour felt suffused with energy, as everyone recognised that we were present at the moment a genuine superstar was being born. David was so confident in who he was during this phase of his career that being around him motivated us all.

On our day off, I hired a car and drove up the coast one hundred miles or so with Denis and Glenis Daly, David's hairdresser on the tour. David, it later turned out, had done the same thing – he was often in the habit of hiring a car and just taking off. That evening he joined Wayne, Coco and me for a Mexican dinner. He was tired and, when we couldn't get a table at first, irritable. When we finally sat down, a pair of autograph hunters came up to the table and started with the classic 'I hope you don't mind', but David interrupted, 'Actually I do mind, I'm just about to start my meal.'

He brightened up during dinner and talked expansively about his love of skiing and of the thrill of a freshly powdered slope. The conversation switched to precious stones, about which he was very knowledgeable. He explained, presumably referring to diamonds, how you had to be careful what you bought in Hong Kong. Unsurprisingly, I hadn't bought any diamonds on my last visit there so wasn't unduly worried.

On the way back to the hotel, we mused on whether Duran

Duran were just the new Bay City Rollers. David felt they should probably grab the money while the going was good. Japanese synth-pop band Sandii and the Sunsetz were a current favourite of his in more ways than one, so the story went. He was disappointed to hear that in England things weren't really happening for them. His other current listening was the new Stones album, *Undercover.* I gave him a tape of Big Country and he remarked on them being something like the Who. He didn't make any more comments about the Scottish rockers, although I did hear him whistling the single 'In a Big Country' one afternoon.

By now I was beginning to be driven crazy by the Sydney press, ahead of us arriving there. Unable to get interviews with David, they harried me for background bits. What does he do on his day off? The *Sun*, like their British counterpart, got very creative. I had given them some pretty innocuous stuff about David doing some boxing training. I opened the paper next morning to see a full-page news story inviting *Sun* readers down to the beach to 'watch him train'. I regretted talking to them at all and I didn't include this gem in my regular press newsletter for the tour. There was also a racy story about some girls trying to book fifteen minutes with Mr Bowie because they were professional groupies. Tour manager Arnold Dunn added that he sometimes rescued girls from band members' rooms at 4am. I made an executive decision and mislaid that story too. A couple of days later, Coco made some joke about my memory going and me forgetting to show her certain newspapers. For once I hoped the UK media didn't pick up on coverage around the Bowie Australian tour.

The backstage scene at Sydney Cricket Ground was wild. About ninety-nine per cent of the Australian film industry had been invited. I was sent around beforehand with Denis to identify the movers and shakers so we would recognise them when it came to captioning the pictures. By now I was an old hand at preparing for these meet and greets. Everything happened in a blur and you had to have your targets and little one-liners worked out in advance. I noted down simple descriptions of the local VIPs, such as glasses, hair colour, weight and style of clothes. These aides de memoire enabled me to swan around gracefully, introducing David to people. Great importance was placed on the whole event because David was clearly in the market for interesting film roles. Even when *Mad Max* director George Miller showed up late, he was ushered backstage to David's caravan. Rarely had I seen David so deferential.

It wasn't all glamour behind the scenes, though. In Perth, David had taken the time to meet with three young people with short life prospects. He talked with them for ten or fifteen minutes and happily posed for their snapshots. No press photographers were present at all.

Balancing the demands of the tour with those of the media was a challenge – and this was when I decided to put in the hard yards 'as' Bowie for one of the radio interviews. David fetishised print, but wasn't so worried about radio as there wasn't a physical product afterwards. To his mind, it just aired and was gone. But I knew local radio was especially important. Australia, like other geographically large countries like the US and Germany, had well-developed federalised local news markets. This went back to the days of newspapers, when you couldn't physically distribute a single newspaper across such vast distances, and it carried over into radio. So, as a band, you could be big in Sydney, but if you didn't put the time in, this meant nothing in Perth.

No one was especially looking forward to New Zealand and, on the plane, tour manager Frankie Enfield told me about his last visit there with Joe Jackson. 'Deadly dull, wet and ultra conservative' is how he described the country. It sounded as exciting as a trip to the Falklands. We made jokes about doing a concert in Goose Green next as the plane lurched in through the thick cloud cover.

As Frankie predicted, Wellington was cold, damp and cheerless, with high winds under oppressively low grey clouds, and the Park Royal, the city's best hotel, was dreadful. Room service that never came, tea without milk, a phone that stuck so when you lifted the receiver it just carried on ringing, a key that broke in the lock, chambermaids who left your room door wide open after cleaning, a missing pair of shoes mistakenly returned to the wrong room – and that was just the first day.

The following day, David received a traditional Māori welcome at one of the local marae. There was a meeting with an elder, and every second of the proceedings was carefully planned. We sat down to watch a children's dance and listen to speeches. There was no press allowed, only TV, and in any case Denis was in the doghouse for having failed to shoot enough colour on the tour so far. He was also pilloried for having his back turned whenever David arrived at the venues and failing to take the all-important 'fans go crazy' images, which I would then send out suitably embellished.

David was in a good mood when I went back to see him in his hotel room to approve the latest press release. He had enjoyed the day and knew that we had some strong publicity material to disseminate. He was lounging in front of a video player watching a dramatisation of President Kennedy's life, which he told me he found highly amusing. We checked the press release together. Focusing momentarily on my appallingly bad spelling and poor punctuation, he muttered something about real writers not needing to bother with that sort of thing. Maybe his love of William Burroughs' stream-of-consciousness style of writing inspired that comment, but right now, as I try to pen this book, I couldn't agree more.

Backstage at Athletic Park, the rugby ground in Wellington where David was playing, I'd lined up interviews with a radio station, a TV show and a freelance journalist. He came out of one TV interview chortling, having outwitted them and dodged questions he didn't fancy. Out front, the 50,000 audience were drinking, fainting and throwing up – not necessarily in that order. The concert was marred by bottles being thrown and fans being passed over the crash barriers. On several occasions, Bowie stopped the show.

Auckland was more interesting. The tour was nearly over and the concert, at a speedway stadium called Western Springs, looked set to become the biggest-ever concert in Australasia. Seventy-eight thousand tickets had been sold, easily breaking the previous record of fifty-eight thousand, held by Dire Straits. It was a good way to conclude the tour. Most of the band members were doing interviews, which also boosted morale. It can get depressing for the backing band when they don't get their moment in the media spotlight too. A paper had even been found to talk to backing singers Frank and George Simms, although apparently not to saxophonist Stan Harrison, who was the only person bar Coco not to be interviewed on the whole tour. Coco would never have dreamt of talking to the press. She and I were good chums by this point, and we often wandered out in search of adventure. On the evening before the Auckland show, Coco recalled how the trendy place we were dining in had been home for David Hemmings when he had been filming in the country. Later that night, we wandered into a rowdy pub and watched a long-haired band pump out blues at top volume.

Back at camp, an irritated member of the production team informed me that there would be no photo passes tomorrow. It was a decision aimed at preventing photographers from regaining access to the site after taking their agreed three shots. Wayne asked me to accompany Denis down to the site in the meantime to get snaps of the $40,000 video screen that had been flown in from LA. Eventually Denis and I found some time to go over all the photographs from the tour. It was 2am by now and we could hardly keep our eyes open, but tomorrow would be too busy. Everything was getting intense because I would be off to the US in a couple of days to finally join Big Country out there. I seemed to spend my entire time frantically typing out copy or making calls to the office, having sweet-talked a receptionist susceptible to an English accent. Though we had several people in our office, there was no one qualified to make the big decisions on anything PR-related, so I would be faced with a long list of things to approve every time I phoned.

The Auckland show was memorable, mainly for David releasing two white doves and making a short anti-war speech, which was definitely a theme with him at the time. On returning to the hotel, I found there was a party. A troupe of indigenous dancers took the floor and the band sat around cross-legged, watching this ancient ritual intently. David moved onto the dancefloor for a samba-style rhumba. A cake was wheeled in and David unceremoniously chopped at it with a carving knife before members of the crew joined him. He made a short thank-you speech, and I slipped upstairs with promoter Michael Gidunski for an end-of-tour smoke.

The next day, I furiously tied up any loose ends and got a call from Coco, who briefed me about an inaccurate story describing violence at the show that David had been upset by. I went up to his room, where I suggested I assemble a counternarrative emphasising the comparable trouble that happens with football crowds. David and I had come to know each other well by this stage and he wandered around quite unaffectedly in his dressing gown talking to me. When it came to the parting of the ways, he said, 'We'll be working again next year, so it's au revoir and not goodbye.' I took a moment for a deep breath. Then it was time to head to America.

9

A Big Country

'Hello gentlemen, how may I help you?' A large Italian-American gentleman is at the door of the Portacabin wearing an intimidatingly well-cut suit.

I look at Ian and he looks back at me. We are in a breaker's yard on the outskirts of Philadelphia, surrounded by hundreds of piled-up cars in different states of destruction and a serious-looking wrecking ball; something about the place suggests it has probably been used to compress more than just cars in its time. Our limousine, paid for by the record company, had left us at the gate and we'd trodden gingerly over broken glass and metal to reach the cabin.

I hold up the bag full of hundred-dollar bills and point at it. 'We'd like to discuss a chart position.'

The guy beckons us in. I am twenty-eight years old and, all of a sudden, this feels a very long way away from music PR. Welcome to music management in the '80s.

I had come off the Bowie tour in New Zealand and gone straight to New York to join Big Country on tour. While I'd been away, their single 'In a Big Country' and the album it was from had been picking up serious attention. I was re-energised by being back on the crisp, busy New York streets trying to drum up more enthusiasm for the band, and I was also doing a bit of Bowie work, including a visit to MTV, where David had recently given an interview in which he took them to task for not playing videos by African-American artists.

The main man in Big Country, Stuart Adamson, who I hoped would take the media by storm Bowie-style, was in a dark mood, talking to no one. I went for a coffee with the bass player and guitarist, and on the way over to the NBC TV studios, I told them a few Australian tour yarns. Their *Saturday Night Live* appearance went well, although the group were visibly nervous, a bit dour – lots of expressions of concentration. I wrote an altogether more upbeat version of events for the press release.

Backstage, the record company was out in force, although the executives seemed to spend most of their time taking coke. Although I'd fallen in line a couple of times, I didn't do coke. In fact, I'd grown to almost despise it. I hated the way it turned some musicians and executives into irrational egomaniacs. I was also frustrated at seeing all that valuable cash that could be used for tour support and videos for my bands just going up people's noses.

I spotted world heavyweight boxing champion (and fellow guest) Larry Holmes, accompanied by seven massive bodyguards, all dark glasses and suits, and I joined their procession until the seven non-dwarves halted at the door of Holmes' dressing room. One by one, they turned their heads in my direction. I introduced myself and asked whether Larry would be willing to meet an exciting new British band, all of whom were big fans, and have his picture taken with them. The big man was very gracious and the band were thrilled. One of the guys took great pride in getting an autograph for his son – he'd already got those of Kenny Dalglish, Cliff Richard and Paul McCartney. Later that night, they met Muhammad Ali in the foyer of the Berkshire Palace Hotel. After *Saturday Night Live*, we had gone back to the hotel in a limo and I'd read the football results aloud. No one bothered to go out that night; we'd probably had enough rock and roll lifestyle for the time being.

Big Country came out of a Scottish punk band we had managed called the Skids, who hit the big time, briefly, in 1979 with the song 'Into the Valley'. When I went to see them at Hammersmith Palais, I realised that the real star of the band wasn't the charismatic frontman but the keyboard player – the quiet guy hanging back in the shadows. That man was Stuart Adamson, and it turned out that Ian was right across this already.

As the Skids began to disintegrate, Ian started putting a band together around Stuart – and thus, in 1981, Big Country had been born. One of their early gigs was supporting Alice Cooper at the Brighton Centre. Even though the line-up wasn't fully settled, you could see something special was happening.

Their sound was blue-collar Scottish rock and, following the release of 'In a Big Country', when I had been over the other side of the world with David Bowie, they had started playing to 2,000 sweaty people a night. That they weren't flashy or showbiz was part of the charm and *Melody Maker*, the *NME* and other music papers rallied behind them.

With their working-class appeal, they found a natural fit on the East Coast and started performing in places like New Jersey, Boston, Cleveland, Philadelphia and New York, which made sound business sense, but led to a series of very samey postcards to my mother. They were suddenly getting a lot of attention and airplay, so we wanted to ensure maximum support from their label. However, we didn't think the record company was doing enough and decided to try to terminate the contract. Shep Gordon recommended we go see a lawyer called Allen Grubman because 'he's a guy who gets things done'.

We duly went along to Mr Grubman's office for our first meeting. On my right in reception was a quiet, punky girl who went by the name of Madonna. Allen yelled and bawled and was incredibly entertaining; we could already hear him from where we were sitting. On that occasion, he was in the process of switching Joan Jett from one label to another.

Allen represented half the executives in music and worked with industry legends like Warner chief executive Mo Ostin. He certainly seemed like a man who got things done and, by the sound of it, things were being done constantly. It was thrilling and a far cry from a staid English solicitor's office with chiming clocks and chaps in pinstripe suits. Allen seemed to literally slobber with excitement when big deals were going down. His right-hand guy, Paul Schindler, was relatively mild-mannered in comparison. Paul's PA, Barbara, was brilliant and made sure that we always got a spot in his diary.

Despite Allen's stature, his support couldn't get the band off their label. What we did do, however, was negotiate a guaranteed advance against a quarter of a million albums in the US, regardless of how many we actually ended up shifting.

In the UK, promotion just meant buying adverts in newspapers or taking Radio 1 DJs out to dinner and encouraging them to support the latest release. In the US, we discovered the word had a whole different meaning. The beginnings of 'promotion' went all the way back to a rock and roll DJ called Alan Freed. Freed wasn't in it for the love of music. There's a famous story about a young, naïve plugger bringing in a record for him to spin. Freed looked at him quizzically and shook the disc sleeve. Still, the wide-eyed promo kid had no idea what was going on. When nothing fell out on the table, Freed fixed him with a knowing look and said, 'Son, this record isn't a hit.' What was missing, of course, was a dollar bill. This system had evolved into what was known as 'payola'.

Payola had a strong hold on the entertainment business in the US, and on record promotion in particular. The mob had live music promoters onside; they controlled jukeboxes and owned record pressing plants. They had American radio locked down and if you wanted airplay, you had to deal with them. We would soon learn how the system worked.

Around the US, there were about three thousand radio stations making up a very complicated patchwork that wasn't really regulated at all. Some of these stations were very small with just a couple of guys working there, spinning the latest local country or bluegrass track. They were very easy to 'get at' and definitely open to persuasion and extra incentives to say that they had played a record they'd never even heard of. Unlike the British charts, the American hit parade was partly compiled from airplay. This was extremely hard to monitor. The more 'adds' you got, the more stations were playing your song. We started hearing whispers about something called 'paper adds'. Could this have something to do with newspapers, I wondered. But no, it referred to phantom plays of records that, in many cases, hadn't even been pressed yet. All the radio station manager had to do was say he'd played a record in the middle of the night and, lo and behold, an envelope would turn up on his desk bulging with cash – or there would be a 'delivery' of whatever got them through the night, be that coke or hookers. When enough mythical plays of the record were reported from around the country, the record label would then press up some copies and distribute them to retail. Crazily, the record often showed up high in the charts before the single had even been decided on.

A week or so before we were due to make our trip to arrange our own bit of payola, we went in to meet the record company, where somebody told us what it would take to get what we wanted. A few days later, we went to the Manhattan Bank on 7th Avenue. The cashier didn't blink; maybe we weren't the first young music people to request a massive amount of cash at this branch of the bank. We put carefully counted dollar bills in a holdall and wandered out into the bustling street full of folks getting their lunch in a hurry, like all this was perfectly normal.

We decided we should keep the bag close to us at all times. Leaving it in a hotel like the Mayflower, where we were staying, would have been more than risky. It would have been a lovely surprise for one of the chambermaids or an enterprising junkie, though. So, we went around town with our luggage in hand, making our way through the crowds on 8th Avenue to get into Polydor Records or turning back down to West 56th to go into ICM and meet our agent, Marsha Vlasic. Marsha always seemed to be yelling, 'Get me Bill Elson on the phone!' followed by, 'I want to speak Seth in Cleveland, now!' She would then shout into the receiver that they didn't know what was really happening with new bands and that they should book our acts immediately. Everyone stood to attention and, as we got to know Marsha, we realised she was really a nice lady – and just very good at her job.

We plonked the valuable bag down beside us wherever we went. Only once did we forget it altogether, and it wasn't until we were down on Broadway that we remembered we'd left it in a record shop a few blocks back. Nobody thought to mug a couple of rock guys who probably didn't have two cents to rub together. The cash was hidden in plain sight.

Later in the day, we'd go up to our favourite restaurant, Nirvana, on the thirtieth floor of a building overlooking Park West. Ian loved it because John Lennon used to go there, but I was just pleased to eat good Indian food, which was hard to find in New York at that time. The whole place was decorated with curtains and carpets hanging on the walls, so it was like walking into a Sgt Pepper video. From there, we'd go on to CBGB to see who was playing, or Danceteria, where we once met members of Big Audio Dynamite.

When the day of our trip to Philadelphia finally dawned, we stepped into our limousine, which seemed almost as long as the city blocks we passed on the way out of town. Soon we were thundering down the freeway, music blaring, shades on and generally living the dream. And then we arrived at the Portacabin.

We followed the big guy inside and, to our astonishment, found the cabin had been transformed into an oak-panelled boardroom. There were oil paintings of racehorses on the walls and a luxurious, thick-pile carpet. We'd come out of bright sunshine and suddenly it was all shadows and low mood lighting, like we were in the back room of one of the better restaurants in Little Italy. There were three or four guys there, all wearing beautiful silk suits. My eyes also registered the bulges in their jackets, and even I knew those weren't wallets. These geezers were the real deal and all had names like Joey or Big Tony.

Everyone was very civilised. The big man behind the desk said, 'OK, limeys, so tell us what you want.'

'Ummm, we would like number twenty-three in the alternative, thirty-two in the rock charts and twenty-five in the pop charts,' I said, as if I was reading out something in front of the class at school. 'Please.'

The guy behind the imposing desk, who seemed to be the top don, looked us up and down, not taking his shades off, and said, 'OK, that'll be $70,000.' We opened the holdall and stood there while they counted the money out. Neither of us had dipped into it and, luckily, no desperate band members had helped themselves in the middle of the night. The money was all present and correct.

There were no further niceties, the meeting was fairly brief and before we could say 'Godfather', we were picking our way a little more speedily back through the wreckage in the breaker's yard. At no time were we actually nervous. It's incredible how we felt we had some sort of invisible protection around us. It must have been the arrogance of youth or the fact that we were living in a rock and roll bubble. After all, we were just the bagmen.

We got back to New York that night and we hung out late, although the next morning I was up early, as always. I went for a run in Central Park and then to a health food café on West 57th, where they served granola and bananas. I'd got into eating healthily in the late '70s after my first trip to California. You soon realise that if you want to stay in this business, especially on the road, you'd better keep yourself in good condition.

From there, I headed over to 7th Avenue for a meeting at Big Country's label, which is what I mainly did in New York.

The following week, we eagerly awaited the arrival of the *Billboard* chart. Although there were other tip sheets and trade magazines like *Cashbox*, *Billboard* was definitely the bible. It's a massive beast, over a hundred pages. We scanned to see what position our proteges have reached in the charts, if at all. And there it was: exactly what we'd asked for. The new Big Country single in at number 23! It was proof indeed that, in the American music industry, money talks and bullshit walks. Of course, it's possible that the guys we did business with had somehow got the chart positions a week early from an insider at the magazine and we were just unwittingly paying a tribute. Anything was possible – only in America.

It all seemed completely normal – and it was then. This sort of 'promotion' was above board. Or, at least, everyone did it. The whole industry was run on it. However, because it was a grey area, it was also kept a little vague in terms of accounting. It was only in later years that record companies realised quite how much money was disappearing. One business was allegedly losing $7m a year on 'promotion' and most of it was being siphoned off in ways that couldn't be explained. There was definitely no paper trail, only green things with George Washington's face on them. To quote Bob Dylan, somebody better investigate soon.

Eventually the industry tried to clamp down. A guy from a radio station in Florida became a whistleblower and started talking about what was going on. Unfortunately, he just happened to get mugged and shot six times in the legs on his way home from work. Bill Clinton did get the whole thing to court in the end and a few people were punished. Someone probably went to jail.

When we were dealing with the record company in New York, the head of promotions was widely supposed to be working for the mob. He left suddenly one day and his boss found millions of dollars' worth of unpaid bills for hookers, cocaine and even foreign holidays for radio executives in his desk drawer. This was a very big and dangerous business.

Returning to the UK after this stint with Big Country, it was a relief to be meeting a Radio 1 person for a cup of tea and cheese roll at the Great Portland Street café.

However pleased I was to be back on home soil, I was almost immediately required to fly out to the States again, this time with my PR hat on. Hall & Oates were a band who suffered from a lack of credibility, despite a string of excellent hit singles in the US. Daryl Hall was tall with blond flowing hair and John Oates shortish and dark with a moustache. They could have been a comedy duo. I had been hired to try and change this situation. A press trip to Florida was arranged to see the band in action and convince journalists that there was more to them than met the eye.

On arrival at the venue in Miami, we bumped into the band's manager Tommy Mottola backstage, a real music industry legend. He was wearing a fur coat and had a girl on each arm. He asked me what were we doing there. I reminded him that we had come to interview his band. He looked surprised. Evidently there had been a miscommunication somewhere and we weren't expected.

The next day I received a call from the always amusing

Randy Hoffman, who handled the band's day-to-day affairs. He told me to entertain the journalists and wait to be summoned. The interviews would happen soon, I was assured.

None of us had ever stayed in a hotel like the Fontainebleau, which was Miami's best. We gorged ourselves on endless room service and then, to our amazement, we found a shopping mall downstairs with high-end clothes which we could also charge to our rooms.

The bills mounted and there was no sign of an interview. Had we had been forgotten? Were the band still in town? I thought I had better come up with an itinerary of activities for the press. Otherwise, the saying that the devil makes work for idle hands could come true and we'd end up with press stories about the trip being an expensive fiasco. We spent the day at the beach, but on returning to the hotel, there was still no news about our chat with the band.

The next day I organised something more adventurous, hiring a car and driving down to the Florida Keys. We spent the day looking for crocodiles and hanging out at Hemingway's bar. Days turned into nearly a week and I couldn't let things drift any further. I spoke to Randy Hoffman, explaining that I couldn't control the situation much longer and that the journalists would be heading back to the airport soon, interview or no interview.

That did the trick and within hours we were sitting down at the swimming pool talking to Daryl and John. Barry Cain from *Record Mirror*, Hugh Fielder from *Sounds* and Rick Sky from the *Star* were lined up for what would be innocuous chats squeezed into the bands' busy promo schedule. Rick Sky's interview seemed a bit off the wall, but by this point I wasn't going to make any fuss.

Everything ended on a positive note and we flew back to London, sorry that our unexpected vacation hadn't been permanent, but glad to have got the interview in the bag. I assumed that the insightful articles about how Hall & Oates were part of the great American song tradition might deter the label from examining our expenses too closely.

Even by the *Star*'s outrageous standards, Rick Sky's story about how Hall and Oates' hit singles were chosen by a parrot was a bit much. Daryl had let slip to Rick that he owned a parrot and that it would often chirp along whilst he was working on the songs. He explained that the parrot was particularly expressive when it was a hit tune. Rick had turned that nugget into an article suggesting that the parrot was in fact fulfilling the duties of an A&R man, selecting the singles. For a group that lacked respect and were seen by some as an industry-manufactured outfit, this was the last sort of publicity we wanted. Secretly, though, I wondered if the parrot might do just as good a job as some of the real A&R men I'd met.

The decade so far had been a blur. I sometimes felt that I spent most of my life in airports or at the side of the road, shouting into payphones, and spent the rest of it at parties being shouted at by music executives who went to the toilets every five minutes. I dreaded to think how many complimentary packets of airline peanuts I had consumed. The whole thing felt like a fairground ride I couldn't get off.

Then, one night, I was standing in Middlesex Hospital in London, holding my and Valerie's first daughter, Josey. As I stood cradling her, looking out over the city, I felt as if I'd stopped moving for the first time in my life.

10

Electric

'OK, Alan. Tell me what's up.'

It was 1986 and I was sitting in a hotel in California, telephoning a UK A&R for his opinion on his stateside execs before we went in for a meeting with them. The label he worked for were one of a number of US outfits who wanted to sign our band, the Cult, and they were competing with Seymour Stein – the legendary founder of Sire Records – and the execs at Chrysalis, among others. One executive at Geffen had flown to London by Concorde to woo us, taking us out to La Gavroche, one of the fanciest restaurants in town, only to be turned away as he wasn't wearing a tie.

PolyGram, who hadn't even been remotely interested some months earlier, suddenly came storming in with a very punchy six-figure offer. It was hard to know what to do with all the contracts that were now on the table, so Ian and I needed someone who would tell us the truth, hence my call to the A&R man. I set out the situation and then asked for his honest opinion. What were the US execs there like?

'Scumbags!' was his fervent response.

The Cult had emerged out of a post-punk band called

Southern Death Cult when, in 1983, the lead singer Ian Astbury had decided to form a new group under the simplified name.

The first time I saw them play, it was obvious to me that their image was great and that they'd be really newsworthy. Ian was mesmeric as a frontman. The lead guitarist, Billy Duffy, was a traditional rock god on stage who was, offstage, very down to earth and the perfect foil for Astbury. They had started gaining traction as a live act in the UK at about the same time as Big Country had. Whenever I was in the UK, I seemed to be touring with one or the other. Bradford, Newcastle, Edinburgh – the novelty quickly wore off. The accommodation was always dismal, often a run-down B&B with chintzy curtains and a creaky bed. Breakfast was usually cold toast and weak tea, with an orange juice out of a tin if you were dead lucky. I often felt homesick, even though home was often only a couple of hours' drive away. Strangely, I always felt happier abroad, particularly in France – it seemed exotic, with the warmer climate and different cuisine. I had developed a familiarity with the more casual French lifestyle on school exchanges. However, the bands loved the northern itinerary and the wild audiences – much of them female – that came with it. They would party into the night and I would retire to my hotel room and read.

Ian Astbury came from a working-class background, growing up in Cheshire, then Ontario, Canada. Nobody could ever accuse him of being bland. The band had a predominantly gothic image, although Ian was very into the psychedelic thing too. Native American history and culture were his main passions, as well as a fascination with a German naval commander called Otto Kretschmer, who had sunk forty-four Allied ships during the Second World War.

Ian had a habit of getting into 'misunderstandings' with the security guards at venues. One night, this memorably led to him having to be smuggled past them by the then unknown support band Guns N' Roses. Patience wasn't one of his virtues, as he demonstrated once in the reception of the Holiday Inn in Portsmouth. It was during the summer holidays and families were checking in: children with buckets and spades, tourists in lurid shirts. Ian, irritated by how long it was taking, pulled a bottle of whisky out of his bag and smashed it over his head. Glass shattered everywhere, and the smell of alcohol saturated the air. It was his rather unique way of saying he wanted to check in as soon as possible, please.

On one occasion, Ian daubed paint all over the walls of his room at another Holiday Inn, this time in Swiss Cottage. The tour manager realised we were in a lot of trouble so, using his initiative, he went over the road to a hardware shop and bought a tin of paint to cover it all up. As he was wrapping up his brilliant DIY, the hotel manager knocked on the door. Other guests had complained about the raucous behaviour and noise in the room, and he had been sent to investigate. He couldn't see anything amiss but wondered why he could smell paint. Unknowingly he leant against the wall and, when he turned to leave, discovered he was covered in the stuff. He was furious. The Cult were banned for life and that was the end of our Holiday Inn stays.

But just a few years later, we found ourselves regularly in the US and the Holiday Inn ban became less of an issue. It had become customary for us to stay at the Sunset Marquis, the legendary rock hotel in West Hollywood, or at Le Parc around the corner. There was a global touring circuit by then and each city seemed to have a specific watering hole for bands. In London, it was the Montcalm or Royal Garden. It was the Sebel Townhouse in Sydney, the Kempinski in Berlin, the Warwick in Paris, the Mayflower in New York and the Sunset in LA – unless you were a metal band in which case it was the Hyatt (known as the Riot House), while cooler film-industry types plumped for the Chateau Marmont. The choice of hotel was partly driven by the enterprising deals of various travel agents, but also by the proximity to the venue or record company. The liberal attitude of certain hotel managers, who could be relied on to turn a blind eye to funny cigarettes being smoked and women being smuggled into musicians' bedrooms, was also a deciding factor. The one thing I noticed at all these establishments as I checked into a room was the fruit wrapped in cellophane with knife and plate. If it was an especially upmarket place, there would be a cookie and card from a general manager who, although offering every assistance, I knew I'd never meet.

I was no stranger to the Sunset Marquis, as I'd first stayed there on an odd adventure in 1979 with a singer called Hazel O'Connor, when for a brief moment it looked as if she was going to become a real global superstar. Also staying there at that time was a reportedly hell-raising David Bowie, though I never saw him.

Hazel was a bubbly Irish girl who worked on our reception. She knew David Bowie's producer, Tony Visconti – in fact, she sometimes cut Bowie's hair as she was adept with a pair of scissors – and she persuaded Visconti to produce some tracks she had written. I started to manage her. At the same time, she was cast in a film called *Breaking Glass* about a young singer in the punk scene. It was funded by Dodi Fayed and shot in north London, mostly around Cricklewood Village, with a cast including Jonathan Pryce, Jon Finch and Phil Daniels, who was playing a music manager. Phil actually came and watched me in the office for a couple of weeks and, when I saw the rushes, it definitely felt familiar. It started to get attention in Europe, especially at the Cannes Film Festival. We'd signed a big deal with Derek Green at A&M and then we got the call that Paramount wanted to distribute the movie in the States. They flew us to New York on Concorde, drove us around with limos full of champagne and we met with top executives. When we said we needed some time to come up with an idea for Hazel's next film, they provided a car for us to drive across the country to LA. One of the execs from Paramount arrived, gave me a holdall with thousands of dollars in it and said, 'We'll see you in four weeks in California.' I'd never driven in the US before, let alone *across* the US. When we arrived in LA, we had a series of high-powered meetings, only memorable because I turned up in shorts and a T-shirt and at one point had to tuck 'myself' back inside my shorts.

Paramount screen-tested the film and found audiences in the US couldn't understand a word anyone was saying, so they subtitled it and changed the ending. It was like the sun going behind a cloud. We were downgraded to a very second-rate motel. When we arrived, there were no flowers to be seen. Our flights back were economy. The executives who had wooed us were permanently out to lunch.

In the end, *Breaking Glass* grossed just £2,471 in the US, which even in those days wasn't a lot of cash. The *New York Times* described it as 'lively and involving'. It was just unfortunate that its life in the US didn't involve an audience.

Back in the UK and licking our wounds, it had then been my bright idea to book an unknown band called Duran Duran as one of the supports for Hazel's upcoming UK tour after their manager sent me a cassette in the post. I had put it on, listened to a couple of songs. 'Not bad,' I thought. 'Let's book them.' After the first gig on the tour, there was a bit of buzz around them. By the fifth, it was a clamour. By the end of the tour, it was obvious most of the audience were there to see them. It became clear that there was only one artist heading for superstardom and this was a real blow to Hazel's live career. I didn't have much involvement with Duran Duran along the way, barring a short period as the band's PR. That didn't go according to plan, and I remember Simon Le Bon taking exception to a press release I'd written and sending it back to me marked out of ten. His markings were those of a minor public school headmaster, referring to bad grammar and poor punctuation, which was anathema to my punk sensibility and built-in rebellious instincts. It really pissed me off and I suppose it was meant to. Years later, though, I have to admit it was quite funny and, in retrospect, a witty P45.

As Ian and I shepherded the Cult through life as a big band in the US – where they had eventually signed with Warner – despite the superficial glamour of the lifestyle, I was busier than ever. There were endless appointments with the record company, promoters and agents, on top of all my PR meetings. The country was massive and each state had a different demographic. An act might break through in New York, LA, Toronto and Chicago, but struggle in conservative middle America. It was very different to getting started in the UK and it required a lot of patience and legwork as one place blurred into another. Kansas was just plain dull, so I wasn't upset to fly down to Dallas and meet a journalist from Scotland who had come to interview the band. The weather was warmish and the joint was jumping. After the gig, we went to a party in a plush apartment full of super-wealthy but deeply uncool Texans snorting coke. After the gig in Houston, we headed up to Austin, a sleepy town with a university feel. The club the band were booked to play was tiny and it quickly became apparent that the local promoter had been telling fibs about the stage size. Regretfully, we pulled out. However, Ian Astbury had disappeared and we were forced to languish in a grotty hotel, debating whether to stay or go and leave him behind.

After Texas, I flew up to Denver, which was crisp, clean and scenic. There was a lot of excitement at the hotel and the receptionist told me that I'd just missed Elton John. Apparently, the Eagles were checking in the next week. The gig I brought the media to didn't go according to plan as one of the group kicked a flight case and collapsed in pain, clutching his foot. There was no encore, just an ambulance to the hospital surrounded by fans in cars. It was time for me to get on the phone and start issuing statements about the UK tour still being on despite the cancelled US gig and hospital trip. It was the middle of the night at home, so I left messages on the answering machines of journalists who didn't even know the band were coming to the UK. Having got a bit of hype going, I felt my work was done and I flew off to LA for more endless record company meetings.

Warners were massively backing the Cult at this point and within a few months they were playing venues on the West Coast – such as Long Beach Arena, which held 10,000 people – and touring with Guns N' Roses and Aerosmith. For the band's third album, 1987's *Electric*, Ian Astbury was insistent that they brought in a brilliant young producer called Rick Rubin. He had made waves working with Russell Simmons developing Def Jam Recordings while still in college, and was developing a reputation among people in the know as the guy you worked with to give a record that contemporary feeling of rap and rock coming together. He'd recently worked with the Beastie Boys, Run DMC and Public Enemy.

At the same time as managing the Cult and guiding Big Country through the next phase of their career, I was trying to keep up with my other PR commitments which, in January 1987, involved rounding up some of Fleet Street's finest and flying them out to Barbados to try to get Jerry Hall off drugs charges.

The actress and model, who was Mick Jagger's girlfriend at the time, had been arrested on the island on 21 January. Mick and Jerry were regular visitors to the Caribbean as they owned a villa on Antigua, and Mick would often travel over to Barbados to record. Jerry had received a call to say a parcel addressed to her had arrived at Barbados' Grantley Adams International Airport, which wasn't unexpected as she was waiting on some personal items her butler had shipped over. On arrival at the terminal, she was handed a parcel and asked to open it to double check it was hers. Alas, she discovered 20lbs of marijuana tucked inside where her delicates should have been. She had been well and truly set up.

Jerry vehemently denied the drugs were hers and insisted that it was a mistake. Unfortunately, the authorities didn't believe her and she was subsequently arrested and put in jail, with bail set at $10,000. At the time, Mick and Jerry were the equivalent of Posh and Becks. Putting her in jail was like putting the

Queen behind bars. The papers made their feelings known with headlines like 'Jerry Hall in Hellhole!' and 'Jerry Hall in Kidnap Hell!'

Mick asked me to take a party of media out to Bridgetown, the island's capital, to cover the outrage. The plan was to fight the PR war and whip things up in the court of public opinion. My job was straightforward: plead her innocence and reiterate what a disgrace it was that she had been arrested in the first place. It was slightly complicated by the fact that Valerie was due to give birth within a fortnight, but I reassured her it would be a straightforward trip and I would be back in plenty of time for the due date. I phoned Josey from the hotel and told her about the palm trees and the parrots I could see from my window.

Given the January weather in the UK, journalists didn't need much encouragement. The flight was wild, with some of them downing bottles of whisky before we'd even landed.

Barbados didn't have a big tourist industry then, so our arrival therefore didn't go unnoticed. We were all staying in one of the best hotels in Bridgetown – at Mick's expense of course – and once checked in (after I'd sent my mother a postcard of some beautiful brightly coloured buildings around the harbour), we headed straight for the bar and pool. For the first few days, there was little more to our routine other than sleeping in, swimming and drinking cans of ice-cold Red Stripe while we awaited further instructions.

The courthouse was located in the coincidentally named town of Worthing, a short distance from where we were staying. It was an old colonial-style building, and the oak-panelled courtroom had a whirring fan overhead. Despite all the distractions, we managed to drag ourselves there.

In retrospect, Fleet Street's attitude was full of colonial undertones. There was no respect for the Barbados judiciary and the resulting coverage was undoubtedly patronising. The judge was an elderly man who was less than impressed with how the case had been – in his view – distorted in the press. He said that if the media continued to present such biased stories, they wouldn't be allowed to attend the case any longer. From there, things tumbled into farce. On one of the days, the judge ordered the marijuana be brought out. 'Bring out the exhibit!' he boomed. As one of the guards carried the box over, it fell apart and lumps of weed fell out and journalists scrambled to pick them up in front of the stony-faced judge.

Days soon started to merge into each other as we waited for the trial to restart and a verdict to be returned. Everyone was on tenterhooks, as the ramifications of being found guilty were potentially severe: the judge could hand down a two-year prison sentence. After two weeks, it started to feel like we might be here forever – although in the Barbados heat, frankly nobody was complaining.

In the end, the case, like the box of grass, collapsed. All the charges were dropped against Jerry. Her actual belongings were reportedly found stashed in a locker at the airport, allowing the judge to rule that the whole thing had been a mistake. Either way, it was a win-win for everyone involved. Mick's girlfriend was safely returned to him, Jerry's profile was bigger than ever, her reputation was intact, and I came home with a rather impressive tan.

Interestingly, I had briefly represented Bryan Ferry a few years earlier, having been hired by the very smart Mark Fenwick, who was his manager. It was fascinating to find out who the real Bryan was: I suppose I expected a very confident, charming man in the ilk of Humphrey Bogart or Sean Connery, but in reality he seemed surprisingly brittle and strangely lacking in confidence.

His attention to detail was so extreme that nothing ever seemed to get approved. I would sit there with piles of contact sheets and interview requests endlessly awaiting sign-off. Deadlines came and went, but still Bryan was debating whether the look was right. After a while, I slightly lost interest as I couldn't see how we were going to take things forward. I concluded that he lacked the ruthless ambition and drive of Bowie and Jagger. On the subject of which . . .

Bryan didn't seem entirely happy during the time I spent with him and later he confided in me that he was still raw about the way Jerry Hall had left him for Mick Jagger back in the late '70s. He filled me in on some of the background, and there was no doubt that from his point of view, Jagger had behaved like an absolute cad. I couldn't help but feel a bit sorry for Bryan.

A few days after we got back from Barbados, I went round to Mick's house for a debrief and I was telling him I'd just had a new arrival – a baby daughter – and that Valerie and I were scratching our heads for an appropriate name. 'Well, it's Tuesday, innit?' he said. 'Why not call her Ruby?' And that was how my youngest daughter came to be named.

A few months later, I was delighted when an artist I had long believed deserved superstardom played a record-breaking ten nights at Wembley Arena. I came to Luther Vandross initially through Teddy Pendergrass, as they had the same manager, Shep Gordon, though I'd had a passing introduction to Luther when, along with Ava Cherry, he was part of the David Bowie touring party staying at the Sunset Marquis. As with Teddy, the media had put up barriers – a Black soul singer trying to gain respect was much harder work than it should have been. But eventually it happened. He became a major crossover star, selling out arenas around the world and producing for other artists including Aretha Franklin, Diana Ross and Dionne Warwick.

Luther lived the high life. On one occasion, during a casual walk down London's Sloane Street, he popped into a jewellery shop and spent £14,000 on a watch. Another time, after I'd accompanied him to a morning radio interview in London, no sooner had I left him in the hotel lobby and returned to my room than my phone started ringing. It was Luther. He wanted to know: did I have any cash? I happened to have £500 on me, which he asked me to bring downstairs. I duly went to meet him in the foyer, where he announced he wanted to go to the Palm Beach Casino in Mayfair and play blackjack. In all the time I'd known him, gambling hadn't really come up. It was chilly as we made the short walk to the casino. On arrival, the doorman let us in with a familiar 'Hello' to Luther and we checked our coats. It was the smallest gaming establishment I had ever seen; it looked more like a soap opera set. Luther made his way over to the only blackjack table in the room, and sat down, waving for me to hand him the £500. He put it on the nose for the first hand. The cards were dealt. Luther drew two sixes, and the dealer had an ace up. The dealer turned over his second card: blackjack. Game over. We quietly left the table and made our way back to the cloakroom, where they hadn't even had time to hang our apparel. It was probably a good thing; I had no money left for a tip anyway.

Over the last few years, I had also been developing more and more relationships with reggae artists, including Bunny Wailer and Gregory Isaacs, and then Smiley Culture and Maxi Priest, who was the cousin of Inner Circle's frontman, Jacob Miller.

Reggae artists often found it hard to get PR support, as the scene had a reputation for violence and unreliability. I was determined to fight this narrative. Everywhere I looked, it was impossible not to notice how differently Black artists were still being treated by the media. And there was still a huge amount of naked racism in the industry. I had once stood in astonishment as the manager of a hugely successful traditional rock and roll band held forth with his National Front-esque opinions. The promoter John Giddings took great delight in telling him that my partner and the mother of my child was Black, at which point the manager went very quiet.

I really loved the fight against the establishment at the core of reggae. It was also a way of keeping my eye in when I was spending so much time on the music management side of things. The challenge of trying to get people coverage when really nobody wanted to know reminded me of my early days in the music industry. The more journalists said no, the harder I knocked at the door. Having mainstream clients like the Stones, Bowie and Blondie gave me leverage. I supposed Bunny Wailer and Gregory Isaacs and their management sensed that I was so determined to get their clients recognition that they had to hire me. But it could mean a lot of banging on doors for not much reward. In fact, one time, after being promised payment by Bunny, I received a call from someone at Gatwick Airport, where it transpired his tour manager had been caught with a lot of furniture filled with marijuana that was parcelled up and addressed to me. The tour manager was arrested and I didn't get paid.

Throughout this time, I felt like whatever I did, it was never quite enough. It never felt like Ian and I had got to a place where we could take our foot off the pedal. It was still hand to mouth. It wasn't that I had forgotten the money; it was just that it appeared to have forgotten me. Every time I came back from a trip, I had missed something in Josey's life – the first step, the first word. And now in Ruby's too. I was deeply uneasy that here was the tribe I had always been looking for, but it seemed I couldn't actually be part of it.

I would promise myself that I would travel less for a while, but then the phone would ring and I'd close the door on the sounds of my family, and go to find out what had happened.

11

You Can't Always Get What You Want . . .

'So, how much money did we make, then?' Stuart Adamson and the other members of Big Country are looking at Ian and me expectantly. That autumn, 1988, the band would release their fourth album, *Peace in Our Time*, and it was clear we needed to try a different tack. Interest in the group had been waning since its high point two or three years earlier, so Ian came up with an attention-grabbing idea to whip up a media storm around the album launch: a gig in Moscow.

It made sense thematically because the title was a reference to improving relations between the East and West, and the album cover showed a giant American flag with a hammer and sickle in place of the stars. While it was getting very rusty in places, the Iron Curtain still hung, and though things had thawed a little from the days of Burgess, Maclean, Blunt and Philby's defections, it was still highly unusual for a Western band to play in the Russian capital. Big Country would actually be the first to do multiple performances there.

It wasn't easy to pull off. The usual route for a band to get into the USSR was to be invited by the Kremlin. Unfortunately, no such invitation had been extended. But we were in luck as a recent change in Soviet laws meant private, Russia-based bookers had the power to arrange such gigs independently. President Gorbachev was trying to liberalise society and normalise relations with the West. Our timing was good. Through word of mouth, Ian made contact with a well-known Russian rock figure called Stas Namin, who was only too happy to help. It worked in our favour that Stas's grandfather had political ties and was able to pull some strings on our behalf. We were in.

A few weeks after a boozy gig and press conference at the Russian Embassy in Bayswater, London, a planeful of media was flown halfway around the world for a week of cultural activities. In total there were over two hundred people on this trip into the unknown – journalists of all stripes, plus assorted label execs and promoters.

Our hotel, the Moskva, was situated next to Red Square. In the foyer, a fierce-looking woman sat at a desk by a lift that smelt of cabbage, while shifty leather-coated men faded in and out of the background like characters from a John le Carré novel. Switching on the ancient TV in my rather sparse room, I discovered there was only one channel, in black and white no less, showing combine harvester racing in Ukraine. Rather than settle down and watch that, I put on my Arsenal top and went for a run around Red Square. People stared at me in utter disbelief.

Most of the work on the trip itinerary had been done by Ian. First on the agenda was a formal reception at the British Embassy, where vast quantities of vodka were consumed. The next day was a shopping spree at Tsum, Moscow's iconic department store, with promoter John Giddings (whom I had always said I had been introduced to by a hooker in the mid-seventies – Jake Hooker from the Arrows). I came away with a fur hat and a bootleg Led Zeppelin album although there were no luxuries bought by the hard-pressed Muscovites. I noticed a crowd outside gathered around a window display admiring what turned out to be a toaster. I also found some excellent postcards to send to my mother.

Returning to the hotel, John and I bumped into the band in the foyer, unaware that they had been doing an impromptu gig in Gorky Park for veterans of the Soviet war with Afghanistan. They weren't impressed that we'd spent the day shopping as opposed to watching them. John and I must have been getting a reputation for being rather casual by that point, although, to be fair, arrangements were chaotic and no mention of this show had appeared on our itinerary.

Finally, it was time for the run of concerts – five dates at the Moscow Palace of Sports, beginning on 30 September 1988. Inexplicably, it was scheduled to start in the late afternoon rather than the evening, and the crowd seemed to be comprised mainly of soldiers. The band launched straight into 'Peace in Our Time', only for the sound to die a minute into the song. As Stuart positively roared out the lyrics, all you could hear was a horrible noise, like stuff going down the plug. He stood there transfixed, not believing what was happening. The crowd, thinking they had heard all they were getting, made their way to the exit. Departing soldiers were overheard saying they were surprised at how short Western concerts were.

This disastrous situation had been caused by a power cut – apparently not an unusual occurrence, typically caused at this time of day by too many people simultaneously putting the kettle on. The promoter tried to console us, pointing out that it was midwinter and the first thing people wanted when they opened the front door was a nice cuppa. Backstage, the mood was glum and Stuart sat with his head in his hands wondering what to do. After a forty-five-minute delay, the gig resumed. The band were nothing less than superb as usual and, by the time the concert finally drew to a close, everyone was really pleased with how it had gone. Even the members of the military, who despite having left, had somehow been rounded up and persuaded to stay. The tour finished on a high.

But when the dust had settled, it was time to look at the accounts.

'Well, as you may or may not know,' Ian said hesitantly, 'there was the, um, unexpected issue that laws in the Soviet Union mean that profits can't be sent out of the country as money. All profits must be donated to the local music scene.'

'Well, what exactly can they be sent back as?' Stuart asked.

'They suggested tractors.'

The meeting went downhill from there. The band's label had sunk a lot of money into the concerts – accommodation, crew and staging – hundreds of thousands of pounds that would ultimately be placed against the band's royalties. They'd assumed some of the costs would be recouped from selling out the gigs. On top of the lack of gig revenue, the album sales were disappointing. Stuart would later say, with the ghost of a grin, 'It's a Scottish trait to have a sense of humour in times of adversity.'

As often tends to happen, bad news all came at once. First, the Cult sacked Ian and I as managers, deciding they wanted to go with a big LA manager instead. I was relatively sanguine, but Ian chased them down the street with a bit of scaffold pole and eventually decided for his sanity he needed to retreat temporarily from the music business.

Within a couple of months, I finally succumbed to the politics of working with the Stones and was very good-naturedly let go.* I think, for them, the psychological games were all part of the fun. Keith was so black and white, while Mick was always thinking about what made the best sense for him and the band, with no room for sentiment. As Ronnie Wood once famously said about Mick, 'He's a nice bunch of guys!'

At the same time, I'd come to the decision that it no longer made sense for me to manage Maxi Priest as he was surrounded by voices that made the job impossible. It all came to a head when a notorious US music figure – once rumoured to have been tied up by one of his bands, who said they would only release him if he paid the money he owed them – threatened me. First, he'd accused me of repeating slavery, as a white guy managing a Black artist. Then later, at a gig at the Brixton Academy, he'd pulled a gun. As a circle opened up around us in the crowd, I suddenly just felt tired. I didn't run away and made sure to hang about and go backstage after the gig, though admittedly not for long.

---

* Years later I was able to laugh about it. I had been invited to a Queen's Garden Party at Buckingham Palace and was surprised to see Jerry Hall, her then new husband, Rupert Murdoch, and former right-hand man to Mick Jagger, Tony King. I decided to wander over. Jerry was very welcoming, introducing me to Mr Murdoch, who I had met at a few News Corp events over the years but didn't really know. Jerry fixed Rupert with a mischievous look and said, 'You know, Rupert, we've all got something in common.' Rupert said, 'What's that?' She replied, laughing, 'We've all been fired by Mick.'

Grant Edwards had never been the most strategic business – it was a kind of Heath Robinson contraption, built from different roles with different bands and artists, mainly chosen because we had a connection to their music. And with the drop in income from groups leaving us, or simply not doing the kind of numbers they had done previously, and many of the groups I worked with on the PR side just not paying us enough to justify the time we put in, there was suddenly a financial black hole. As black holes do, it started to pull everything into it. Within a couple of months, I was forced to put the Notting Hill office on the market and even sold the furniture to a junk shop.

All I could hear was Shep Gordon's voice in my head. 'Alan, what did I tell you about forgetting the money?' As all this was happening, I had to stay cheerful – nobody is interested in a miserable publicist. I felt like an actor in a play that I knew was about to close. I had a young family to support, so the show had to go on. John Giddings helped me by offering me a room at the back of his office in Putney and I re-focused on PR. It was a tough experience. I had gone from being Mr Big of rock and roll to being Mr Nobody of Putney High Street. I put significant time and energy into convincing our clients not to leave us, trying to keep the company from going under while putting on a front for the media.

In the summer of 1989, I joined David Bowie again for the Tin Machine tour. It was a relief to be away from London and the constant firefighting. One day, David stopped the tour bus outside a pub. We all trouped into the bar and he ordered 'a pint of your best mild' for everyone. The landlord looked a bit nonplussed. The pub had long switched to lager and Premiership football. Even someone as future-proof as David had found himself a man out of time.

We got back on the coach and I sat there staring out the window. Another bus, another band, another town.

I was thirty-five years old and it felt like I'd been working non-stop for the last fifteen years. The last few felt like an endless succession of trips. They had become so frequent at points that I didn't even unpack my suitcase. Other times, I kept one packed and ready.

I had sacrificed so much to the job, first as a romantic partner, then as a father over long-distance telephone calls, snatched at the side of a freeway or from an airport lounge or hotel lobby. I worried that being named by Mick Jagger almost certainly didn't make up for your dad stopping just before blowing out the candles on your birthday cake to take an emergency call. The girls weren't babies any more. They were starting to ask questions about why I was so often away. I wasn't even sure I knew the answer myself. But then David was beckoning and it was time to talk coverage strategy. The engine started and it was on to the next town and the next gig.

Part 2

12

Spice Up Your Life

'OK, so dark hair is Posh, curly hair is Scary, blonde is Baby, then ginger is . . . Ginger and that leaves Sporty. Yes, thank you, girls.' I whispered goodbye to my daughters, hung up the call in the nick of time and was brought into a meeting room. In it were five young women surrounded by more suits than I had ever seen before in a record company meeting.

'Girls, this is Mr Edwards,' said Paul Conroy, the head of Virgin Music UK. 'He's worked with some of our most established acts, like Janet Jackson and David Bowie, and we'd like to employ him on your behalf. Is there anything you want to ask him?'

It was 1997 and these five girls were arguably the biggest music story in the world. There had been news helicopters hovering over the building when I arrived at the Virgin Music headquarters. I had the sense, as I had only a few times in my career, that what happened in the next few minutes was going to change my life. A lengthy silence followed. I braced myself for a bombardment of technical questions about the media, just like Mick Jagger had unleashed before he had hired me.

'Yes,' said the sleek brunette I had recently learned was

known as Posh (though in that moment Scary would have worked equally well). 'We have one question . . .'

Forty-five minutes earlier, I'd been in the offices that I had, until a few months before, shared with fellow music PR Chris Poole. Over the last five years, we'd built a list of clients together as I recovered from the unravelling of Grant Edwards, and I'd recently bought him out. The '90s had so far been a chance to refocus. I had also become increasingly involved in David Bowie's career, as I acted as a kind of management consultant. Not manager, though. That was a dirty word around David after his experience with his former manager Tony Defries. Apart from the fact that Defries' percentage was ridiculously high, it was based on gross – an initial payment of money without any costs factored in – so after high expenses and management commission, the artist never made much money. David felt that if he lost money on a tour, the manager should share that cost because, after all, they were building a business together for the future. That was not how management contracts in that era were interpreted, however. The letter of the law was that the manager took his money first as a 'tour cost'. Their argument was that as they had to invest their time in a project, they should be paid whatever the outcome, just like any other service, such as crew, trucking, lights, etc. But, in fact, the manager, unlike the crew and support, was also on a percentage of future earnings, so this was a rather disingenuous position. David was still paying this off in the '90s, a couple of decades after he'd parted ways with Defries. Though my work with David was just as intense as it had been, it was a different kind of deep work on fewer projects. I was his guy when it came to record companies, marketing and, of course, publicity; every day there were meetings with execs, promoters or tour managers. This was now my world and, in all honesty, at that point I really didn't miss a lot of the frantic PR stuff.

It meant I had to spend big chunks of time in LA, sometimes two months at a time. I'd hang around the Warners office at the end of the day hoping chief executive Mo Ostin would tell me stories about the early days of the music industry. He told me how he'd get to the office very early on Monday mornings to open up, around 6 or 6.30am, and he'd often find Frank Sinatra sitting there on the steps – hat tilted to shield the already hot sun, tie askew, suit crumpled – wearing a slightly guilty expression. He'd been in Vegas and was flat broke and in need of cash. Mo would always bail him out, but each time Frank had to give away a bit more of his ownership of the Reprise label, which is how Warners came to own Reprise and how Frank Zappa and Frank Sinatra became unlikely bedfellows.

Occasionally I was required to go to LA for a single day. Now, that would be unthinkable. You'd be lucky to get through security and check-in in that time and, of course, there's the damage to the environment. But then it was possible to do the whole journey in fewer than twelve hours.

Aside from my time in Bowie world, I was still taking on clients. Robert Palmer had always seemed every inch a *GQ* model, so I was quite surprised, when I started working on his publicity courtesy of managers Dave Harper and Mick Cater, to find that he was quite an easy-going chap with a passionate and encyclopaedic knowledge of music. He certainly liked the good things in life and his time in the Caribbean had turned him into something of a modern-day Noel Coward. He loved good food and fine wines, and knew how to look crisp in a suit. We launched one of his albums at Cliveden, a wonderful country house infamous for the swimming pool antics that ended up being part of the Profumo scandal. The managers had done a deal with Jaguar and all the journalists were driven there in top-of-the-range cars and afterwards whisked off to dinner at Le Manoir, which was then considered the best restaurant in the UK. Robert had style, but it was his observations on music that inspired me. For instance, he told me the reason Ghanaian highlife music had random Hawaiian-style guitar was because all the young musicians flocked to see the Elvis films in open-air cinemas in Accra and picked up the style there.

He could sometimes appear out of step with current trends. I remember he once played a concert of standards at the Albert Hall. The fans hadn't really read the small print and were expecting a night of soul-rock tunes like 'Addicted to Love'. After a few songs, they became restless and, as the evening wore on, it got worse and some audience members started to drift away into the Kensington night. It got so bad that the managers locked the exits so people couldn't leave. The bloke next to me was reading Dostoevsky, he was so bored. There was one point where Robert asked, 'Have you got any requests?' and someone shouted out, 'Yes, when is Robert Palmer coming on?'

Most of the time, though, it was refreshing to be able to think deeply about one artist. David didn't want to chase attention and when he did do press, he liked to play things as cool as possible most of the time – even if, in 1992, I'd found myself organising a *Hello!* wedding shoot for him and his bride, the acclaimed supermodel-actress-entrepreneur Iman Abdulmajid, who he had met in Los Angeles a couple of years previously. David was completely in love with Iman and had wooed her single-mindedly. Soon a wedding date and location were decided on and arrangements were made. The ceremony was to take place at the secluded Villa la Massa in the beautiful rolling hills of Tuscany, and a £250,000 deal was struck with *Hello!* for exclusive rights to the wedding. I suspect the deal was pushed along by Iman, as this wasn't in keeping with Bowie's typical media positioning. It was my job to make the whole arrangement work smoothly without drawing unnecessary attention to the *Hello!* connection, which might undo a bit of his street cred.

I arrived the night before the wedding with Brian Aris, who was the number one magazine photographer in the UK at that point. There were only sixty-eight guests, a select list that encompassed both David's mother Margaret and Yoko Ono. I was simultaneously a guest and a member of staff, which meant I had a slightly confusing dual role. In fact, I also had the honour of being the chief usher. In my ushering capacity, one of my biggest jobs was to identify the fourteen members of the Abdulmajid family who had flown in from Somalia. They were adorned in beautiful flowing fabrics and looked fantastic. Unfortunately, I embarrassed myself by mixing up Iman's mother with her sister when distributing name tags.

As is the way with this sort of exclusive, if someone else got photographs, the whole deal could collapse. At one point during the ceremony, as David and Iman left the church, there was a flash. I went and got the seating plan, and Brian and I worked out where it had come from and immediately both said the same name: a prominent New York fashionista. We went to tell David what had happened and who we thought it might be; David wanted to sort it immediately. We found the guy sitting on a sofa in the reception venue in his topcoat. David went up to him and quietly demanded his camera. The guy didn't respond. 'Camera. Now.' And the guy meekly handed it over.

As soon as the wedding finished, Brian and I flew to the *Hello!* headquarters in Madrid by private plane. For the next four hours, we chose the pictures, while I wrote captions and made the print deadline with minutes to spare. Then we were straight off to London. We arrived back at Heathrow looking pretty battered with coffee and tea stains on our shirts, bleary eyes and hair all over the place, and we bumped into other guests arriving back from Tuscany, still looking immaculate, all discussing what a beautiful wedding it had been.

A few months after his wedding, I was with David for a gig in Rome. As usual, he wanted to see some art so we went to visit the Vatican. David didn't like people making a fuss over him and often used to move about incognito wearing a cap and carrying a Greek newspaper. This visit was no exception and David, Coco, me and a few others from our party arrived unnoticed at the Sistine Chapel. David was a mine of information, especially on how Michelangelo came to take on the job, apparently reluctantly as he considered himself a sculptor. Pope Julius XI told him he had to do it and, in those days, you didn't argue with the head of the church. David was bringing the story to life, not only for us but others. I noticed a few people hanging on his every word as he explained that, contrary to popular myth, Michelangelo didn't lie on his back to do the painting but built his own scaffold. Still, it was exhausting work physically. David said it was so stressful that the great man even wrote a poem about it. I wondered if he could relate to the experience in any way to being told by record companies that he had to do something and finding the whole process wearing. Either way, it was an extraordinary behind-the-scenes look at one of the wonders of the world. When I looked around, there was a growing line of people behind us and I realised they thought David was the official tour guide.

Naturally we had become very close over those years. Often the phone would ring when the family were sitting down for dinner and Josey would pull a specific face as she announced, 'That David Bowie bloke's on the phone again!' Bryony once whispered to me that he was like his character in the film *Labyrinth*. Lola did some work in the office and told me that, though he was shorter than she expected, he was the only artist she was ever in awe of.*

It wasn't all plain sailing. One time, in New York, I received a spectacular rollicking when David played at Radio City Music Hall as part of a co-promotion with *GQ*, who had made his new album available as a free download. The only catch was that he had to do a concert for *GQ*'s executives and advertisers, to which he somewhat grudgingly agreed. Come the night, it was exactly what you'd expect. A slew of smartly dressed couples, in a beautiful theatre, not breaking a sweat but having a swell time all the same. They weren't exactly hardcore Bowie fans, but it wasn't one of those nights where only the clanking of jewellery can be heard between songs. I went to the bar and got talking to the *GQ* editorial staff about things we could do together in the future. After the show, I made my way backstage through

* All four of my daughters even ended up singing on a couple of Bowie songs, including 'The Hearts Filthy Lesson', which was used in the soundtrack to the film *Seven*.

the maze of corridors to David's very modest dressing room. I walked in. He asked me what I thought. I went into autopilot, said what a great show it was and how I thought everyone had loved it. He looked at me and just flipped. 'It was the worst gig of my life. I can't believe you said that – the audience weren't interested. I couldn't hear the sound at all, couldn't hear my own vocals.' And that was just the beginning. Though it probably happened to me few enough times to count on the fingers of one hand, when David let rip, you really knew it and so did everybody else. You could hear this tirade reverberating through the Radio City corridors. Outside the dressing room was a who's who of the New York music industry – people like Tommy Mottola, head of Sony – and embarrassingly they could hear every single word. The evening was only saved when I realised that the extremely attractive older lady with long blonde hair I'd got talking to at the afterparty and assumed was an executive was, in fact, Lauren Bacall.

The worst time of all was when I had convinced David he should have his photo taken on a ferry on his way to the Isle of Wight Festival in order to get into the *Sun* because, quite simply, we needed to sell tickets. He didn't love the idea, but we came up with an authentic 'Bowie' angle. He wasn't flash and never took helicopters to gigs – in fact, he was travelling to the island on the ferry with the rest of the public. He agreed and I set up celebrity photographer Dave Hogan to take the shot.

On the day itself, I went to meet David in his tour bus on the ferry. We enticed him out, then Dave gave him a few directions for the shot, at which point David completely flipped out at me because he hadn't realised we were doing this sort of shoot. The telling-off went on for about a quarter of an hour, and people all over the boat could hear it. Eventually some fellow passengers gathered around to watch the drama. It was one of the most painful, humiliating experiences I have ever had in my whole professional life. I didn't go back to the Isle of Wight for ten years, as I didn't want to relive the memories.

But almost all of the time, working with a mind like David's this closely was an immense privilege, even if his restless creativity did throw up some major challenges. One of his tallest orders came when he decided he wanted to release a drum and bass record in China. Apart from the fact that the single, released under the pseudonym The Tao Jones Index, wasn't exactly mainstream, record shops didn't exist in China in the same way they did in the West.

However, David was sure it would work and he wanted the song lyrics immediately translated. I couldn't think of anyone who could do this. After racking my brains, I went down to London's Chinatown and asked one of the waiters in a Chinese restaurant on Gerrard Street if they could help. Fortunately for me, they obliged. When David called the following week, I was at least able to say, 'We've had a version done with the words in Mandarin.'

We got the record pressed, but there was a new issue: I didn't know what to do with it. I spoke to senior people at labels for advice and soon found out there weren't really any Chinese 'charts' – or, in fact, an established market for international music at all. Helpfully, an exec from BMG, Christoph Ruecker, was on hand to help. Christoph and his colleague in marketing, Gabby Sappington, had been loyal supporters of David's and they pointed me in the direction of a distributor in Hong Kong. He turned out to be a tailor who also supposedly distributed records, but in desperation I had a few boxes of vinyl shipped out to him. The reality of the situation began to dawn on me. Every week, I'd get a call from David: 'How are we doing in China?' I couldn't tell him that the records were languishing at the back of a shop in Hong Kong. I had to start being imaginative and would say things like, 'Oh, I think they're having a distribution meeting' or 'I think they're deciding how to market it'. I was still holding out hope that someone would discover the record, word would spread and it would become a hit. I dreaded this whole episode blowing up into a big row, but there was no turning back and I had to keep the charade alive. One day, three months after I'd first sent the records to Hong Kong, David called. I held my breath, fearing the worst, but he made no mention of 'Chinese sales'. In fact, he never mentioned the subject again. Maybe the tailor had contacted him directly asking if he'd mind taking the box of records back.

Another time, David casually asked me to collect an art student who was arriving from Leeds at King's Cross station and drive him around for the day. We had a hilarious time screeching around the West End in my old Merc stopping at specialist shops. I'd just park the car on the kerb and wait for him. On one occasion I went inside with him and was astonished to find him buying all sorts of medical equipment. He muttered something about the pharmacy, so I presumed he was opening a chemist's or something. It turned out that the art student was Damien Hirst, and the Pharmacy was a trendy restaurant that he was opening with the PR genius Matthew Freud in Notting Hill.

I had also started working with another inimitable rock genius. In the spring of 1991, I received a call from Prince's office and was advised that if I was interested in doing his PR, I should fly to Minneapolis as soon as possible.

On arrival, I was collected by limo and driven in near silence for half an hour into the countryside. It was winter and everything looked very featureless and flat. Suddenly there was a clearing and an extraordinary, futuristic building popped up like a UFO. It was Paisley Park, the recording complex that Prince called home.

I was taken to the entrance and walked in – but nobody said anything. The staff showed me upstairs to a room, which seemed suspended in the air, with glass on all sides including the floor. I sat there waiting. Ten minutes passed, but still nobody came in, not even to offer tea or coffee. The whole mood was peculiar.

Suddenly, music started playing. Although I didn't know it at the time, I was listening to what turned out to be *Diamonds and Pearls*. I was conscious of being observed in some way, like I was an animal in a zoo, so I thought I'd better show lots of emotion as it might be the difference between getting the account or not. Never has a face telegraphed such enthusiasm, or an air guitar been played so passionately.

But at the end of the playback, nothing happened. Just more silence. I assumed, perhaps, I was about to meet Prince. Then an assistant came upstairs and said, 'Your car's outside.' I'd flown halfway around the world for this? I got back in the limo and we headed off. But this time, the chauffeur started firing questions at me. 'What do you think of the album? What do you think of that track? What about the guitar?' I'd been completely bowled over by what I'd heard, so was being incredibly effusive. This was lucky, because after a few minutes of interrogation, the penny dropped. The conversation was either being taped or fed back to Prince, so he could find out what I really thought of the record. The driver deposited me at the airport without even saying goodbye. Several days later, back in London, I received a phone call from a member of Prince's team, the lovely Jill Willis.

'If you want to do the PR,' she said, 'you're hired!'

That was my introduction to the world of Prince. It was a strange and wondrous place – a place where visiting celebrities backstage would be asked to wear latex gloves, a place where his PRs were expected to have a dedicated hotline in our office on Charlotte Street just for him (we called it the 'Batphone'), and a place where everybody on his team had to turn up suited and booted for concerts. I guess, being the consummate professional, he wanted to see that everybody was taking the endeavour as seriously as he was – that it wasn't 'just another gig'.

It would be easy to misconstrue Prince's idiosyncrasies as diva-like. But the idea of the 'diva' is one of the biggest fallacies in how people view celebrities. It's a way to simply dismiss the unusual patterns of behaviour you see among the rich and famous – and generally it's a misreading. While some Z-listers might act like that deliberately because they think that's how celebrities 'should' act, for any serious star those behaviours don't spring from self-importance. They spring from having to live a life that most people simply can't comprehend. To spend time with artists like Bowie and Prince was to glimpse into an entirely different world.

In 1994, I had taken a major career left-turn, going to work as general manager of PolyGram, the company that had recently bought Island Records and A&M. PolyGram was a major record label employing hundreds of people and with superstar acts like Elton John signed to it. The company would later morph into Universal, the biggest record group in the world. Howard Berman, an old friend from United Artists and the Stranglers who was now the MD of Phonogram (part of PolyGram), fought hard to convince me and had incredible faith in me, but it was almost immediately clear I'd made the wrong move. I had enjoyed the salary hitting my bank account and the unfamiliar stability this brought to our family finances but, beyond that, I merely turned up at PolyGram's large but rather soulless UK headquarters down by the River Café in Hammersmith and sat in my office. I was so unhappy, even from the first day. I had done my best and tried to knuckle down, and there were some good moments. I got to know Jon Bon Jovi, who had quickly advanced from being the work experience kid (but never stopped being very nice) and I helped organise some things for Plant and Page, who had a record coming out, which was great. But back at the office, it all felt very drab. It was almost like being in a factory, really. I felt divorced from the artists and was missing the action. I was more of a front-line person – talking about units and sales projections didn't work for me.

One day, I went to the company's chairman Roger Ames with my concerns. He told me to meet him that evening in the pub, where I found him playing pinball. I explained everything to him. To me, it was a massive deal, but to him it was just a tiny detail in his day. He looked at me and, after a while, somewhat quizzically, said in that wonderful Trinidadian accent of his, 'Well, I could never understand why you came here in the first place, Edwards. Don't worry. We'll sort it out.' As quickly and simply as that, I was free. But I will always be grateful to Howard for his faith in me and sorry it didn't work out.

At the same time as rebuilding and recalibrating my working

life, I'd been dealing with a trip to the Catholic Children's Adoption Society, where I'd arranged an appointment to try to learn more about my birth mother. It had been a strange meeting from the first moment.

'Ah, Mr Edwards. We knew you were a good communicator. If you weren't, you wouldn't be alive today.' It became clear that what they meant was that my parents had chosen me from a kind of beauty parade among many other children.

I was given letters between them and my birth mother, who I discovered was called Mary Duigan. I also learned that my father was from Michigan and had served in the US Air Force. All those times I'd been travelling up and down the Eastern Seaboard with bands, I could have walked straight past family.

From the Society, I learned that my mother was twenty-one years old when she had me, and I spent the first six weeks of my life living with her in Streatham. By this stage, she had already made contact with the Society as she didn't have enough money to look after me, but she was unable to wait for them to find adopters. In one report, they showed concern for her lifestyle as she was 'hanging about with Americans'. So, in September 1955, I was shipped out of London and into care. From there I was sent from home to home like a grim game of human pass-the-parcel.

First, I was taken in by a Mrs McDonald, who lived in Deal in Kent. My mother was based nearby in Margate and was able to visit when she could afford to pay the bus fare, which wasn't often. Her finances were very tight and, over the coming months, she found herself changing addresses frequently and struggling to contribute to my costs. In January 1956, she wrote a desperate letter to the Society. 'With regards to the adoption, can you give me some information as to how soon the adoption could take place and what arrangements need to be made? I'm finding it a great strain paying every week for him and he is now six months old. Trusting you can help me.' When Mrs McDonald fell ill and I had to move in with another family sixteen miles up the road, my mother stopped visiting. She would never set eyes on me again.

The following month, I was meant to be adopted by a Mr and Mrs Cook. I stayed with them for just three days, as they didn't like the fact I screamed so much. Even though it was explained to them that I was likely just upset with the recent upheavals in my life, they asked for me to be moved. Into another foster home it was, then. I was placed with a Mrs Meadows in London for three months. According to the records, I seemed happy in her care. And then I was plucked out of the care system by my adoptive parents. A letter dated a couple of months afterwards reported that I was 'growing into a lovely boy, and the adopters love him dearly. They will provide well for him.' The reports say I cried all the time for the first year and then never again. I can probably count the number of times I've cried since.

When I first received the reports, I shut them away in a cupboard. But gradually, over the years, I began to get them out and read them. All through this time was the plate-spinning act of a busy household with four daughters, who had to be taken to ballet or dropped off at a party or a gig. There were the tears and laughter and shouting of family life and so much music blasting out of every room.

So, bolstered by my daughters' expert knowledge of the Spice Girls, in that room at the Virgin Music offices, surrounded by those suits, I felt strangely calm. I had recently renamed the company Outside, after first checking with David Bowie that he was OK with us sharing a name with his new album. A few months previously, I had also been hired by Virgin, through Nancy Berry in LA, to work on Janet Jackson's album *Velvet Rope*, so I was dealing regularly with Paul Conroy, the head of the UK company, and had spent a lot of time with Janet and clearly made a good impression. Although you could probably argue I had taken a step back from my previous volume of front-line traditional PR and the most demanding elements of music management, I felt very equipped to answer any question the girls could throw at me.

'Yeah, we've got a question for him.' I leaned forwards in anticipation. 'What kind of shoes are you wearing?'

There was a sharp intake of breath around the room. I genuinely had no idea. So, I checked and said, 'Hush Puppies?' The girls looked at each other, and one of them responded, 'We can work with that. Let's hire him.' It was a perfect introduction to the Spice Girls and their comic-strip humour. They'd obviously made the decision before I got there, but wanted to add a touch of drama.

And boy was there a lot of drama.

13

Viva Forever

'Ciao Alan, it's Alexis. How's Rome?' This was a surprise. Alexis was a lawyer who I'd known for many years and who looked after, among others, Lemmy and John Lydon. But I hadn't spoken to him for a long time and I certainly hadn't told him I was in Rome.

'Hello Alexis. Long time. How do you know where I am?'

'Because you're on a live broadcast on Sky News.'

That was the moment I truly processed the scale of it all. In November 1997, even the Spice Girls just sitting in a car going through Rome was a breaking news story worthy of rolling TV coverage. A few hours later, they would hold an impromptu concert on their hotel balcony that made front pages around the world.

Within twenty-four hours of accepting the Spice Girls' offer, there had been thousands of phone calls coming at me. The sheer volume of requests was so overwhelming, I realised the only way to do the job effectively was to be on the road with the band, so I flew out to Rome, embedded myself with the group and had a crash course in getting to know them.

The relationship between a PR and an artist is an unusual

one. On the one hand, you are in a service role, often just one of many people they employ – along with gardeners, chefs, masseuses, accountants, promoters, agents, you name it. If you're working on a big stadium tour, there might be as many as four hundred other people on the road: you're a cog in a very large – albeit precision-engineered – machine. Developing instant relationships with your clients is an art. You often have only a few seconds to convince someone you're the right person to be working with. Of course, it helps massively if you're genuinely interested in and know something about them.

Often, I've had to find that connection under pressure. One year I took my client Lou Reed to the GQ Awards, which were being held at the Royal Opera House in London. We were in the lift heading up to the drinks reception, with about half a dozen other people, including the musician Ray Davies. I was briefing Lou on what to expect at the event and Lou said to me, completely deadpan and within full earshot of everyone, 'Who are you?'

You could hear a pin drop in the lift. And I could see Ray Davies was smirking.

'I'm your PR,' I replied.

Lou obviously knew who I was and just did it to put me in my place – but why? I figured our relationship needed to be improved and fast, because we were about to have a conversation with *GQ*'s editor Dylan Jones, who was welcoming people at the other end of the corridor. I had a hundred yards of corridor to turn things around with Lou, but I knew from experience you can say a lot in a hundred yards. I wanted to show how well I knew his work; I knew he wanted to be respected as an artist, not just a 'legend', and began talking in some detail about his largely forgotten first album, *Lou Reed*. You had to be a real fan to know it and I even quoted a few lyrics from its relatively obscure songs. He started looking at me with surprise. Seconds later, we greeted Dylan, and Lou was all sweetness and light. 'Oh, here's my PR Alan,' he said. 'He's a great guy.'

Another time early on in my relationship with the legendary Shep Gordon, he had called me into a meeting after struggling to get any interest in Alice Cooper in the UK, where even the record company boss wouldn't meet with him. Shep sat in reception for three days straight until he was finally ushered in to see him via a back corridor. I was called into a meeting to discuss Alice's PR and marketing with a tableful of suits. Shep sat there in a Hawaiian shirt smoking a massive spliff and making his displeasure known. I sensed an opportunity to make a mark and suddenly stood up and went to the telephone. Everyone just stared. I picked up the receiver and demanded in a loud voice to be put through to the editor of the *Sun* immediately. Then, after a short delay, I started telling the poor editor that I wanted an Alice review in the paper and that it better be big, before slamming the receiver down theatrically. Shep Gordon stood up and said, 'At last, someone in this country with red blood in their veins.' I was hired to work for Alice for life. What nobody had realised was that, as I was dictating the copy to the editor, what I could actually hear in my ear wasn't a whimpering scribe but a voice saying, 'The time, sponsored by Accurist, is fifteen minutes past four precisely.' I left the meeting in a hurry, as now I had to get back and ring a mate at the *Sun* to ask very nicely for a review of Alice Cooper.

Client relationships are so many and so varied that there isn't really a rulebook of how best to make them work. For a start, these relationships are dependent on all kinds of things, from the physical circumstances you find the client in to their state of mind, which in some stars' cases can be variable. If there are multiple layers of people in between yourself and the client, it's a lot harder. One American artist we work with has so many publicists, assistants and agents that I've lost count. There could be as many as twenty people on an email. That makes for a very non-creative type of relationship. In fact, I was so discouraged from talking to this star, even though I technically represent him, that when I found myself standing next to him in the toilet backstage at a media event in the West End, I hesitated to say hello. It means that the campaign will probably be technically proficient, but lacking in soul. Often the media can smell that, which ultimately affects the type of review they give.

One of the trickier things to deal with is selective memories. This tends to happen when the shit hits the fan and the blame game kicks in.

One famous sports client tipped me off about goings on at his club and asked me to leak it, which I successfully managed to do. I thought I'd got a result when the story popped up on the front of one of the tabloids and the client was happy. However, when the person upstairs decided to take legal action about the story, my man conveniently forgot the conversation with me. I know it happened and to this day I recall every detail – how I pulled my car up by the Roundhouse in Chalk Farm and took the call on my mobile phone. Suddenly I was faced with a court appearance as the source of the story. Seeing as it was going to the High Court and I was going to have to face a household name, this was an incredibly stressful episode.

So-called 'crisis management' is often the first encounter with a client. At that moment you're like a dentist helping someone with a toothache and can be incredibly important to them, but quite likely you'll never hear from them again.

If the person you're trying to deal with is drunk or on drugs, then the problems multiply. There are wild mood swings and pauses. When I worked with reggae singer Gregory Isaacs, he was doing so much freebase that he passed out during an interview I'd set up for him in Kensington. The journalist and I carried on chatting and wondering what to do. Extraordinarily, Gregory suddenly opened his eyes and answered the question forty-five minutes later. In his mind, there hadn't been any gap at all. A similar thing happened with Ronnie Wood in Paris when being interviewed by Robin Denselow of the BBC. Ronnie nodded off at one point and I could only conclude that the question had been dull. It was unlikely that he had smoked a funny cigarette; more likely he had jet lag, I argued. That old chestnut.

Sometimes a client is very shy, as with Prince and David Beckham, and that poses different problems. You have to chivvy information out of them bit by bit, as well as being as upbeat and confident as possible. One interesting conundrum is when a musician says that they won't deal with a particular news group. Or, as in the brilliant Nick Cave's case, media in general. He makes it clear that he doesn't like doing interviews, yet he is one of the most interesting and fluent conversationalists out there. When he talks about his late son to a packed hall, or writes about it in his book, you are moved to tears. Yet he still doesn't 'do interviews'. More politically minded clients sometimes don't want to talk to either the *Daily Mail* or the *Sun* – and even News Corp in general because of Rupert

Murdoch, although that's increasingly rare. There are still clients who just want to talk to the *Guardian* or outlets they feel are sympathetic. Elton used to be wary of the *Daily Mail* back in the day, but he had every right to be concerned about their obvious homophobia at that point, something that would later change under subsequent editors.

Touring is the best way to get to know a client as you have lots of dead time on your hands. Sitting on buses or in hotel rooms for hours, you end up chatting about all kinds of stuff. I was lucky to have relationships that developed along those lines with Mick and Keith, Jon Bon Jovi, Daryl Hall, and David, of course. They tend to be much deeper and long-lasting relationships, and can even end up being described as friendships.

My time with the Spice Girls began like a rocket taking off. I went from not knowing which one was which to knowing everything about their lives. I discovered that Victoria was very funny – I immediately christened her Witty Spice. Geri was a genuine believer in Girl Power. I'd spend a long time talking to Mel C about football. Mel B would always ask about my daughters. And Emma Bunton was the most eternally good-humoured person I'd ever met.

The Girls were in Europe gearing up to release their second album, *Spice World*. I then joined them for their major world tour in 1998, including the American leg where they would fill stadiums with 70,000 people a night. That was Beatles-level. Big Country or the Cult were pleased to get 10,000.

One thing I enjoyed so much about working with the Girls was the sheer intensity: it was like driving a car very fast, screeching around bends with your adrenaline pumping. And I had a lot of freedom. There wasn't a manager as such, as they'd left Simon Fuller by this point; there was the triumvirate of their lawyer Andrew Thompson, the financial guy Charles Bradbrook and me. We all got on very well and were able to make decisions independently. Leaning on my management experience, I was able to do what I felt were the right things for the Girls. Having said that, we were directly accountable to the group, and we held regular, sometimes daily, meetings at which we explained and discussed strategy. They had the final word but, by and large, they let us do what we did best. With some acts, you had to convince them to do press. Getting them to engage was like pulling teeth. But all of the Girls had grown up in households where newspapers were read every morning. They had strong opinions and their favourite columnists and interviewers.

The other thing I loved was that working with the Spice Girls had a family vibe. I didn't realise how much I yearned for it until I was unexpectedly planted in the middle. Not only the Girls, but the parents: Jackie and Tony Adams, Andrea and Martin Brown, Sandra and Ted Beckham. It's strange because I had my own beautiful family, but I still craved being part of this close-knit unit, even though I so often thought of myself as a loner.

Incredibly, despite the constant public attention, the group remained down to earth. One time, Victoria and I wanted to have a meeting somewhere discreet, so we went to the first-floor café of the local Heal's furniture store – you had to walk through the carpet section to get there. The shoppers never bothered us because obviously it couldn't be Posh Spice – it must be someone who looks like her. This was very much my style too, although my habit of turning up for meetings with a Tesco carrier bag eventually got on the Girls' nerves to such a degree that they bought me an expensive Gucci briefcase. Most of our interactions were very casual, whether it was going round to David and Victoria's house in Hertfordshire and having a takeaway, or Mel B turning up unannounced in the office and turning it into a playpen for her kids. My role felt like being a father figure at times.* I certainly felt protective of the young women at the centre of this media storm.

I'd always had a lot of female clients. One of the first was the wonderfully talented Joan Armatrading. It took me a little while to click with her, especially after I'd taken Simon Kinnersley from the *Daily Mail* to Munich to meet Joan and see her play. The resulting 'Joan Armour Plating' headline wasn't what we were looking for, but Joan and I became friends over the years. She's a great writer and her catalogue deserves to be revisited.

Another early female client was Joan Jett of 'I Love Rock'n'Roll' fame. She was a lot of fun and quite punky before the fact. Not long after that, there was Pauline Black from the Selector, who once described me as a 'shaggy-haired, charming facsimile of a vertically challenged David Essex'. Then there had been Debbie Harry and punk, that strangely asexual movement that really gave women a platform to be central members of the band: Poly Styrene, Tina Weymouth, Gaye Advert, Chrissie Hynde, the Slits, Patti Smith . . .

But it was the Spice Girls who changed my life. After leaving the Virgin offices, I had gone from being a relatively backroom

* When one of my daughters, Ruby, was reluctant to go to school for some very understandable reasons, Victoria insisted on calling her. At this time, getting a call from Posh Spice was akin to being phoned by the Pope.

'David Bowie guy' to what felt like the most high-profile PR in the world. And when I got back to London after the tour, the phone was still ringing off the hook. It wasn't just media requests. As with footballers or actors, musicians like to go where the heat is, so within weeks seemingly every pop star in the UK wanted to work with us. I'd pick up the phone and it would be Westlife, put it down and Atomic Kitten would call, or perhaps All Saints – and we signed them all up. It was unreal.

It totally changed the direction of my company too. Suddenly, we were the pop people. Over the years our roster would come to include Boyzone, Leona Lewis, Steps, Ronan Keating . . . It was a golden age for pop, thanks to a large extent to the Spice Girls' original manager, Simon Fuller. He showed record companies how to work out what the public want and design groups to fit – which saved a fortune on sending A&R people down to pubs to get drunk on expenses and come back with bands that flopped. Fuller also reinvented something from the '50s and '60s: the band as a brand. Very cleverly, he saw that commercialisation – sponsorship deals, marketing deals, the kind of things that most musicians deemed uncool – ought to be embraced. He wanted more deals, bigger and better – and that became part of the marketing.

The company grew quickly, as the work kept on coming in.*

Given that I used to be 'the punk PR', naturally the music

* I would go on to work with a tremendously talented team, including Chris Goodman, who has run the music side of my company brilliantly for twenty years, and Suzie Fellows, who would develop the events side of our business. More recently, David Lim, who is the number one pop PR in the UK.

wasn't always to my taste. But the thrill of it all was intoxicating. And I was the boss, the one who the younger team members would often feel like they had to explain the modern world to.* Representing all those high-value pop groups was like having ten horses in the Grand National. I loved the competition of it and was fiercely loyal to my acts. I really wanted to make sure they sold more than other bands and got more front covers, and I tried my hardest to out-do the other PRs and agents.

I had done my time knocking on doors and trying to get people interested in artists they hadn't heard of, as well as working with icons and learning how to tailor parts of their story to different media audiences, but this was something else entirely. There was such an appetite for news around celebrities. And for many of these pop groups, a substantial chunk of their audience were children, so their brand had to be absolutely squeaky clean. Suddenly a large part of my job became working out how to keep things out of the papers (which is, of course, how PR started in the Hollywood studio system). These stories then set the agenda for TV and radio. Good coverage could launch a career and indeed the opposite was true.

---

* I once got a call asking if I would show a new American artist called Jay-Z a few clubs. At that point I wasn't really aware who he was. He was a nice enough guy and we were getting along fine. I suggested that we visit Browns in Covent Garden, which was hot in those days. As I entered with Jay-Z towering over me, the entire club seemed to stop still. I remember that Julian Stockton from our office, who happened to be there, was literally open-mouthed. He couldn't figure out how his boss was hanging out with one of the fastest-rising hip-hop stars on the planet and hadn't even mentioned it. I took the kudos and my street cred was great for a while.

A new generation of showbiz reporters – led by the *Sun*'s influential Bizarre column, which was fronted by people like Andy Coulson, and the *Mirror*'s 3AM Girls, who were launched with great fanfare by Piers Morgan – ushered in a period of incredible competition to bring in more and better stories and exclusives. The temptation to exaggerate and not always verify a story or, as it later transpired, even question what the source of the information might be, was significant. The pressure from editors was unimaginable. On top of that, it was really exciting work. Money was no object. If a journalist needed to try to get a word with a pop star on holiday in the Caribbean, they'd be whisked out on British Airways at the drop of a hat.

Paparazzi like Jason Fraser or Darryn Lyons could earn £50k to £100k a night by selling photographs of the Beckhams at the Ivy or of a pop star falling out of a nightclub. The auctions would happen late in the evening, perhaps 9pm or 10pm – you'd see photographers on their mobile phones in pubs near News International, pushing the papers to go higher to secure the images. Even if they were quite mundane photos, it still made sense economically. A good shot of a major star might mean an extra 100,000 sales for the next day's paper, which was in turn perhaps an extra £1m in ads and also a jump on its rivals.

With such towering sums of money involved, the pressure on the PR became enormous, especially to help protect the exclusivity of the photographs. Journalists and editors were like rock stars. They'd have limos and drivers, which would park up outside Scott's or the Ivy, and nobody would think twice about spending £1,000 on the best bottle of Château Margaux.

This wasn't an entirely new fascination. When I started out in the '70s, I had been warned to be wary of talking in front of waiters or taxi drivers, as they would often pass information to the papers in return for money. The tabloids had already started covering pop stars, of course. The *Sun*'s Bizarre column had been around since 1982. As Kelvin MacKenzie, editor of the *Sun* from 1981 to 1994, put it, popular music had become so important to people that they would even read about it in a national newspaper. But things went into overdrive from the mid-'90s onwards.

It would be a mistake to think the stars didn't play along and often enjoy this cat-and-mouse game too. Sometimes I'd get a call from Geri or Mel B from the Spice Girls saying, 'Look, if we give them a picture, will they leave us in peace the rest of the holiday?' There were unspoken rules and if I could broker the arrangement, then it suited everybody: the paper got their story and the pop star got a mention for their solo album or whatever it was. The way this would work is that a pop star would let me know that they were going to be shopping in Harrods at 11am, say, and they'd give me the authority to tip off a specific photographer on the understanding that they would get to see the pictures before publication. Some stars even wanted a share of the revenue generated. There had been rumours this was something Princess Diana had done, but I don't know for sure. Either way, this system meant they ended up with controlled images of them looking good and avoided the rest of the pack. The PR's role in all this was vital. These things had to be set up carefully without anybody knowing, and there would be clandestine agreements in place about the pic and what the accompanying copy would look like. Sometimes the whole game started to feel like a spy thriller, full of shadowy deals, fast cars with tinted windows, and pop stars travelling under false names or flying to unexpected destinations in order to throw the press off the scent.

At other times, it was truly surreal. Photographer Jason Fraser once called me from the South of France to say that he had just come across two members of All Saints bathing topless and that he wanted to warn me that he was going to take a picture. I called the group members to tip them off, but they laughed at the idea and said there was no need to worry as the beach was completely empty. Jason, however, did get the pictures. It turned out he had holed up in a disused lighthouse at the end of the beach and was using a telephoto lens.

Newspapers and magazines were prepared to go above and beyond to maintain relationships. There was often an understanding that if a star gave the title exclusive stories, the papers would give them favourable coverage in return. Sometimes, as a favour, the publication might make unflattering or commercially unhelpful pictures disappear, or buy the pictures off the market, paying perhaps as much as £100,000 for exclusive rights. They would then destroy the photographs or, more likely, keep them in the safe in case the celeb didn't play ball in the future. As I've mentioned, crisis management is a big part of PR. Typically it's about keeping a story out of the press – showing it's not true, putting forward sympathetic interviewees, picking enough holes in the journalist's version of events that they lose confidence in it, or praying a bigger story comes along and sweeps it off the front page. I became used to responding to a crisis by finding somewhere quiet and boiling the situation down to its essence on a bit of paper. Then it was back into the fray.

Within weeks of taking on the Spice Girls, I quickly had an endless diary of late-night dinners with editors. We would meet after the paper had been put to bed, often about nine o'clock. The favoured restaurants for such meetings were the Ivy and, later, the Ivy Club and Scott's, but there was a whole circuit. Copious amounts of alcohol were consumed and the best food was ordered. Discussions would be had off the record about which celebrities were 'playing ball' and which ones weren't. I spent a lot of my time defending my clients.

'You've got to understand that she is under a lot of pressure and of course there's a baby on the way, so we really have to give her a break,' I'd say. 'Honestly, she's ever so sweet and she will talk to you, but let's park it for a couple of months.' My relationships with editors would help ensure that there was less heat on my clients – though they would, of course, have to deliver the goods eventually, at a time and a place that suited them. Remembering those first principles learned with Keith, I knew that you're only as good as your word, and I tried to make mine absolutely dependable. My instinct was always to play it straight. I would never knowingly lie and would studiously avoid ever playing papers off against each other; that sort of trickery and double-dealing always comes out and only ends in tears. I tried to keep careful notes and not drink too much.

There were some celebrities who would cheat, saying one thing and doing another – for instance, promising an exclusive to the *Star* and giving it to the *Sun*. Sometimes it was accidental, but some people just couldn't help themselves. Often they were the same ones who left a trail of unpaid PR bills and there'd be an agreement that they deserved what was coming to them: bad press.

On reflection, this stuff could get quite heavy-handed. The PR might quite innocently tell a client that if they didn't cooperate a bit more they were probably going to get negative coverage. I suppose one could say there was a whiff of blackmail about that, but the truth is it was just the reality of the situation. The PR was simply being the messenger and such is life: if you work against people then they are likely to say negative things in return.

It was a very rough-and-tumble world, but also highly charged, hilarious and in many ways a lot of fun. Everybody got to know each other well. People moved from one paper to another, married, fought over stories, attended funerals and weddings, drank together. It became a pack. I don't think anybody really sat back and thought about how much power they were wielding and whether or not the influence was getting out of hand.

Sometimes it did get sinister as the pressure for more stories led journalists to resort to ever more extreme measures. I found this out to my cost when I came back from a family holiday in Sardinia and was told that a newspaper had 'acquired' recordings of some telephone calls involving a client I had made, which they were going to use as the basis for a story. I remember once turning up to a Spice Girls meeting at lawyer Andrew Thompson's house and noticing a car parked a few doors down with a couple of shifty-looking characters inside. On closer examination, I noticed there was an aerial protruding from the back window pointed at the upper window of the house. They were clearly listening to our conversation. I alerted everyone, who – to my surprise and relief – found it funny.

In the middle of this Spice-mania, my adoptive mother Elizabeth suffered a serious stroke and spent about a month in hospital. I visited frequently, keen to let her know that she wasn't alone and that I loved her. The last time I saw her, she had this look in her eyes as if she was floating off into space, like an astronaut whose cord had become unattached and had no way back to the ship. It is an image that will never leave me.

The Girls were often in touch, looking out for me. The funeral was at St Mary's in Worthing on 6 December 1998 and was a modest affair. I'm not sure that anybody looked at the card attached to the huge bouquet of flowers that was sitting in the church that day. But if they had, they might have been surprised to see the names Victoria, Emma, Melanie B, Geri and Melanie C.

When I was helping to go through my mother's things with my brother and sister, I found an album she had kept of every postcard I had ever sent her. Page after page of them, from all around the world, neatly ordered. I cried for the first time since I was a child.

14

More Money, More Cash

'The offer,' said Richard Desmond in his typical no-nonsense way, 'is one million pounds. World rights, exclusive. And it's on the table . . . until you leave this office.' He sat back in his chair and looked at me, as I did my best to look inscrutable. Richard – publisher of *OK!* magazine – had phoned me while I was in my office in Tottenham Court Road. It was well into the evening and at first the conversation was about music, since we both loved blues-rock. He had then asked me to look out of the window. Down on the street below were his driver and his Rolls-Royce. Despite the fact it was already 9pm, Richard suggested I get in the car right away and come over to his Docklands office to discuss a deal.

After a bit of small talk, he came out with it. Editor Martin Townsend had hinted there might be an offer coming through from *OK!* for the Beckham wedding, but I had no idea it would be so big and on such dramatic terms.

Richard Desmond's background was in music magazine publishing: in 1975, he launched *International Musician and Recording World* as a livelier rival to the staid *Beat Instrumental. OK!* was designed to take on *Hello!*, which had been around since 1988 and was quite a 'respectable' publication. It tended to focus on European monarchies – pictures of Danish royalty riding bicycles around parks – so it was very rare that I would ever deal with them in those days, though we'd worked together on David Bowie's wedding. Richard's analysis was that nobody could care less about stuffy old aristos. The real royal family were the likes of Posh and Becks, footballers and all the other newly minted celebrities. It wasn't just rhetoric: 1997, the year he launched *OK!*, was also the year that Diana died and there was a whiff of republicanism in the air, incredible though that may seem now. At the same time, Britain found itself at the centre of the cultural universe. Tony Blair was voted in that May, Britpop dominated the airwaves, Damien Hirst and Tracey Emin were reinventing the art world, the Union Jack had been reclaimed as a positive symbol, and everything seemed marbled with hope. But it was a ground-up popular movement. The country had lost faith in the old establishment and into that vacuum entered pop culture. At the time, the biggest stars in the world were coming out of the UK. Everyone wanted to read about them. It was a genius move.

Even amid this feeding frenzy, though, a seven-figure fee was unheard of for British celebrities from UK magazine titles. There was only one problem: I knew the Beckhams were en route to LA and uncontactable. This one was going to be down to me. Richard had heard rumours that we had a big-money offer from the *Sun*, but in truth the best we had achieved to date was £130,000. It didn't take a genius to work out what to do. We shook hands and I headed back to the West End elated. It was the UK's most lucrative celebrity exclusive ever. But I was also quite worried – what if David and Victoria didn't want to do it?

The next day, as soon as I was able to get hold of her, I spoke to Victoria on the phone and explained everything. I nervously awaited her verdict. Her response was to the point: 'Please tell me you signed the fucking deal!' I swiftly realised I might have been fired if I hadn't.

I had met David through Victoria and soon took on his PR too – although our relationship had begun with a crisis. It was the 1998 World Cup and he had been sent off during England vs Argentina for flicking out a foot at Diego Simeone. It was an extraordinarily unfair decision – I'm not sure he even touched Simeone – but the media backlash was full-on. He was vilified in a way that nobody in sport really has been since. It went way too far.

The day after the match, I flew out to New York for the Spice Girls gig at Madison Square Garden. As I approached the venue, I saw someone who seemed completely out of context: David Beckham. He had come out to be with Victoria and get away from it all. As 'soccer' wasn't as popular in the US, he had relative anonymity out there. He explained that he had forgotten his pass and asked me very nicely if I could get him a ticket to the concert, which I found endearing because if anyone could get a ticket, it was David Beckham. It was quickly obvious that the man was in pieces about what had happened, utterly devastated.

That week, we were travelling up the Eastern Seaboard in a tour bus and, for David, that bus was a protective bubble – he was with the Girls and he was just one of the group. There were no journalists around, nor people on the street yelling at him. And from the US newspapers, you wouldn't even have known that there was a World Cup taking place. You couldn't easily get hold of British papers out there – and, of course, it was in the days before digital editions – but I knew the front pages back in London were horrendous because I had a well-established system for getting my hands on them. In the UK, my team would buy all the papers, photocopy them and fax them over to me. I took it upon myself to help manage the situation.

I realised David was in too sensitive a place for me to show him everything. In any case, nobody can cope with a huge deluge of bad news. Instead, I desperately looked through the UK papers for glimmers of hope. I'd find even just a column or a paragraph that was favourable and gather up all those little nuggets, so that when I showed David the bad stuff, I was also able to present something sympathetic. It wasn't manipulative. It was more a case of looking after a client's well-being and judging how much bad news a person can take in one go. I was also having constant phone calls with British journalists to gently remind them that there was a human being underneath this story.

Eventually, writing something positive became the more interesting angle for the press and slowly things calmed down. The incident with Simeone didn't dent his image in the long term. In fact, his brand was just getting started. In those days, footballers were largely just blokes who kicked a ball around on Saturday afternoons. They didn't grace the pages of fashion magazines like *GQ* or have opinions on global issues. David, however, was determined to change that. My job was to build Beckham's brand outside football – an ambition that burned deep within him.

One of the first non-sport pieces we had done was when I took *Esquire* journalist Ian Penman up to the Malmaison Hotel in Manchester to interview David in December 1998.

Afterwards, David invited me back to his house for dinner. He was living in what footballers used to call 'digs' in a terraced street in Salford. It was a modest affair. The first drama was that we couldn't get the lights on until I found a coin for the meter, followed by a kerfuffle while he looked for a can opener for the baked beans, which transpired to be the only food he had in the house. At last we settled down and I asked him what he wanted from his PR adviser. Usually, the first question young stars would ask me was 'Can you get me a Ferrari?' or 'Could you get me into this nightclub?' I realised straight away that David had a different agenda. He told me that he felt very strongly about developing women's football; he hated racism and homophobia, and wanted to fight against it; he thought soccer in the US was underdeveloped and wanted to be part of taking it forward – and all that was just for starters. He clearly had a vision that went way beyond kicking a football.

David also had strong views on the development of his own image, suggesting we do an Elvis-esque, '50s-style shoot for an upcoming *Sunday Times Style* interview, with him sporting a quiff. His attention to detail was extraordinary. On the way back to London, I scribbled notes down on the back of a train ticket. This contained the seeds of the 'Brand Beckham' PR plan.

David's footballing and commercial interests at that point were managed by football agent Tony Stephens at SFX Management. Together, David, Victoria, Tony and I – along with Andrew Thompson, Charles Bradbrook and later an up-and-coming PR working for me, Caroline McAteer – formed a tight team. Often an agent wants to control everything, PR included, but Tony just let us get on with it, which turned out to be a good thing.

David and Victoria were obviously very much in love and when they decided to get married, it was such a happy time and no surprise to anyone like me who was around them so much. I don't think any of us realised this was the beginning of Brand Beckham the business.

The day they announced their engagement had been organised with military precision to maximise it as a media moment. However, it was becoming increasingly tricky to balance the Spice Girls' interests against David and Victoria's. The Girls' relationship with the *Sun* needed to be maintained as the paper had been supportive all along. Victoria had promised Andy Coulson, editor of the paper's Bizarre column, an exclusive on the engagement when it happened, so we had to ensure that they got some special treatment. At the same time, as always, it was vital that I kept the rest of Fleet Street supplied with stories, otherwise they were likely to become hostile. This way everybody got a bite of the cherry. The *Sun* would get the exclusive – the interview and pictures of David with Victoria – but the rest of the press would be alerted to a photo call just after the *Sun* had done their bit. That was the plan.

Unfortunately, from a logistical point of view, Victoria and David could only do the engagement announcement on Sunday 25 January. There was no way that giving the *Sun* a little teaser in advance would work, as they wouldn't be able to hold it over for Monday's paper, when it would no longer be an exclusive.

Help was at hand in the guise of an incorrect news story: the *Sun* was convinced that there was a Beckham wedding list at a branch of John Lewis outside Manchester. Victoria was appalled. It wasn't so much that the paper had a private story about the wedding, but more that anyone thought the wedding list would be at John Lewis. Not posh at all. She exploded when I told her. 'John Lewis! It could be fucking Gucci at least!'

The *Sun* duly canned the story and I continued my conversations with Andy Coulson, who was trying to take a holiday in rain-soaked Florida. He wisely gave up the ghost in terms of trying to get something exclusive ahead of everybody else on the Saturday. It just wouldn't have been practical. David – probably mindful of the wrath of Sir Alex Ferguson – was nervous about the whole media circus. He was wary about talking to the *Sun*. Victoria was getting jittery too and was now suggesting a phone call with Andy rather than a face-to-face interview. When I explained that just wouldn't work for them, she suggested a quick ten-minute chat before David arrived.

I tried to keep all options open. My thinking was that if I kept the arrangements a bit vague, by the time everybody turned up at the hotel in Cheshire, there wasn't going to be any alternative but to do the *Sun* spread with Victoria on her own. This would get David off the hook and should work for everybody.

I got up at 5.30am on the Sunday morning to head for Heathrow and the short hop to Manchester. On arrival, we grabbed a taxi and drove through sunlit fields out towards Chester. Andy Coulson, legendary photographer Dave Hogan and Sharon Hanley from our office were packed in the back, bouncing around along the country roads. It all seemed a bit surreal but then being in the middle of these dramatic news stories always is.

On arrival at the hotel, I called Victoria and David. They weren't up, judging by the noises coming down the phone line, and weren't in any hurry to join us. I sat with the media in another room. We read newspapers, drank tea and watched bulletins about Bill Clinton's latest exploits on Sky News. Just as we began to worry about the time it was taking, there was a knock on the door and in wandered Victoria and David. She looked absolutely fabulous, and he seemed so sweet and very shy. I left the two of them with Andy while I went in search of the rest of the newspaper pack, who were hanging around in various country lanes waiting for more information. Our mobiles were ringing off the hook all the time and everyone was trying to find where we were. I was shaken for a minute when a cavalcade of cars drew up in front of the quiet country hotel and sixty people got out. Was this the whole of Fleet Street arriving en masse? Luckily, they were old ladies on a day trip.

Victoria, Andy, Dave, Sharon and I settled down to wait for David, who was going to be featured in the exclusive after all. To help pass some time, I explained that the word 'Posh' originally came from a phrase used by colonials sailing to and from India. Their tickets would state 'Port Outboard Starboard Home', ensuring they got the best cabins. Victoria looked less than interested.

Finally, we got going and Hoagy started taking the photographs, which included some great set-ups in front of the hotel. Victoria was concerned that the whole thing didn't come off too cheesy, so we steered clear of the really corny stuff like the two of them holding up a glass of champagne.

A bit later that morning, when the rest of the media had started to gather outside, I went out the front of the hotel with the friendly security guy Vernon to tell the assembled throng that David and Victoria would be out in a minute. In the meantime, we sent out some soft drinks to keep everyone relaxed. Unbeknown to me, as I was delivering the drinks and chatting to the media, Sky News had been filming me. Quite soon I started getting calls from family, saying they'd seen me in a country lane in Manchester, with a mob of strange men in raincoats holding microphones.

After posing for the media outside the hotel, the couple sped off in a nice Jag and we started figuring how best to get back to London in a hurry so that the copy, pictures and everything could be filed. In those days, it still wasn't done remotely. We packed ourselves – Andy, Sharon, Vernon and me – into a car provided by the local minicab company. The driver hit the pedal and screeched his way down the motorway to the airport, trying to catch the 4.30pm flight back to London. He was a bit of a geezer and looked like someone who might have sold the Happy Mondays something dodgy at the Hacienda. In the name of sustenance, we managed fish and chips on the way.

In the whirlwind around the engagement, Victoria was getting agitated because every time she left the house, photographers were chasing her. She believed someone had tagged her car so that they would know exactly where she was. That's quite possible given everything that was going on. The media were always looking for bits of new technology which would give them the jump on competitors. Fixing a tracker to a car would be no big deal. Victoria was also upset that the *Mirror* had printed a picture of her and David's new cars without the number plates blacked out, which meant that fans could recognise them wherever they went. We got onto that straight away.

There were some ongoing arguments with the *News of the World*'s editor, Phil Hall, at this time. He suggested that we weren't being straight with them and were favouring the *Sun*, which was not true. The stakes were high: the paper put on an extra 235,000 copies on a Sunday if there was a Spice Girls cover and when you added to that the advertising and everything else that goes with it, it was probably an extra £1m in revenue. That's just for one story, so you can see how the pressure was on everybody to get something and why nobody cared too much about the consequences.

Nowadays, technologies like X (formerly Twitter) and other platforms enable stars to communicate directly with fans. Everyone has become a citizen reporter and photographer thanks to their mobile phones. David Bennett, who along with Richard Young can be considered the godfather of party photography, recently told *The Times*: 'The iPhone killed rock'n'roll. A party will get really good, but there's so much organisation. Too much . . . control. And how can you be "extravagant", shall we call it, when anyone can photograph it? Because even a dodgy phone picture is enough. Let alone a video. Plus, social media changes fame and now everyone wants to be seen. A photograph of a celebrity went from being worth hundreds or even thousands to two or three quid today.' Ironically, the Beckhams – and myself in my own small way – contributed to the explosion of celebrity media in the UK while simultaneously sowing the seeds of its downfall. Did we kill the golden goose?

Much of the direction in those days came from David himself, whose approach was two-fold. On the pitch, he trained harder and longer than everyone else, while off the pitch he relentlessly cultivated his personal style. He was acutely conscious of the way he looked and was determined to be original. He wasn't copying the other players; he took his cues from American rap music, fashion and beyond. It marked him out from his teammates.

The fashion focus of Brand Beckham hit the headlines in 1998 when David went out to the Chevre d'Or restaurant in Èze, during the World Cup, dressed in a sleeveless t-shirt and a Jean Paul Gaultier sarong. The look divided opinion. Many admired his 'metrosexuality', while the traditionalists in the football community were predictably scathing.

Beckham's bravery increased his global recognition. Speaking later to the *Daily Star*, David said: 'Maybe I've sometimes overstepped the mark with something that a footballer in the past wouldn't wear, and that's led to trends or people trying new things. Everyone should be allowed to be who they are and dress how they want.'

By now, Brand Beckham was in full swing. The plan wasn't written down but was clear to all involved: to develop him as a global brand that existed beyond the world of football. It was all very informal. The meeting notes were often written on the back of a Chinese takeaway carton lid on a Friday night at Victoria's parents' house in Hertfordshire. Years later, Brand Beckham ended up being studied on university courses and occasionally I'd hear learned professors of pop culture pontificating about the phenomenon on Radio 4. In all honesty, it was simpler than that and was built on perpetual motion, instinct and remorselessly hard work. David and Victoria both practised harder and wanted it more than the rest.

Like the Spice Girls, David was very decent to everyone who worked with him. When he and Victoria were done renovating their new home, Rowneybury House – or 'Beckingham Palace' as the press called it – David wanted to do something to say thank you to the builders. The grounds of the house were so extensive that he had full-size football pitches installed, so he organised a tournament. But this wasn't just any old kickabout. All the builders were divided into teams peppered with professional footballers whom David had enlisted. He played as well. He called it the Rowneybury Cup and had a trophy made in the shape of a silver boot.

I took part and my team made it to the final – but David was on the opposing side, so we had a battle on our hands. We decided to really go for it. We played out of our skins and tackles were flying in – this was the cup final of our lives. David was being kind letting us get a couple of goals ahead so that we could enjoy the moment, but in the second half he suddenly didn't want to be on the losing team and started playing properly. He began spraying shots from the halfway line, but they kept hitting the bar or the post. He was not laughing. So somehow, despite being massively outclassed, our team managed to win it. I've still got the trophy.

Little more than a month after David won the Premier League/FA Cup/Champions League treble with Manchester United, it was time for our main event, which was to take place at Luttrellstown Castle on the outskirts of Dublin. The wedding itself was spectacular. It was almost as if it were in a Hugh Grant film (indeed, the florist had worked on *Four Weddings and a Funeral*). Everything was perfect, from tiny details like the cutlery up to the small but perfectly formed guest list, which contained mainly friends, family and bandmates (plus pretty much the entire England team).

One of the highlights of the evening was to be an exclusive performance from the couple's close friend Elton John, who was flying in unannounced from the South of France. As the wedding got underway, I was on high alert, taking phone calls from the world's media, trying to tell them something but nothing, which is a skill that takes years to perfect. The questions came at me from all angles. Many of them I could answer, but there were other details that had to be kept secret, one of them being the surprise performance. My head was working on all kinds of different levels as I moved around, looking as relaxed as possible but making a million mini calculations and decisions all the time.

Then I received a call from someone in Elton's management: Elton couldn't come after all. They said something terrible had happened and I wondered at first if this was just the normal PR spin, and maybe he was feeling a bit tired. But, no, there really had been a near-tragedy: Elton had suffered a heart attack and wasn't going to be performing today. I knew this was going to be a shock for David and Victoria, but at the same time nobody could have anything other than sympathy for Elton. It was him that we needed to think about.

David and Victoria were at the top of the steps outside the castle, looking beautiful, waving and talking to guests as they came down. I made my way up gingerly, trying to be as unobtrusive as possible, edging up step by step, squeezing past footballers' wives until finally I was up next to them.

I had to keep it pretty succinct; I cupped my hand to my mouth so that no one could hear and explained that Elton wouldn't be performing. After the initial shock and disappointment, when I explained what had happened, they understood instantly. What could you say? The show more than went on.

For Richard Desmond, the gamble paid off handsomely, despite one hair-raising moment when a messenger handling the images disappeared for about three hours and a conspiracy theory emerged that he was in the pay of Max Clifford and had got the images to sell to a rival. In reality, it was a new messenger and he got lost, but our worries weren't that fanciful – people have done plenty of underhand things for much less than £1m. *OK!* sold 1.5 million copies of that issue. They literally couldn't print enough.

The Beckhams were several full-time jobs on their own, but I had to make sure I had enough time and focus for all my other clients too. As the millennium drew to a close, I found myself wearing many hats. This all came together in October 1999 with Net Aid at Wembley Stadium, a noble but odd endeavour organised in collaboration with the UN and backed by American tech providers Cisco, who put millions into the event. The line-up featured George Michael, U2 and David Bowie. The intentions were good. Well, fairly good. I suppose the underlying aim was to promote Cisco Systems – it's just that we didn't talk about that side of things. It was a bit of a mess from the beginning, with jostling over most aspects of the event. At one point, Bono had to get on the phone and act as a peacemaker. At the same time as these preparations were going on, David was meant to be introducing Lauryn Hill at the MTV Music Awards, after the label made it clear they wanted him to. There was jostling there too, with rows between the record company and Coco, which I had to get involved in. What became clear is that, for whatever reason, David was seriously considering whether I was up to the job.

I spent these weeks ducking in and out of different rooms with multiple clients, trying to make each one feel like they were the only one who mattered. It was like something out of a French farce as I went from chatting in Lenny Kravitz's dressing room to bumping into the Aerosmith boys in the corridor. I had to introduce various clients to David Bowie without anyone feeling my true attention was on anything other than them.

In the middle of all this, David called and he was grumpy because I'd got an author to write a book to tie in with his new record. The idea was that it would be more exciting than your standard biography. However, there had been some spelling mistakes in the book and, when David asked me if I'd read the whole thing, I had to admit that I had only skimmed it. He told me in no uncertain terms that he thought the book was 'a crock of shit'. This was extremely unusual for David, who was unfailingly polite and almost never lost his temper in this way.

While I was dealing with the fallout from the book, a story broke about kidnap threats made towards Brooklyn Beckham, which naturally freaked Victoria and David out. I was also due in Germany to see the Eurythmics about working with them. Dave Stewart was a stream of madcap ideas, whereas Annie Lennox clearly didn't enjoy PR and felt she had to save her energy for the shows. Nothing came of it in the end, as is the case with so many conversations of this sort. But I was left with a brilliant story about when Bob Dylan went to see Dave at his studio in Crouch End. Dylan went round to the address he'd been given, knocked on the door and asked for Dave. An old lady answered it, showed him in and said Dave would be home quite shortly. Many hours later, Bob was still sitting there having a cup of tea in the front room when the door opened and in walked a bloke called Dave, back from work. Only it was Dave the local plumber. Bob had been given the wrong address.

As people's thoughts began to turn to celebrating the millennium, I found myself in a debate with David about a big piece of television. Usually, he was up for anything that would promote his new music, but occasionally he went the other way. When I suggested he go on *Newsnight* to be interviewed by Jeremy Paxman, I thought it was a masterstroke. He thought I'd gone crazy and was nervous that it would be a car crash. I was convinced he would be fine and couldn't see any reason why Jeremy, a big fan of David's, would want to stitch him up on TV. David told me that I would be fired if it wasn't a good interview. I quickly realised he wasn't joking.

The interview turned out to be lively and insightful, and David and Jeremy got on very well. They talked about all kinds of things, from alcoholism to bond deals, and there was a particular focus on the internet and all the possibilities that would come with it. After the recording was finished, David came over to me, made an imaginary tick in the air with his hand and said, 'One to you!' before walking out.

More than twenty years later, the conversation is still circulated on social media and is considered one of the most influential interviews David ever did. Three years before, I had attended – on David's insistence – the launch of the first-ever downloadable single by a major artist. David, Coco and I went over to the deserted Apple offices in New York; it was midnight and they had opened especially for us. I didn't really understand why until I watched 300,000 young Americans download the song. Something had changed in the world of music and, as usual, David was pointing the way forward. In the *Newsnight* interview, David had accurately prophesied the future once again. It didn't seem that big a deal at the time. I was just relieved not to get sacked.

Early PR in motion, around 1975. Marc Bolan was playing a college in east London and his parents, Mr and Mrs Feld, had popped in on the way to bingo to wish him luck. Cigarette dangling from my hand, I'm introducing Marc to the gentleman from *Sounds*. Unbelievably, journalists wore Afghan coats in those days!

Not so *High and Mighty*: Uriah Heep on the slippery slope in Switzerland.

Using the one phone in my one-room office in the squat in Covent Garden. I was just excited to be running my own show at last.

Reading all about it to the original members of Motörhead – Eddie Clarke, Lemmy, who is clearly not impressed, and drummer Phil Taylor – somewhere above the English Channel in Gerry Bron's plane, before we hit turbulence.

The Stranglers sign up to United Artists in December 1976 over a pint at the 100 Club in Oxford Street. Left to right: Hugh Cornwell, PR with silly braces, Ian Grant, Dave Greenfield, Jean-Jacques Burnel, Jet Black, Andrew Lauder and Derek Savage.

Always looking to create a new angle, we took Blondie to watch the then highly successful Queens Park Rangers play at Loftus Road in 1979. Debbie was game for a laugh and enjoyed meeting the players after the match, and I got a plug for the band's album *Eat to the Beat*.

Mick Jagger attended a packed press conference at La Beat Route in Soho on 28 April 1982 to announce the band's European tour. I can be spotted to the right in a Doctor Who-style scarf.

Having a laugh with Keith Richards outside the band's hotel in Nice. 'Keef' was generally very relaxed, especially when talking about music.

Mick looking pensive, shielded by security man Carl and resigned-looking publicist, probably at a club gig. Mick was always keen to check out new bands.

Probably trying to convince someone that client Hazel O'Connor was about to become a big star. She did in the end, but unfortunately it was short-lived.

A suited and booted mullet moment with Big Country. Left to right: myself, Mark Brzezicki, Stuart Adamson, Bruce Watson, Tony Butler, Ian Grant and promoter John Giddings.

On the road, things happened in a hurry, and often I'd make notes on my hand. In this instance they look like briefing notes for a rock star staying in room 599, whose interview was likely to include a question about drugs and was possibly with a journalist from the *Telegraph*!

I felt very close to David at times, and this picture captures something of the magic. He was a great influence on me as a person as well as professionally, and I was very lucky to have learned at the feet of the master.

David, Coco Schwab and myself in Bromley, David's teenage stomping ground, around 1993, when his album *The Buddha of Suburbia* was released.

In typically surprising fashion, David asked my four daughters, Lola, Bryony, Josey and Ruby, to add backing vocals to a track called 'The Hearts Filthy Lesson' that he was working on with Brian Eno. The song went on to be included in the hit movie *Seven* and the girls had something to tell their school friends about!

Briefing David about what to expect from the media at Cork Street Gallery before the opening of his first major visual art exhibition in 1995. Iman is very much part of the conversation.

Backstage at Wembley Arena with Labour Party leader Tony Blair prior to a Bowie gig in 1995. He was a genuine fan and stayed for the entire concert, which was over two hours long.

A media moment with soon-to-be global superstar Usher in 2001. Al the journalists wanted a picture wit him because he was so charming

The Spice Girls returned for a press conference on 28 June 2007 to announce a world tour, and we used flags from all the different countries they were playing in to emphasise that this was a global event.

A classic PR and client photograph, capturing the red-carpet aspect of the role perfectly. Here I'm escorting Naomi through the photographers on arrival at the prestigious Serpentine Summer Party.

15

Fame

'Hello Alan. I would like to make an offer totalling a quarter of a million pounds.'

I was pretty sure this was the highest-ever offer for interview rights with a hairdresser from Wales. But in our brave new world, that's what happened when you came second in *Big Brother.** It was the morning after the second series had finished and I felt like an auctioneer as the media offers came in. First it was £80,000, then £100,000, £105,000 and £125,000. Eventually someone bid £200,000 for the interview alone.

Helen Adams was already dreaming of the flash cars and foreign holidays, but everyone kept changing their mind on the deal. News International came in at £150,000 but they packaged it up with additional offers from *FHM* and *Hello!* – carving up subtly different forms of 'exclusive' between themselves – that took the total value above £200,000. Helen was keen to be in *Hello!* because she deemed it classy. But then the ever-powerful Richard Desmond went up to £200,000 for *OK!* and promised

* Our team were handling exactly the same process for the winner of that year, Brian Dowling, who went on to have a career in broadcast.

a run of further coverage afterwards. Helen picked up £250,000 for media deals overall, but in the days that followed, she started questioning whether she could have got even more money.

This was the moment that I seriously wondered how long this dance could go on. It felt as if, in our desire for famous people, we were now reverse-engineering famous people out of thin air. I had no problem with it on one level. I'd much rather Helen got £250,000 than some former Eton schoolboy, but there was something about how febrile and desperate it felt that rang warning bells.

When *Big Brother* had launched the previous year, in 2000, it had been a national event. There had never been anything like it before and some observers described it as being a serious experiment in human behaviour. It was like a zoo and everybody was looking in. Those hungry magazines and newspapers smelled an opportunity. The papers were desperate to get exclusives with the contestants. By the time of the second series, Channel 4 were concerned that the contestants, who were young and not necessarily media-savvy, might sign up to things that weren't in their best interests, so they asked me as a neutral party to guide them through the process. It ended up needing a huge team of us, including Julian Stockton and Stuart Bell, because there was just so much press attention.

The first person to be evicted from the house was a teacher by the name of Penny. Six hundred thousand people called in to vote her off the show. Immediately, she was propelled into the clutches of the media. My job was to handle an auction between the *Sun*, the *Mail*, *OK!*, the *Express* and other publications. Everybody wanted her story and the money was going up, up and away.

The country was gripped by the show and the papers were backing contestants like racehorses. Paul, Liz, Dean, Bubble . . . everybody had a favourite. Seven weeks after Penny left the house, we were down to the final two contestants: Brian and Helen. Brian was backed by the *Mirror* and Helen by the *Sun*. I headed down to the house to watch the final. Various former housemates wanted to talk to me, including Bubble, who called me over conspiratorially. I assumed he was looking for a newspaper deal. No, he wanted a pair of tickets for England vs Germany.

That summer came to an end with horrific finality with the events of 11 September. I was out at lunch with Jodie Dalmeda from BMG discussing the MOBOs and Usher when one of the waiters mentioned that there had been 'some sort of attack in New York', but nobody had any extra information and we carried on eating. It was a beautiful, warm September day. As I got into a minicab to head back to the office, news of what had happened in New York was coming over the radio. By the time I arrived and switched on the news, there were images of the planes crashing into the Twin Towers being shown repeatedly. We all stopped working and gathered around the television. Everybody sensed that the world had changed for ever.

Though it paled in significance, the music world was experiencing a sort of epochal crisis of confidence of its own that winter. When Paul McCartney and Mick Jagger released albums that underperformed in quick succession, the industry was suddenly gripped by the idea that people didn't want the old stars anymore. As the free file-sharing service Napster had begun to take bigger and bigger bites out of record company balance sheets, there were rumours of redundancies and huge cuts to their expenditure. In some ways, it appealed to my punk roots: the old order was being shaken up. But I couldn't escape the nagging feeling that our new focus on fame in and of itself wasn't making anything worthwhile and was going to eat its own tail.

Record companies had started to think that having an act plastered across the newsstand was brilliant marketing. Musicians were turned into 'celebrities', with the consequence that artists who didn't want to play the game found it harder to get traction. The labels would pay through the nose to win and retain the most tabloid-friendly acts. This trend even dragged someone like David Bowie into it when word came that Virgin EMI weren't going to release his new album.

It started when I received a message from Ashley Newton, head of A&R at EMI, referring to 'bad news'. I'd suspected that this might be coming, but it was still a shock. Sales hadn't been what they were for a while, but this was David Bowie! Only the previous summer he'd played an astonishing Glastonbury set, which reminded everyone he was one of the most iconic British songwriters and performers ever. But I'm sure the accountants had pointed out that they weren't making any money from sales of the songs featured in that performance. David hadn't wanted to do Glastonbury and Michael Eavis wasn't at all keen either (possibly worried that David would do a drum and bass set), but John Giddings and I both passionately believed that this could be an amazing reminder of David's brilliance and significance in the culture. So I got something going with the *Sunday Times* to try to stir some speculation, which I hoped would show David there was hunger for him to perform. I wanted to be extremely subtle about it. However, not for the first time, I overplayed my hand. The next morning's *Sunday Times* headline was 'Bowie to Headline Glasto'. Apparently, the Glastonbury ticket office was inundated with ticket enquiries like never before in their history.

After a few days, neither Julian Stockton or I had heard from David and we were worried that he was annoyed. Then we got a message from him: 'You're very naughty boys. Don't ever do that again. Well done.' David once told me that the first time he'd played Glastonbury it was to 2,000 people and the backstage catering was the farmhouse kitchen where you'd go for your milk and eggs. This time, there was such a clamour to get in that the fences fell down. He walked out at twilight to an audience of 120,000.

David didn't want the entire gig to go out on TV, whereas the head of music at the BBC could see how enormous this moment was going to be. The argument was still going as David took to the stage. In fact, I was still having the argument with him at the side of the stage for the first three songs of his performance. In between songs, we put a compromise position to David, but he wouldn't budge and the BBC weren't able to broadcast the whole set.

After hearing the news about David's album, I immediately started putting feelers out for interest from other labels, but surprisingly there wasn't much. It was more the end of an era than the end of David. In fact, he'd been here before when he was let go by RCA. David's next release, this time on EMI, had been *Let's Dance*, which went on to sell 10.7 million copies, so beware men in suits.

The reality, though, was that David was without a record contract. Time waits for no artist. I supposed he had based his career on sudden left turns; Tin Machine, for instance, had been one twist too many and the fans didn't follow. God only knew how David was going to react to the news. To add to the stress, I was in the middle of navigating my own difficult separation from Valerie. I had moved out of our family home and into a flat.

I worked out how I was going to tell David about the label and the bigger picture context I was going to frame the news in – how it was shaping up to be a horrible year-end for the record industry with further firings and droppings to come. The unapproachable A&R departments, the heads of promotion missing in action, the MDs that weren't MDs and couldn't even sign off on a meal ticket, the massive costs involved in promoting records, the short-term emphasis on pop and vanishing margins had all contributed to the downward spiral. 'Even Rod Stewart has been dropped, but we've been here before, David. This is just a blip. In fact, it can be good news and free you from the restrictive constraints of a record company – although unfortunately it also liberates you from their cheque book, which may be less appealing.' I wouldn't place any emphasis on the latter point for now. I may not have been to university, but I surely qualified for honours in the art of diplomacy by this stage. David would have time to think of a new strategy, or maybe he'd just walk away from music and concentrate on his art or being a father or . . .

David was understandably a bit shaken when he heard the news. After all, he *was* David Bowie, and he had been with the EMI group for nearly twenty years. I hoped he would stay positive and that we'd go ahead with setting up the small label – focusing on cool new acts and following David's own artistic direction – that we'd been talking about for a while.

All was quiet at the record company. Not even a call from the UK MD. It seemed the decision was made a while ago and everyone had just been going through the motions. Ashley Newton told me that everyone felt the album was really good, but that it lacked an obvious big hit single, the inevitable conclusion being that there wasn't enough financial return for the time that would need to be invested.

David was already on the front foot. He was incredible when there was a crisis. He wanted us to hit the press before EMI did, avoiding the 'EMI drop Rod' type of story. No, David was going to 'leave' EMI, not get dropped.

We concocted a hard-hitting press release about how David was forming his own label, had signed acts and acquired a studio. I was a little nervous about the reaction from EMI, especially because of a sentence we'd cheekily inserted suggesting that David was free to leave because the label forgot to review his option. We suggested toning it down to David, but he wouldn't hear of it and put the phone down.

It was the time of our office Christmas party and everyone was headed into Soho, beers in hand. I was going to make the annual fun speech, but the Bowie announcement had to come first. If we were going to beat EMI, who would also be beginning festive celebrations, we needed to get in there first. So, we went in strong and, by the time the first editions dropped, we had a 'furious Bowie quits label' type of story popping up all over the place. There wasn't much subtlety in national tabloids when placing a story like this. The papers were either on your side or not, and that's where the PR really earns their money. They sure as hell were on our side now.

David was a bit freaked out at first by how hard we were

pushing it, but he of all people understood how important it is to control the agenda. Virgin were also upset – both in California and London. They were reeling from calls from the *LA Times* and *Sunday Times* business sections chasing them for comment. Ken and Nancy Berry, the heads of Virgin, hadn't reacted yet. Nancy had gone above and beyond in her support for David, and I'm sure she was as upset as I was that it had come to this. I recommended to Virgin that they keep quiet and let David 'get it off his chest'. Hopefully, wise counsel would prevail and they wouldn't retaliate.

In the end, the story came out pretty much as we planned it. Even Ashley Newton called from LA on the quiet to compliment us on the stylish spin. David seemed on top of the world to be out of his contract with Virgin and was making plans left, right and centre.

While running his own label would have been a great creative trip, the news that Columbia, a division of Sony, wanted to sign David could only be positive. Despite the disappointment at the way Virgin had treated him, David had had a couple of tentative conversations with other labels. He and his super-smart business manager Bill Zysblat had gone for a meeting with the Sony exec Donnie Iner. David went dressed classically in a tailored suit and Church's shoes – somewhere between Lawrence Olivier and Frank Sinatra. He was in the best mood afterwards, cracking jokes and generally smokin', convinced that the company would support him. And with the Meltdown Festival and some European dates to come, we were looking at a vastly different scenario than the depressing one that had confronted us a mere few weeks previously. I was thrilled for him in this moment of triumph. He deserved it.

Meltdown was a brilliantly mixed arts and music festival on London's South Bank that David was curating the latest iteration of. I had spent all week preparing and was up and about early on Saturday, but dozed a bit in the afternoon and subsequently felt a bit too laid back for comfort on my arrival at the Royal Festival Hall. Jonathan Ross was just getting out of a natty sports car with a handful of Bowie records that he intended to spin later that evening. I went about my many little duties, such as checking which media were in the house and making sure the photographers could get clear pictures.

Just to confuse matters, one of my other clients, Victoria Beckham, came on the phone right in the middle of it all and I had to find a quiet place to speak to her. I was never entirely sure what David Bowie thought about the Beckhams. Victoria was complaining about a particularly vitriolic piece in the *Mail* by Jeff Powell about her husband. The article was harsh, even belittling the bottle it required to take his celebrated penalty against Argentina at the 2002 World Cup. Victoria was also concerned about a *Sun* piece saying that David had skipped Elton's party and was holidaying instead. He was indeed holidaying – at Elton's place.

As I wandered by the other David's dressing room, he was in the mood for a bit of banter. I really loved our off-the-cuff conversations and I like to think they relaxed him. Maybe that was one of my roles – to bring a bit of ordinary life into these pressurised situations. He looked at the hi-tech Nokia phone I was using and laughed loudly at the image of a toilet I'd assigned to the phone number of a manager I didn't like. We were agreed on that one – as we know, David didn't like managers at all.

David was interested that the Who were carrying on without

John Entwistle, whose death had just been announced. He figured that Pete Townshend had realised something like this might happen, hence he'd rehearsed another bass player, Pino Palladino. Pino was in the wings and, only a matter of days after the Ox's death, was playing the Hollywood Bowl and presumably doing 'Boris the Spider'. Ironically, the tour had supposedly been planned to get Entwistle out of a financial jam in the first place.

Pete and David were friendly with each other and David even referred to him during his headline Meltdown set. He recollected them both being on the famous 5.15am milk train after the clubs had shut one night. 'We both wrote songs about it, completely different of course.'

The show itself was nothing short of stupendous. David played the whole of *Low*, which came to life in a wonderfully unexpected way. I remembered it as the album you put on at 4am coming down from speed in the punk days – deeply atmospheric and darkly moody. The Pistols' drummer Paul Cook, who was at the show, noted it was the only album from the older generation of rock stars that you were allowed to play back then.

As I often did, I felt so lucky to be working with David. So much of my company's work with pop artists felt like a firework: bright and loud but gone in a burst. With the best will in the world, I didn't think much of the work we were doing with *Big Brother* contestants was going to echo through eternity. But here was David in his fifth decade as a songwriter, in conversation with the past but not as part of some misty-eyed nostalgia.

His new album, *Heathen,* released by Sony, was doing better than anything he had put out for about fifteen years and would hit gold status in the UK within the next few weeks. As ever, the media were fascinated by him. Victoria Beckham herself called me to say that she and David had noticed the amount of publicity Bowie was getting and that it reassured them that they were in good hands. It's rare to get that kind of feedback, but it made me laugh that the Beckhams should be taking comfort from the level of publicity David Bowie received. In many ways though, the clout that I had with many of the tabloids because of clients like the Beckhams did mean I had been able to keep focus on David during a period of his career when otherwise he would have been less culturally visible. I also felt fortunate that I had a view across the whole of the media, because it meant I had the confidence to say no sometimes.

This is exactly what I did when it was suggested that David do a round of regional TV shows to help sell *Heathen*. Lots of record companies were looking at the media environment and the sorts of stories and artists that were getting attention, and then trying to force all their acts into boxes they didn't fit in. But I felt strongly that doing this with David could devalue him and make it harder to get bigger TV appearances when we needed them. David listened to both points of view before agreeing that we shouldn't do the regional TV. He understood that the thing about being in a media bubble is that the bubble eventually bursts.

However, some people very much made that media environment work for them. If Robbie Williams had started his career ten years earlier, he might not have had the success he did. But in the early 2000s he was a global celebrity, hanging out with the Spice Girls and Oasis, and appearing on the front pages every day. I decided to pitch to be his PR.

It was a Monday afternoon in late 2002 and I was having a last-minute meeting with Robbie's managers, David Einthoven and Tim Clark. Although Tim and David were very friendly, I mistakenly thought they were just going through the motions with me. The next day, I was surprised when I got a call telling me that I was hired. Before you could sing when you're winning, I was talking to Robbie's personal manager Josie in LA and being lined up for conflabs with his team. I was thrilled – but secretly I was also daunted by my workload. I was stretched thinner than a Rizla paper.

The first proper strategy meeting was via conference call, and I had to tell everybody about our media plans. Josie was on the line from LA and the thought crossed my mind that Robbie might be listening in. There was no evidence of this until near the end of the call, when I heard a mumble of assent from a voice that sounded remarkably like Robbie's.

The approach we wanted to take with Robbie was to maintain his visibility and image as a credible, cool, respected singer, but also make him a little bit inaccessible – not least because Robbie didn't want to do lots of interviews.* Much of our strategy was about keeping him in the press without having to give access: providing a picture of him kicking a football or in rehearsals and supplying a light-hearted story that was appealing to the news editors. The quid pro quo was that in return they would mention the tour or the album somewhere in the story.

There was big Robbie news on the horizon. He was in talks to sign a major six-album record deal with EMI. Tim Clark had

---

* For a very brief period, I also worked for Gary Barlow and was tasked with making him more edgy.

pledged to Dominic Mohan, editor of the Bizarre column in the *Sun*, that next time a significant Robbie story broke, he would tip him off ahead of the pack.* Tim asked me to let Mohan know that the EMI deal was about to be done, so I phoned him and dropped a few hints. The story went from there and, by the time he rang back, it was obvious that this was going to be a splash – 'splash' being newspaper terminology for a front-page story. He had exaggerated the story out of all recognition, adding a lot of conjecture about the type of deal and quoting a massive signing figure of £80 million. This would make it the biggest British record deal in history.

Rather awkwardly, while I was talking to the *Sun* journalist, I was standing outside the MOBO Awards where reporters from all the other tabloids were taking their seats, a few feet away from me, unaware of this skulduggery. It was imperative that I kept my voice low, secret agent-style. I knew the other writers would be annoyed when they got calls later that night from their news desks telling them about the *Sun*'s exclusive.

I was worried about how everyone was going to react – and I was right to be. Tony Wadsworth, CEO of EMI, saw the front page of the *Sun* when the next day's papers were revealed that night and he called me in a rage. They hadn't been planning to spend that much on Robbie's deal, but suddenly £80m was the going rate. Tony was certain it had been leaked from our side. I promised to investigate but couldn't very well tell him I was acting under instructions from the management.

The next day, my alarm went off at 6am. I struggled out of

* Tim, who recently retired, was immensely respected and popular in the music industry.

bed and pulled myself together before heading off to Notting Hill to write a statement about the Robbie EMI deal at his office. I sat there, shattered, trying to work out the wording – lots of stuff about the deal being 'innovative', 'ground-breaking' and 'a watershed', all of which was true. This agreement meant that EMI would participate in Robbie's touring, publishing and merchandising, effectively making them not just a record company but an entertainment business. Robbie Williams was committed to them for the foreseeable future.

I organised a press conference for Robbie at the office and duly set up the photographers and cameramen. Robbie arrived, stood in front of the cameras, and leaped in the air with both his arms up like a footballer winning the World Cup. 'I'm rich!' he shouted. 'Beyond my wildest dreams!' I caught the eye of Lucy, Tim's assistant. It was a wonderful moment that perfectly captured the UK's confidence at this time.

16

Get Up, Stand Up

'What do you think?' said Victoria, her eyes bright. For one of only a few times in my life, I had no idea what to say.

'Play it again,' I said to buy time, hoping that maybe I hadn't heard what I thought I had. But she pressed play and there it was again, the familiar drums, bass guitar and organ. It was like a karaoke version of 'Get Up, Stand Up' by Bob Marley, barely any different from the original. I couldn't quite believe what I'd just heard. It seemed that producer Damon Dash had recorded her vocal over a thrown-together backing track. I didn't really know how to break the news to her. I knew she was genuinely excited at the thought of pushing the pop boundaries and exploring a type of music she found so much more exciting. People still had this idea of her as that stand-offish caricature, but she was actually incredibly warm and funny, and deeply invested in trying to make music she felt passionate about. It was the kind of music that she and David listened to, but stepping out of that pop bubble left her vulnerable. Victoria had an authentic interest in where urban culture was going and I would never want to trample on that. But I feared this was not the move. I went through the motions of getting clearance from

Island and Chris Blackwell's office. They must have thought we'd lost our marbles.

We had been pootling along, making a dance-pop album with A&R man Pete Hadfield and collecting some nice songs which were going be released on Jeremy Marsh's Telstar label. The sales of Victoria's 2001 debut album hadn't been mind-blowing, but they were prepared to go again. But then Victoria decided she should be making a much more urban record. It was a bit startling, really. She introduced me to an American rap entrepreneur called Damon Dash, whom she had met in New York.

He clearly wasn't convinced that we knew how to make a record. Things became more and more difficult for us as the process was fraught with creative differences and tensions. It was upsetting, but I had to try to contextualise it. You can't do this job if you don't take the artistic temperament into account. It's just a fact of life: we are dealing with highly strung, creative individuals. You have to find ways of managing it in your own head, otherwise you can't carry on.

Once, a particular client had really been on my case, complaining endlessly and being quite aggressive about it. I thought back to school days and remembered how insolence drove people over the edge. Maybe this approach would work with my client. And sure enough, the more polite I was, the more upset he got. I even decided to turn it into a bit of theatre one day. I knew he was calling, so I got a few people up from the PR floor and had them sit around in my office as I put the call on the loudspeaker. The client was on fire that day. 'This is the worst fucking PR campaign I've ever seen. You don't know what you're doing.' I would politely interject with comments like 'I say, that's a jolly shame', adding that 'everyone here is trying their best, you know, old chap'. This English gentleman persona was working a treat. The politer I got, the closer he came to combustion. He would have really exploded if he'd known he had an audience listening to this performance and practically wetting themselves. Thank you, ex-client, for a ruddy good afternoon's entertainment and not getting under my skin at all on this occasion. Must run, old chap – afraid I've got another pressing appointment.

When we were working with Dash, the *Sunday Mirror* ran a story about Victoria's fury at the suggestion she should get rid of him. 'Posh won't ditch Dash' screamed the headline. I was trying desperately to make sure there was the right sort of coverage of Victoria and her album too.* It seemed to me there was more than a hint of racism involved in the glee the press took documenting the tensions between her and Dash instead.

Later in the year, this tendency was even more prevalent when the press went to town on a story about a police raid on an aftershow party for the MOBO (Music of Black Origin) awards. The MOBOs had been first launched by Kanya King in 1996 as an antidote to the Brits, which seemed to honour the same few artists year after year. Annie Lennox had won British Female Solo Artist for as long as anyone could remember, yet Black

* While I would obviously in no way compare our experiences, I don't think there was anyone working in PR in April 2003 who didn't have a shiver of recognition in the midst of the invasion of Iraq, when the Iraqis' spokesman, who would become known as Comical Ali, claimed on TV that the Iraqi army had repulsed the Americans. Unfortunately for the hapless comms man, some American tanks rolled up behind him, with guys chewing gum and smoking cigarettes. He carried on broadcasting regardless. If you wanted to find a more perfect image for a PR person left out to dry, it would be hard to find.

singers like Mica Paris, Beverley Knight and Des'ree rarely, if ever, seemed to pop up. There needed to be an alternative that recognised how much great Black music there was around. A glance at the charts should have been enough, but some people were still living in the past.

I had handled the publicity for all the MOBO shows as it evolved from being a night of specialist music awards into a global brand and one of the most hotly anticipated events on the music calendar.

The MOBOs were also incredibly glamorous: as well as the performers, the audience made a real effort to dress up and became part of the show. It wasn't one of those corporate things with lots of executives in suits talking business and disappearing off to the toilets with alarming regularity. It was more of a celebration of music, style and culture. Victoria Beckham performed one year; another time, Mel B presented. Many big US stars turned up too. I once went to a soundcheck with Usher and he insisted that I get up onstage and that he'd teach me a few dance moves, much to the amusement of the small crowd milling around. I was terrified because Usher, now up there in the hall of fame as one of the true greats of R&B, was widely recognised to be the best dancer in the world and I may well have been the worst. Young, glamorous columnists like Eva Simpson, Sarah Tetteh and Jessica Callan from the *Mirror*'s 3AM Girls got what the awards were all about, filling their columns with fun stories, pics and gossip.

The show had many rivers to cross – last-minute pull-outs by acts, resistance from the industry, a lack of funds – but it was its reputation for 'trouble' that I wanted to address. After the show, people would organise their own MOBO parties, which would become part of the story. Gun crime was rife in the early 2000s and inevitably it spilt over into the music world sometimes. There was a shooting incident at a post-MOBOs boat party one year. The tabloids loved this and pretty much had the headlines pre-written: 'Trouble at Black Music Event' or 'Riot at the MOBOs'. It really got out of hand to the point where if somebody as much as knocked over a drink at the party afterwards, more lurid front pages would pop up.

Much of my job was firefighting these stories, year in, year out. The conversations went on late into the night. I felt so sorry for Kanya, who worked incredibly hard in the face of resistance all around and on a shoestring budget only to have to deal with this. She was a mixture of sad, philosophical, hurt and angry as we seemed unable to stop the tide of nastiness. Her team members, like the brilliant Vannessa Amadi, would painstakingly relay to me what had really happened and I and my team – including our head of music Chris Goodman and our head of pop David Lim – would battle to get the headlines changed. Many a night after the show I'd be remonstrating with a hard-bitten news editor or trying to contextualise. We'd all been at plenty of shows with pretty much entirely white audiences where there was trouble and they were never described in anywhere near the same way. Some of the reporting was just lazy, but underneath there was definitely a racist agenda with some of the writers.

In 2001, our client Asher D from So Solid Crew had got into a silly argument with a traffic warden at Hanover Square that escalated and resulted in police finding a converted air gun in his car. At no point was the weapon shown or used, but nonetheless it was a gun – and given the current context, this wasn't going to be a slap-on-the-wrists job.

Asher was the approachable one from So Solid, always friendly and with a background as a respected actor – he would go on to star in the ground-breaking TV series *Top Boy*. It all seemed so unlikely and everyone hoped he was going to get lenient treatment. The initial signs were promising with the judge pulling the half-hearted Crown Prosecution Service up on a few points, but he still remanded Asher inside for three weeks until sentencing. Asher's mother was very upset, his girlfriend cried and he looked bewildered. After all, he was only nineteen years old. Nina Santiago from the office handled the press conference on the steps outside and I endeavoured to stay in the background, not sure if being seen to be involved with this case was a great association for the company, especially given the number of pop stars we were then representing.

The case had become high profile and the court was packed for sentencing with much more media than last time. The prosecution pointed out that the police found Ashley's attitude 'refreshing' when he admitted possession of the gun and explained that he was 'relieved that the gun had been found'. I really felt for him, as it was clear he had been caught in a situation that had spiralled out of control.

Simon Pendol, the defence lawyer, took centre stage, and strong use he made of it too. He supplied the judge with letters from the great and the good of the entertainment world, including us. He then took the unusual step of playing part of Ashley's initial confession at the police station back to the court on a tape recorder. This was definitely the voice of a young man caught up in a mess and very regretful, not the bravado of a would-be gangster.

The judge refrained from making an example of the rapper.

The sentence of eighteen months, with only nine to serve if he behaved well, was painful, but the courts were under pressure. The truth is that many people wanted to sweep largely Black-on Black crime under the carpet, with disastrous results for all concerned. Ashley served his time in exemplary fashion and went on to revitalise his career, closing the book on this whole experience. I wasn't at all surprised by his deserved rise as an actor.

The press no longer told you that the ink meant they couldn't print photographs of Black artists, but there was still a hell of a long way to go. I would often think of my daughters and what it meant to them to see artists who looked like them, and I felt committed to making progress wherever I could.

Sometimes I wondered if the reporting would ever improve but, bit by bit, it started to become more balanced. Nowadays, the MOBOs are viewed in the same way as any other music awards show, but it's been a long road and Kanya massively deserves all the accolades that have been bestowed on her. It's taken a quarter of a century, but the awards have helped change perceptions and launch waves of new talent, including Stormzy, Headie One, Central Cee and Little Simz, to name just a few.

Soon after the Dash drama, Victoria came to see me to tell me she had decided she wanted to make a change, meaning we'd cease working together. I was both her manager and PR, so this was a big deal. I appreciated the fact she gave me the news face to face and gave up a few hours of her busy time. Soon after, her new manager called me to make a settlement. David Beckham called a few weeks later, knowing how upset I was about the loss. It was incredibly thoughtful and caring. Unfortunately, I'd smoked a strong joint just before picking up the phone and couldn't get many words out. He must have thought I was that devastated. Still, it was a classy thing for him to do.

What did the Spice Girls really, really mean, if anything? Was Girl Power a real thing or just a marketing slogan? For me, I suppose they represented family as opposed to so many of the acts I'd worked with whose main interests were getting smashed and moving on to the next town. As the father of four strong daughters, I thought it was great to see a group of similarly strong-willed women conquering the male world of the music industry, although the irony of me being a white middle-aged male (one among very many surrounding them) was almost entirely lost on me at the time. By this point, of course, punk had been so thoroughly absorbed and processed by the mainstream that any association I had with it meant practically nothing. Representing the biggest girl group of all time was certainly great cachet for me with the younger members of my family and friends. It's odd to think now, as each band member with their 'character' seems decidedly old-fashioned, but I remember looking out into the crowd at Spice Girls concerts and watching the faces of the thousands of young women who were energised by them and their music. It wasn't revolutionary, but they represented a multicultural, young, buzzing and fun London. Sometimes a band being packaged can actually tell us more about the time than an 'authentic' group. The pop mainstream was so ready to embrace these young women and the audience were so passionate. I know that for my daughters, it meant a lot to see Scary Spice reclaiming the stereotype of the 'angry Black woman' – and wearing a sexy leopard-print outfit while doing so.

I would go on to work with the other members of the

group in various capacities over the coming years, but stopping working with the Beckhams was very much the end of an era. What I always tried to keep in mind was that there's always another chapter. But being fired is never pleasant, however the client does it.

One household name didn't call me when my time was up, but just sent an email, which in turn was circularised. I tried calling but nobody was home. It wasn't like this was a massive financial loss. In fact, I had recently told the artist that I wanted to increase our fees by five per cent, which was well under the rate of inflation. Seeing as they were probably our lowest-paying client, we're talking only a few hundred pounds extra. They baulked and said they would need to consider it. Then there was a piece in the paper about the artist needing to 'make a change'. I couldn't help but cattily wonder if it was loose change.

I was fired by Nick Faldo for a line he didn't like in the *Sunday Express* about him reuniting with a caddy named Fanny. Some writer had made an inappropriate joke. In view of the great work we'd done turning around his image, getting him on the cover of the *Sunday Times* and the *Observer* magazine, I was disappointed to receive a four-letter voicemail early Sunday morning.

The following Thursday, I got a call from Faldo's agent, reinstating me, which wasn't surprising seeing as there had been a fabulous feature in *The Times* on the Tuesday, set up by us. On Saturday, Faldo's ex, Gill, talked to the *Mail* about his inability to 'communicate with humans'. I understood where she was coming from.

Often there's nothing you could have done differently. That had been the case with Elton John the year before when, after working with him for five years, a negative review was published in the *Independent* slating one of his gigs. Elton was seriously affronted by it. I was summoned down to the Shepherd's Bush Empire where he was doing a show and given a thorough dressing-down, my error being that I should have 'taken more time choosing the reviewer'. If only it was that simple: that decision is left to the reviews editor, not the PR. On this occasion, I survived the telling off, slightly bruised but alive to see another day. Or so I thought. By some bizarre misfortune, the *Independent* made a mistake at the printers and accidentally ran the review again. This time I was 'let go'.

Getting fired simply comes with the territory when you're a PR. A manager might find his or herself on the receiving end of a P45 a couple of times, but for a PR it can be an almost weekly occurrence. We're the easiest to blame, especially if there's been a bad review or a lack of coverage. 'Always shoot the messenger' seemed to be the mantra of certain managers and labels. I had come to process it by seeing it like buses: there's always another one coming along.

In the 2000s, I did some work for Riverdance maestro Michael Flatley and he gave me the bullet for no good reason. A few years later, his manager called and asked if I would do some publicity work for him. I said yes, assuming they were aware of our history. From my perspective, it was all water under the bridge. On the day of the meeting, I turned up to see various people sitting around a table, Flatley at the head of it. When we caught eyes, he did a double take.

'Haven't I seen you before?'

'Yes,' I said.

'Didn't I fire you before?'

'Yes . . .' I replied hesitantly.

'Well, you're fired again.'

I actually didn't mind, as he'd paid me for the work and what he'd achieved with Riverdance was incredibly impressive.

A few years later, it was Paul McCartney. When I got hired to work with Paul after a call from his office, I was honoured. After all, he was a major client to have and a Beatle to boot. His team wanted to know who would work on the account day to day, realising that it wouldn't be me. The way our company is structured is that you have a number of senior publicists, each responsible for their own accounts, with me looking after much of the client relations, strategy and, of course, the heavyweight relationships, such as those with newspaper editors. Some people have criticised my adherence to this way of working, saying that I would be much safer working directly with a few clients. My view was that that would make me vulnerable and ultimately less effective because I'd always be nervous about getting fired. With a bigger spread of clients, you can handle the normal churn of a PR company with clients coming and going. If I had my career again, maybe I wouldn't have spread myself so thinly, but then again, if I had done that, I wouldn't have been able to build a company and wouldn't have had half the adventures and exciting clients I've had.

But I did sometimes come to regret this way of working – for instance, when I'd entrusted a colleague with putting together a press campaign for Robert Smith, the lead singer of the Cure. He is a very gentle soul and an extremely talented man – to me he seems quite undervalued as a great British songwriter. Apart from being very shy, he was just never that bothered about mainstream coverage, although the music press like the *NME* and *Melody Maker* did some great interviews with him.

On one occasion, we decided to try to set up a really substantial media schedule. I assigned an enthusiastic young publicist who had recently joined the company the job of calling up national papers, Sunday supplements, women's magazines, radio stations – the lot, basically. Robert's manager Chris Parry and his lovely PA Ita would check in with me to see how things were progressing and I would confer with the young publicist, who assured me that the interest was really good and we already had lots of commitments for interviews. Apparently, the *Telegraph*, the *Express*, Q and the *Mirror* were already locked in. I relayed this back to the management and all was going swimmingly – until I got a bit more forensic in some of my questions about which journalists would be conducting the interviews. At first, the young PR sounded quite convincing, but after a while the cracks started to show, especially after I bumped into one of the writers who was on our list and he knew nothing about an interview with Robert.

I confronted the publicist the next day in our offices in Tottenham Court Road. He looked at me with panic in his eyes and then, without warning, stood up and ran down the corridor and out of the front door, not saying a word. I was shocked, but it soon dawned on me what had happened. He had invented an entire schedule of interviews. Not one of them actually existed – it was the Mary Celeste of publicity campaigns. Chris and Robert were surprisingly understanding. Maybe they saw the funny side of it, or perhaps Robert was relieved not to have to go through with it all. Last time I heard, the hapless publicist was working in a bar – probably serving make-believe pints!

Paul McCartney's team were very business-focused and we received a sixty-page contract, easily the longest I'd seen. It took months to negotiate and cost a lot in legal fees. Paul himself was always very personable, super charming to be with. Sometimes I'd go around to his office in Soho Square and he'd play me new material. He was very tuned into any feedback and, like all '60s stars, very conscious of the print media. Once I accompanied him down to a public school where he was doing a memorial concert for Linda. Both he and I had arrived early before the journalist from the *Sunday Times*, and were left in the school music room to chat. He got up and asked me if I'd like to hear a song. 'Sure,' I said, before he sat at the piano and launched into 'Lady Madonna'. It was great and even I had to pinch myself. I'd bought the single at school and here was I getting a private performance.

Things began to change when Heather Mills came on the scene. At one media event around a photo exhibition in Camden, she reamed Stuart and myself out, saying that we didn't know anything about the media and should follow her advice about how to organise a press conference. It was all a bit embarrassing, really. Later, it became an acrimonious fight when Paul decided to break up with her and the nasty stories and briefing in the press reached a crescendo. She wasn't exactly popular in the first place and our job was to make sure that that stayed the case with the key writers. We had incredible contacts and, given the fact that we also looked after David Bowie and the Beckhams at that time, considerable influence.

But when a key member of my team left and Paul decided he wanted to go with them, I said I needed a bit of time to find a replacement PR and stabilise the company. This was what the onerous contract guaranteed me. Then one of his team rang up and started threatening me, saying that Paul should be allowed to leave immediately, and swearing and slamming the phone down when I didn't immediately acquiesce. I was shocked. I hadn't experienced this side of working with Paul.

He sent me a persuasive personal letter, but I responded saying that Outside was in effect a small family business and that I couldn't allow it to be collapsed, however important he thought it to have my former PR up and running and fixing media schedules right away. Part of me felt like saying that the Beatles were only the Westlife of their generation or how much I admired Lennon, but luckily I held back. I had to take it on the chin and keep my cool to get through it all.

Even here, I had to pinch myself. Here was I having a full-on personal row *with a Beatle.*

It's not always what clients do but how they do it, and that's so true when it comes to being 'let go'. Fired, given the old heave-ho, given the chop, laid off – there really are myriad ways of dressing up what is always a nasty experience. There are, though, nice ways of doing it and some not so nice. When getting sacked, usually the best outcome you can hope for is a call or email from an agent or manager or, in the very best circumstances, the artist. The worst is when you don't get told at all and instead hear about it through the grapevine – or, God forbid, another PR calls you to tell you they will be looking after your client from here on in.

Invariably, as a PR you spend time with the artist out-of-hours, seeing the 'real' them. Most stars are almost ordinary people, although they live in fantastic worlds, often surrounded by sycophants and totally out of touch with reality. That doesn't make them bad people. They're just in need of careful handling sometimes. They are often victims of the showbusiness system: built up too quickly, money thrown at them and living the dream. Some are generous, like Elton and Debbie Harry. Others, like Mick Jagger, keep a careful eye on their wallet. Some are surprisingly loyal, others drop you like a cheap pair of tights when they realise you can't secure them a *Vogue* cover.

Mick would invite me round for afternoon tea at his house in Kensington to discuss business. Jerry Hall would be there too, and the kids would be playing around us, so you become one of the family. You allow yourself to become emotionally invested. You're lulled into a false sense of security. They confide things in you that you maybe rather wouldn't know. Then the storm passes and they forget the vital role you've played, or maybe want to forget you because you remind them of whatever it was they did. Or perhaps they see you like an unexploded mine that might go off any time, so they decide to get rid of you. You've become too close just by caring and doing your job properly. Now you get the 'Dear Alan' letter.

I don't know if I took these dumpings any harder than other PRs did as a result of the rejection I had when I was young. Maybe I just had more of them. Either way, these enforced falls from grace could take me months, even years, to get over. I'd wake up in the middle of the night wondering what I did wrong. When the relationship comes to an end, it can be tough to swallow. How the artist handles it can make all the difference.

Generally, though, I've managed to deal with it without showing the client the hurt that I was feeling as I didn't want them to have the pleasure of seeing me upset. At school, whenever I got caned, I would never cry and I would never show pain – and if I could manage to smile as they hit me, all the better. So, I would try to draw on that. But I was also under no illusions that this was the nature of the job. You're rolling with all kinds of tough characters and if you can't take the heat, you shouldn't be in the kitchen.

One of the things that made this period easier to bear was the number of new clients in various different worlds we were working with. Outside, which had always been a specialist music agency, was suddenly representing celebrities of all stripes. Alongside models and TV chefs, we took on a considerable number of sportspeople.

In fact, Ian Grant and I had dabbled in football in the early '80s, signing up Spurs captain Steve Perryman, Gerry Armstrong – the Watford player who had sprung to almost overnight fame by having a spectacular World Cup playing for Northern Ireland in Spain – and Steve Foster of Brighton and the England national side.

I'd also very briefly worked with the boxer Lennox Lewis early on in his career. I went to see him fight at Crystal Palace Leisure Centre when his opponent was a butcher from France who'd taken a half-day off. Years later, I tried to broker a deal for *OK!* magazine with Mike Tyson. I ended up downstairs at the Dorchester Hotel with a man called Crocodile. Surrounded by old ladies having scones and tiny sandwiches, he mimed what would happen if the magazine didn't pay.

We started working with Arsenal's Swedish midfielder Freddie Ljungberg, who I had signed by turning up unannounced in Gothenburg at his lawyer's office, which was the only address I could find. Freddie had been sporting a red mohawk recently and I had been become somewhat obsessed with the idea that he was the first punk footballer. However, when I gifted him some signed Sex Pistols albums and was met with polite but total bemusement, I learned the useful lesson that sometimes a haircut is just a haircut. My colleague Caroline McAteer brokered a high-profile deal with Calvin Klein, which featured him photos of him in his underpants. It was an enormously successful campaign and started appearing on the tube and buses across London.

I also once spent a year trying to convince Novak Djokovic to do some press interviews. I liked Novak, and he was clearly very smart, but he was utterly uninterested in PR. The first time I had met him was in a bungalow in Wimbledon, the night before his first match that year. I was earnestly pitching all sorts of PR ideas to him. After a few minutes, I realised he was looking at me nonplussed, at which point one of his aides said, 'Novak only speaks Serbian. We expected this meeting to be in Serbian.' Even I didn't know what to say to this. At this point, Novak burst out laughing: 'Look at your face!'

In those years, it felt as if we were beginning to see a new phase in which the different parts of culture increasingly echoed one another. It didn't seem to matter if it was music, sport or fashion – there were clients who wanted to use the media in new ways to tell a story about themselves. And they would take me to some very interesting places indeed.

17

You Spin Me Right Round

'Alan, could you come in here?' said Tony Blair. 'I need to talk to you about something important.'

It was 2006 and, for a variety of complicated reasons, I was in the House of Commons to introduce the Columbian pop star Shakira to Gordon Brown. It was all part of our plan to make her a bit more credible. Her then boyfriend was the Argentinian finance minister, so I decided that we'd set up a pap picture, taken by my old friend Jason Fraser, of her coming out of the Dorchester with a copy of *The Economist* visible in her bag to really cement this more grown-up image. The next step was to get her pictured with a real politician, maybe one on the financial side of things. How about the chancellor?

Blair clearly had rather a lot going on, so I hurriedly followed him into a room with glass walls, through which I could see John Prescott and Clare Short glaring in at us furiously. I half wondered if the ongoing Alastair Campbell-shaped hole in his team might mean there was a job offer on its way.

I couldn't imagine what he needed to discuss with me so urgently. 'Well,' he said, wringing his hands in that unmistakable way he had, 'there's something I must ask you.' I was still nonplussed. 'It's about David Bowie.' For the next ten minutes, he proceeded to pepper me with questions, more like the editor of *Mojo* than the leader of the country: 'Where is the album being made? Is it being recorded in Switzerland or New York? Who's playing bass?' I updated him as well as I could and he became thoughtful. David had this effect on people. I once handled the PR for a Bill Clinton breakfast, where Bill delivered a typically inspirational speech about the third way in politics to a room of assembled entrepreneurs. Afterwards, I was introduced to him. We had a perfunctory chat until I mentioned that I represented David Bowie, at which point his eyes lit up and he began discussing David's saxophone-playing technique.

I first met Tony Blair when he had just been made leader of the Labour Party. He was famously a big Bowie fan, so I invited him to a gig at Wembley. We were both early, so we just sat down in one of those dull dressing rooms with nothing on the wall, opened a bottle of wine and told stories. Of course, he had been in a band called Ugly Rumours at university and wanted to know about life on the road. I noted that he stayed for the whole show, which was well over two hours. At that point, David was playing a lot of new material and it wasn't always an easy listen, but Tony was a genuine fan.

For some reason, 'Tone' also wanted to know what it was like on tour with UB40. I thought that maybe this was a bit too risqué for someone in high office, as the Birmingham reggae outfit were known for being pretty wild on the road. They had formed out of a sense of anger at being young in Thatcher's Britain. I remember once arriving at a hotel with a journalist who was going to write a piece about them, and the receptionist apologising to us that the bar was off limits because there was a fight going on. Intrigued, we went and had a look. To our amazement, we recognised members of UB40 in the middle of a scene out of a Wild West bar brawl. The behaviour went downhill from there. I censored some of the details as Tony did seem a bit serious-minded and it might have been a bit much for him. But I was incredibly impressed that Blair made the effort to say goodbye individually to all the security staff in a by now-deserted Wembley Arena and I filed away a mental note that he had that natural understanding of people that you can't be taught.

A couple of years later, I saw him again when he presented David Bowie an award at the Brits. Blair took to the stage looking more like an earnest college lecturer than a future prime minister. Many of the music executives at that time lived up to the stereotypes of the pinstripe-suited, cigar-chomping, champagne-swilling fat cat and were decidedly unimpressed, with quite a few boos clearly audible. The thought of those potential extra taxes under a Labour government clearly spooked them. In those days, the Brit Awards were held in the cavernous Earl's Court Exhibition Centre. Alastair Campbell and I were given the task of writing some words for Tony and David. We somehow squeezed into a red phone box outside and wrote a speech on the back of a fag packet. We took turns writing one line after the other: one sentence for Tony, followed by one for David, until we had something that worked for both parties.

Blair was definitely out of his comfort zone and seemed a bit nervous. This was only increased when David came on stage glammed up and wearing high heels. Bowie gave Blair a cursory thank you and launched straight into 'Hello Spaceboy'. I think this was his way of being seen to be irreverent to politics and politicians.

David was normally extremely wary of politicians and, as a general rule, he didn't like to meet them. I quickly learned that on tour with him; often local politicians would want to meet him after a show, but he was very reluctant to be used as a photo opportunity.

Once, in the very early '90s, we were in Croatia for a gig at Zagreb's Maksimir Stadium. The president wanted to welcome David to the country which, on the face of it, was all good publicity. But David had a sixth sense about it. Maybe he had picked up on the undercurrent of hostility that was soon about to explode into conflict. He made it very clear to me he didn't want to meet politicians from any sides, which was very prescient of him. The atmosphere was strange, not like any of the other shows on the tour. You could feel there was a real edge in the crowd, in the city, everywhere; that strange feeling that something was about to happen, but you couldn't put your finger on it. We didn't hang around after the concert. Not long afterwards, the region erupted in a bitter and bloody civil war.

Since the beginning of the decade, David had pretty much been based in New York and had inevitably become more switched on to American politics. Bill Clinton was in many ways an American Blair before the fact: he was of the same generation and well into music. He was a saxophone player himself and, as I'd later find out at that breakfast, a bit of a Bowie admirer too. I sometimes wondered if there were any world leaders who weren't – though I did once hear that Putin was a Beatles fan. Despite David's caution around getting involved in politics, he and Bill were destined to have a meeting with an outcome. Strangely, it came about through events in Somalia, where another dreadful civil war was ripping the country apart.

Iman, whose home country is Somalia, was shocked by the suffering and wanted to do something practical to help, even going there herself. David, while a bit nervous about the idea, was incredibly supportive. I recall one slightly surreal meeting where we went to the offices of *Newsnight* at the old BBC building in Shepherd's Bush. David was taking the whole thing very seriously and was wearing a khaki suit-type get-up. We ended up on the floor, poring over maps of East Africa while discussing the potential trip with BBC reporter Robin Denselow. Staff wandered around being very British and trying not to notice, as if having a rock superstar and supermodel on the office floor was all perfectly normal.

Iman's trip went ahead, but nearly ended prematurely when the Jeep they were travelling in was approached by armed militants right out of the airport. Security legend Jerry Judge, who I had persuaded to go with them, backed the car up quickly and saved the day. The resulting BBC film of the trip gave a genuine insight into the horrors of what was going on in the ultra-violent conflict and ended up making a real difference when David and Iman were invited to the White House to screen the film for the president. I was told that Clinton was so moved by what he saw that it was a factor in his decision to order an American intervention, some of the drama of which was later captured by the film *Black Hawk Down*. Bowie was making bigger changes than he could have ever imagined.

A few years down the line, I wondered if he might make another exception to his 'no politicians' rule for the new leader of the Labour Party. Even before our encounter at the Brits, I had known Alastair Campbell a bit through his work as a journalist and I'd since contributed to a mini report for the party on how to get the youth vote for Blair.

David listened to what I had to say about Blair. He was sceptical, asking why I thought he should even be interested. I said I was convinced that Tony Blair would run the country for the next ten years. As it turned out, it was a pretty accurate guess.

Blair was assiduously using music to court the young vote, which would find its fullest expression in the Cool Britannia reception in July 1997, a couple of months after he was elected prime minister. Creation Records founder Alan McGee was a passionate supporter and Oasis were definitely New Labour too. However, at this point, Blair needed more established music acts to come out for him too. Alistair wondered if David might say a few words of support. I knew that David just wasn't that bothered, and I took from that that I could at least express a modicum of backing on his behalf for Tony Blair.

I was a bit taken aback when a full-page spread in the *Sun* popped up with the headline 'Bowie Backs Blair'. There weren't any direct quotes, and it was very much a behind-the-scenes, 'sources say' type of piece. But the message was clear, and I think it was probably more valuable to New Labour than I realised. David was quite relaxed and dismissed it as being just another newspaper story.

In years to come, David and Tony developed a nice rapport. Occasionally, I would get letters at our office and the address on the back would be 10 Downing Street, and I would forward them on to David. They could be quite random in terms of subject matter. In one, Blair thanks David for sending him a copy of Elaine Pagels' book *The Gnostic Gospels*. Tony goes on to say that he's 'most grateful and much looking forward to reading it when time permits'.

Tony would later say of David in a tribute he wrote in *The Times* that he was 'political but – typically – in a way that was not bounded by any conventional politics and that found its own path with his huge integrity', noting that he had 'a huge impact on the thinking about sexuality and freedom of expression of sexuality'.

On Saturday, 8 September 1998, Tony invited David and Iman to Chequers for dinner. (Chequers is the sixteenth-century manor house where prime ministers traditionally entertain important guests.) The visit was meticulously planned, with David's amiable driver Bill Churchman given instructions about how long to allow for the journey and where to park the Merc. David and Iman were advised to carry ID with them, keep hand luggage to a minimum and not bring cameras or mobile phones. The following Monday, David was due to attend a private screening of *Everybody Loves Sunshine*, the gangster film he'd made with the UK jungle producer and DJ Goldie, so it would be a short trip to the country. The enigmatic and super-talented Goldie and David had clicked, so he was really looking forward to hanging out with him and wasn't going to be late – prime minister or no prime minister.

In his piece for *The Times*, Blair recalled of the dinner that 'the star was so good-looking his features could have been "ordered" by God', and that when he was a student at Oxford and he first saw him perform as Ziggy Stardust, it was 'like nothing else we had ever seen. I went to many concerts at the time. But this was the only one that made me think. I remember discussing it for weeks afterwards with friends.'

For a while, I became something of a regular at Number 10 myself. Some of the situations I have found myself in thanks to those connections still amaze me. One New Year's Eve, many years later, I went to a party in the Cotswolds. We drew up at an editor's house and the prime minister at the time opened the door for us. We got inside and nearly the whole cabinet was there. They were actually in the kitchen, so I guess they were the kitchen cabinet.

One of the most senior ministers was semi-conscious at the table in front of me, clasping the last available bottle of wine. Afterwards, I stayed at a designated country pub nearby. In the middle of the night, two Eastern European girls knocked at my door and asked if I'd like company. I declined but immediately I wondered who had arranged, maybe paid, for this treat – and, more importantly, why. Some sort of leverage, for sure. It was at moments like these that I asked myself how a scruffy kid who liked pub rock had ended up here.

Now, in 2006, I was asking Tony Blair whether he'd like to meet Shakira. He greeted her and said that his children were fans, and that he'd seen her on TV performing at the Brits a few days earlier – which was a bit unfortunate since she hadn't even been in the country. Shakira looked slightly crestfallen. Tony, sensing an awkwardness, went on to say he thought she 'represents many cultures and styles all at once and that's a great thing', before saying goodbye and walking off, the weight of the world on his shoulders. Only a few months later, he announced he would resign within a year. And less than a year after that, he was gone.

Aside from my work with Bowie and New Labour, I've had some rather unexpected brushes with the world of politics over the course of my life. In the early '90s, I was once having breakfast at the Mount Nelson Hotel in Cape Town, where I was staying with David Bowie and Iman, when I became aware of two older guys hunched over the only other occupied table in the dining room. I didn't pay them much attention and carried on eating my cornflakes until I realised they were Nelson Mandela and F.W. de Klerk. They were scrawling on a napkin what I would later realise must have been part of the plans for dismantling apartheid, which they announced two hours later on the terrace to a horde of media.

Perhaps even more startling was an encounter I had in 2008. I was in the office one evening when the phone rang.

'Alan, it's Naomi. Are you doing anything later?'

'No . . .' I said, tentatively.

'Do you want to come to Paris and meet Hugo Chávez with me tonight?' If it had been anyone other than Naomi Campbell, I'd have thought they were joking.

A few hours later, I was sitting in a Parisian hotel function room surrounded by members of the Venezuelan military. The guy next to me was a naval commander with plenty of medals on his uniform and an attaché case chained to his wrist. He was clearly discussing something important. Next thing I knew, someone had brought out some maps of Venezuela's neighbour Colombia and unfolded them on the floor. The military men were on their knees, pointing at different areas of the map while their walkie-talkies crackled away.

Suddenly, there was a tap on my shoulder. 'Do you want to come up upstairs and meet the President?'

After a very thorough search in which they even dismantled my phone, I was propelled into a room: before me was Naomi

Campbell sitting down and talking with Hugo Chávez. I knew I had about one minute to forge some kind of connection with Chávez, because that's the longest time people at that level are prepared to give you before they lose interest and you become invisible. Fortunately, I had done some research and started talking about the Venezuelan revolutionary Simón Bolívar. Chávez's eyebrows went up. Then I started talking about the irrigation systems that the president had recently instituted. Chávez got up and put his arm around me with a big smile on his face. From that point on, we just talked and talked; he was funny and charismatic. Eventually, it was time to leave. Chávez gave me a really warm goodbye but, as I walked out of the room, he said something confusing: 'Make sure that people in America get my message.'

'What?' I asked, suddenly realising his friendliness may not have been entirely down to my charm.

'You're the Editor of *GQ* in America. Please make sure your readers understand how serious I am.'

Suddenly his comment that if President Bush came and attacked his oilfields, he'd blow them all up took on extra significance.

'If President Bush does anything,' he continued, 'I'll react.'

I didn't feel at this stage I could explain who I really was.

'Give my best to the Mayor of London,' he said as I left.

I've worked on and off with Naomi for years. Underneath all the drama and fame, there is a very vulnerable and understandably defensive south London teenager. I don't think it's possible for someone like me to understand what it's like to be a Black woman who has been as high profile as she has. She is incredibly loyal and people have remarked that the dynamic of our relationship is like family.

I played a small part in defusing the ongoing tension between Naomi and Piers Morgan after her privacy action against the *Daily Mirror* was first won, then appealed. It had got incredibly personal after the initial ruling, with Piers saying it had been a good day for 'lying, drug-abusing prima donnas who want to have their cake with the media and the right to then shamelessly guzzle it with Cristal champagne'. However, knowing them both, I suspected they would actually get on. So it was that the three of us found ourselves in VIP seats to watch Arsenal play Manchester United. By the end of the match, Naomi and Piers were firm showbiz friends.

It wasn't long after the Shakira meeting in 2006 that Gordon Brown and I were of use to each other again. My client Jon Bon Jovi was well known for his involvement in politics and I was looking for an extra angle to garner media coverage around his performance at Alexandra Palace, where he and his band were being inducted into the UK Music Hall of Fame. I knew that Gordon was attending and a plan started to form in my head. Before the event, I met Jon at the Mandarin Hotel. He was in a great mood and very pleased with a piece we'd brokered in *The Times* that morning. Neil Sean from Sky was ready to talk to him and all seemed to be going according to plan with the press schedule. This seemed to be the perfect moment to explain my scheme to cook up a few additional column inches.

I then made my way up to the venue as quickly as I could to check that everything was OK on the red carpet before the band turned up. It was absolutely freezing out there and I wondered how many times I'd done this, hanging around like a stage-door Johnny, waiting for the stars to arrive. I remembered the

MOBOs a couple of years earlier in Leeds, where the bitter cold was well below freezing and all our team were huddled up in big parkas trying to usher scantily clad celebs in front of the cameras.

The red-carpet turnout for the Bon Jovi show was pretty weedy; an extra PR angle was definitely called for. A good creative publicist who can dream up an angle that works for the media is worth their weight in gold – not that they ever get paid any gold. Often, good PRs are former journalists, as I was in my own extremely modest way, having written my reviews for *Sounds* and *Record Mirror* back in the early '70s. The ability to know what makes a story is important.

Unless it's an absolute A-lister, or there's some controversy, it can be very hard to get a client in the paper, no matter how many records or concert tickets they're selling. That's why PRs are always saying, 'But we need an angle to get this away.' This is a concept that a lot of managers and artists seem to struggle with. They ask, 'Why do we need an angle? Surely our story is interesting enough.' 'And what is your story?' the publicist wearily enquires. 'Well, we've shipped out a record number of units, are up for a Grammy, and we're big in Japan.'

How many times does the publicist in the politest of terms have to explain that they'll need more than that?

Luckily, on this occasion it seemed we had just such an angle, and also an artist who was smart enough to 'get it'. Jon was a brilliant mix of intelligence and easy-going charm. I thought there had to be a story here given Jon's Democrat credentials and Brown's Labour background. Some sort of leftish transatlantic alliance, perhaps?

Gordon's people were very helpful and fortunately there

was a narrow window of opportunity between arrivals when I could go and grab Jon from the front row of the event and take him back to meet Gordon, who was in a room with his aides. The organisers were twitching and desperate to get Jon back in the hall. I just barged in and got on with it, thick skin being another PR prerequisite. Whether or not Gordon remembered me from the Shakira meeting was irrelevant. I had accessed the inner sanctum. Everybody realised this was a good story, so we just got on with it. A *Sun* reporter was present, doing 'A Week in the Life of Gordon Brown', so this would add colour and we were guaranteed some coverage. Everyone wins – the politician, the pop star and the readers.

When I first came into the music business, politicians seemed very remote to me. I couldn't really have cared less who was running the country and, I am afraid to say, I've pretty much come full circle on that. Growing up, prime ministers were people I saw on the news or read about in my parents' newspaper. I never expected to see one, let alone meet one. I remember Douglas Hume vaguely, but Harold Wilson was the first one to make an impact on me. Like Blair, he seemed to be 'one of us', whoever 'us' was. I remember watching a newsreel of him addressing a large election rally – mostly workers, judging by the cloth caps. He stopped for a minute and asked for quiet as he had an important announcement to make. A hush fell on the gathering. He then proceeded slowly and carefully and one by one to read out the football results. It was a brilliant touch and perhaps my first true exposure to political PR.

The idea of 'spin' and the New Labour government are inextricably linked now, and perhaps that's tied to that ultimate act of unacceptable spin, the 'sexed-up' dossier of claims about

Iraq's weapons capabilities. But even before Blair, I had always thought that an understanding of the relationship between politics and other parts of media and culture was utterly essential. Why would you not give yourself every tool possible to communicate who you are and what you want to achieve as a politician?

A few weeks after the meeting between Gordon Brown and Bon Jovi, in an irony not lost on me, one of the members of a band who were intimately associated with Cool Britannia decided to rough me up for reasons I have never really understood while I was sitting in a café having a meeting about a Tony Bennett record campaign. He punched me in the back and kicked me, shouting that 'I didn't have a good bone in my body' before encouraging me to 'take it outside'. I had no idea what this was about. It's faintly amusing in retrospect, although it certainly wasn't in that moment. He was like the nutter in the pub who you hope will go away and bother someone else. Then he started saying I had been talking behind the back of someone dear to him. I was shaken but didn't want to give him the satisfaction. I hate bullies, so I went outside.

I realised that I was at a distinct disadvantage and likely to get my face smashed in. Still, I had to do it. Suddenly I was eyeball to eyeball with him. He rambled on incoherently, saying he and his mates know that I work on Tottenham Court Road. He said I'm a 'nice guy' but I've 'got so much power' and I think I 'can just destroy people'. At one point, he hesitated and asked me which acts I've looked after. I replied, 'Bowie, the Stones and Prince.' He went a bit quiet but continued to rant at me. I was determined not to flinch, but I was anticipating a blow. Bit by bit he started to run out of steam and his weird monologue fizzled out. It seemed to dawn on him that I genuinely didn't know what he was talking about. He looked faintly embarrassed towards the end. Cool Britannia felt like a very distant memory.

18

Sign of the Times

'Hello Alan. It's Prince. I can't do the conference.'

'What do you mean "I can't do the conference"?' I asked, gripping the phone so hard my knuckles turned white.

'I just can't do it.'

This was very bad. The conference was to announce his Earth Tour, which was actually a slight misnomer: the 'tour' was to take place at a single venue, London's O2 arena, in the form of a twenty-one night residency tying into his *Planet Earth* album. Prince wanted to discuss it with me and Rob Hallett of AEG, the entertainment company that operated the venue.* We had plotted every detail since I had been summoned to meet Prince for dinner the previous year, in 2006. At the time, Prince's standing wasn't quite what it had been. In the '80s and '90s, he was arguably the biggest star in the world – not in terms of

---

* Rob and I had known each other as teenagers through a club in Brighton that he ran. Ian Grant had booked a rock band in there called Tonge, who he managed and I handled the publicity for. I had a lively but very warm relationship with Rob. He could be misunderstood but he was one of the great promoters and was especially brilliant at handling massive US stars.

record sales or tickets, but sheer cachet and cool. And he was a subject of enduring fascination to the press.

One of my first tasks as his publicist had been to take a posse of Fleet Street's finest on a jaunt to Rotterdam to see him play live. I'd been instructed to bring out about ten columnists, including showbiz reporters from the *Mirror* and the *Sun*'s Bizarre team. Inevitably, they were more interested in the glamour of the aftershow party which was being held at a club in town. Once the gig was over, we headed straight there but there was no sign of Prince. I was told he was sitting down with the band and playing the show back – they were going through every single song and anyone who'd dropped a note was in trouble. The problem was that it was fast approaching midnight and the journalists were getting drunker by the minute. One in the morning came and went. So did 2am and 3am.

I kept in touch with Prince's bodyguard for updates, all the while wondering how I was going to keep these journalists from getting too smashed. I had been hoping the writers would do some one-on-ones with the singer. As daylight crept into the club, I began to think I might as well stand down. But then the call came: 'He's on his way.'

Prince arrived and we chatted briefly about which journalists were with me, who they wrote for and what they had thought of the gig. Well, I say 'chatted'. Prince spoke to me entirely through his bodyguard. Prince would talk to him, he then relayed the utterance to me, and I replied back to the bodyguard – even though we were all only two feet apart – as if communicating via translator. Then, just as suddenly as he had arrived, Prince decided the vibe wasn't quite right and he left. From a press point of view, it was anticlimactic to say the least.

Prince's decision to be invisible wasn't some sort of brilliant PR strategy that he had come up with in the '70s. It was actually just him – he was painfully shy. In 1980, he told the *Los Angeles Times*: 'I think other people are more interesting than I am. An interview means I have to do all the talking.' I believe he meant it. He certainly reacted badly to gossip that he considered intrusive. On one occasion, he wanted a retraction from the *Daily Star*, which had run an erroneous story suggesting he had a romantic interest in another singer. I received an all-caps message from Prince by fax: 'THIS IS BEYOND FAKE. TELL ALAN EDWARDS TO GET A RETRACTION.' Seeing as Alan Edwards was me, I did.

Although in many ways he was highly strung, Prince also liked mischief. When he was among those who worked for and with him, he often had a playful smile about his lips. As a PR, I enjoyed rising to the challenge and always had an opportunity to do so whenever a big envelope arrived in the post from Paisley Park. Inside there would be thirty unique 'transparencies': images framed in cardboard that could be reproduced in print publications. The subjects would be completely random: Prince in front of a yellow Rolls Royce, Prince in front of a purple house, Prince shopping. His instructions to us, usually, were to make up a harmless story to go with the photos and do what we wanted with them. As publicists, this was manna from heaven. The more exaggerated and fantastic the story, the more he liked it.

He was the opposite of most clients. You would never hear him complain 'they got the colour of my shoes wrong' or 'they didn't mention the album'. He understood how to keep his image in perpetual motion. Despite the obvious headaches, he was a publicist's dream client – if you could be as flexible as he was.

As a result, by the 2000s he was so in command of his career that he was able to follow any and all of his artistic tendencies. There was a lot of material coming out and the public had lost their handle on him. So, when he pitched the O2 idea, he initially faced resistance – perhaps he could fill it for seven nights, but twenty-one? That would be a record and to the business executives it seemed a stretch. What Prince had confidence in, though, was the power of his performance. He knew he was still seen as one of the greatest live acts of his generation and he wanted to go all-in on these concerts.

The Prince brief to me was straightforward: what he wanted was a big, old-fashioned PR job, so I knew I had to bring my A-game. As he spoke at that initial dinner, in between picking at a tiny dish of what looked a bit like dog food, hardly eating anything, as ever, the conversation was thrillingly wide-ranging. He spoke not just about the O2 plans, but also his frustrations with the record industry system – drawn-out release cycles, restrictive contracts, highly scheduled distribution – and how he wanted to break free of it. That was a perennial theme for Prince and he believed the digital age would allow us to remake the whole thing.

After dinner, he decided that he wanted to go clubbing at Boujis in South Kensington. It was 1am already, but naturally Prince wanted to change outfits again before we set off. On arrival at Boujis, we were taken to the VIP room. But this being Prince, it wasn't a normal nightclub experience. Prince sat drinking Diet Coke, no alcohol, and proceeded to hold forth on anything and everything you could think of – Egyptology, the future of civilisation, the internet ... I decided I'd better start taking some notes because I did work for him, after all, and I wanted to look like I was taking all of this in. I started scribbling stuff down, but it was pitch black. I couldn't really see what I was writing.

'Alan, you write just like me!' remarked Prince.

'Oh, what do you mean?'

'Well, you write in hieroglyphics too.'

We had booked a venue for a lunchtime press conference to announce the O2 shows. The chosen spot was the then trendy Hospital Club in Covent Garden. We had invited 300 people: journalists and TV crews from right around Europe. So to cancel this huge event now would not only be bad for Prince but, selfishly, it would be terrible for my company. I was really concerned, so over the phone I tried to reassure him and chisel out the reason he didn't want to turn up. But he just wouldn't explain what the issue was. He clearly wasn't unwell, so what on earth could it be? And then he came out with it.

'I can't do it because it's a hospital.'

As he was a Jehovah's Witness, he explained, that type of building was off limits. I breathed a sigh of relief. I explained it was just *called* the Hospital Club; it was really an arts complex and hotel. Eventually he came round, but he had a proviso: I had to read out a statement to the assembled throng stating that they weren't *actually* in a hospital. At that point, I would have agreed to anything just to keep the show on the road, so I swallowed my pride and followed his command to the letter. I made the announcement – I didn't play it for laughs – and I could see the crowd looking at me, pityingly, wondering if I had been working too hard.

Thankfully, my embarrassment was brought to an end by a tap on the shoulder. I looked around and it was Prince. He took the mic and did a wonderful press conference. In the end, Prince's O2 gamble was completely vindicated: every single one of those twenty-one nights sold out.

There were strict guidelines for the publicity team before his eagerly awaited O2 shows. He didn't want photographers or TV crews at the shows. He also asked for a fuller meeting with me to discuss how best to utilise his rehearsals for publicity purposes. This didn't transpire, but I did get a cryptic message saying, 'Tell Alan Edwards to be Alan Freed' – Alan Freed being the American radio DJ who would shake the records he'd been sent to check for a cash bribe that would determine whether or not the song was 'a hit'. Presumably Prince was indicating that he'd like great publicity and by any means necessary. He needn't have worried. I would argue that his run of shows at the O2 were the greatest concerts ever staged in London. The band had to know about a hundred and fifty songs and set lists would change spontaneously. I was privileged enough to sit in on some rehearsals and soundchecks. Prince would flick from one song to another and you'd never know which part of the catalogue he was in. He remembered every band member's part inside out and they had to play it perfectly. One day, the drummer messed up, so Prince just pushed them off the kit and showed them how to do it. He was a veritable Mozart.

Before the first show, the nervous energy was infectious backstage. I ran into some people talking about a Prince total resort/entertainment centre that they were planning to build in Las Vegas – and who were mad keen for Bowie to do it too. Further down the corridor promoter Rob Hallett had his suit and tie on. Somebody ribbed me for not having a tie and reminded me that Prince liked his team suited and booted – jeans were not an option. Everybody was a bit on edge. It was only an hour or two to showtime.

Despite being incredibly shy, Prince still wanted to know everything that was going on. Each night the executives were lined up and Prince inspected them. Uniquely, he did this through a peephole in a purpose-built flight case. When it was time for him to take the stage – which was shaped like his signature 'Love Symbol' and plonked in the middle of the arena – roadies wheeled the flight case through the unsuspecting crowd, followed by a parade of awkward-looking music execs instructed to march behind him. Then he was under the stage and ready to pop up out of nowhere. It must rate as the most bizarre stage entry of all time.

Prince was like a fighter before his set, pent up and ready to go. He opened the show with a blistering 'Purple Rain'. The crowd were in the palm of his hand already and the atmosphere was electric. His band, including various horn players and slinky female drummers, kept a tight beat and were brilliantly marshalled. That first night, he told the audience, 'I've got more hits than Madonna's got babies!' Prince was, without doubt, the most accomplished live performer in the world at that time. The reviews were sensational. The man from the *Standard* said he wanted to attend the next twenty shows as well.

Although the audience reaction at the end of the concert was incredible, Prince still wasn't spent. He was addicted to performing and it was clear that, like so many great artists, he lived for it, craving the oneness with the crowd. Maybe onstage was the only time he was truly fulfilled and completely relaxed.

The O2's house lights were on and many of the audience had left when Prince rushed back on stage just with his guitar, launching into a random collection of tracks including 'Raspberry Beret' and a cover of Funkadelic's 'One Nation Under a Groove'. The band were running through the audience clutching their instruments, trying to catch up. He'd already started by the time they reached the stage. The seven songs he performed beyond the encore were like a concert in themselves. The crowd went crazy.

Then Prince left the stage, dramatically disappearing through the floor – there was a secret trapdoor and lift. While the audience were gathering their wits, he was wheeled right through the unsuspecting fans. Nobody realised it was him because he was in the flight case again, which looked like any other piece of equipment. The box had a seat and a fan in it. I was told that on the US tour there was a misunderstanding and the flight case got left in in a corridor next to a pile of other cases ready to be transported to another city a thousand miles away. Unfortunately, Prince was still in it. Luckily, they found him before the cases went in the van.

Backstage after the show was incredibly quiet; it made Barbra Streisand look positively raucous. We nipped over to the smaller Indigo venue where Prince was doing his aftershow bash. The vibe wasn't quite right, though, and he was unhappy that the audience was older and the ethnic mix wasn't right.

I joined the media in the upstairs bar. There was plenty of alcohol and camaraderie of sorts, despite nagging calls from editors demanding the writers get an 'exclusive line'. My team were busy entertaining them and keeping everyone happy until Prince got back on stage for another whole performance.

One of his team mentioned that Prince was coming upstairs

to meet the media, but that never happened. I went down to the dressing room and it was empty, save for a lone promoter who started lurching around, ranting about record companies. He explained that he was going to start a label to distribute Prince's music because Prince was very unhappy that his music wasn't being played on the radio. We couldn't get our heads around why radio programmers were so rigid, refusing to play his songs just because they weren't available at retail. Nobody cared about the charts anymore, but it seemed that radio had long ceased to be about the music and was driven by what advertisers want.

Over the next few weeks, as he played his twenty-one dates, each brilliant show blurred into one brilliant summer of Prince. I served champagne to P Diddy. I kept Kéllé from Eternal and Michelle Gayle company while they waited for a photo shoot with Prince. I met Faye Dunaway and noticed she was wearing a kind of clingfilm glove. I looked after Naomi Campbell and Amy Winehouse, who was looking worse for wear – so much so that Prince commented on it.

I became used to Prince's mastery on stage and eccentricity off it. Each night, the same questions would be posed among his entourage: 'How is he tonight?' 'Will there be an afterparty?' Some nights there were, at the Indigo Club again, and they were thrilling. But often he decided there would be no party.

One night, I was rushing backstage to the dressing rooms when I almost bumped into a man in a black bandana in the corridor before realising it was Prince himself. We nodded to each other silently. On the nights he didn't show at Indigo, we stayed up until the early hours of the morning drinking cups of tea, just in case he decided he did want to go after all. Another night, I was nearly home when I got a call that he would now be doing the show, so I turned back around. I was nearly at the venue when I got another call saying he had made it all the way to the side of the stage, but decided once more that the vibe wasn't right. There was one evening during his stay in London when he had hired out a massive place with bowling lanes, pool tables and a games arcade. After several hours, I was about to turn to the dark-haired man standing behind me and ask him if he thought Prince was going to attend when I realised, like an apparition again, that he had been Prince all along.

Later that night, I ventured into his roped-off corner and we talked properly for the first time since he'd arrived in town for the concerts. He wanted to know what the secret to getting played on UK radio was. I threw my hands up and told him about how Robert Smith of the Cure, frustrated at the lack of airplay for quality music, had started his own radio station, XFM, in our old office in Charlotte Street. We talked about the MOBOs and he was appalled by reports of the violence associated with the show, saying that he thought record labels had made a big mistake by not banning rap music with all its negative messages. I mentioned that I'd met Warner boss Mo Ostin. Prince was off on one about thieves and crooks in the record industry, and how they suck the artists dry. Nowadays, he said, labels offer all kinds of 50/50 joint-venture deals, but it wasn't like that when he started out. He said he wanted us to work on getting a label owned and run by musicians for musicians off the ground. He noted that film stars such as Charlie Chaplin and Mary Pickford set up United Artists on exactly the same premise, even though ultimately they had to sell it to a major studio.

While Prince might have been exasperated at his lack of radio airplay, we managed a media coup when, at his instruction to 'get some music from the show out there', I called up Kay Burley and arranged to have two songs from the concerts go out live on Sky News at 8.30pm. I genuinely believe those shows will never be forgotten. They demonstrated a musical genius at the height of his powers.

Only a few months later, I was back at the O2 for another iconic concert when we were hired to handle the publicity for what was to be Led Zeppelin's last-ever gig. Chris Goodman handled it all and arranged for the band to do their first photo shoot together in decades. We had been a bit nervous, especially after a few 'concerned' calls from Jimmy Page's manager, Peter Mensch, whose reputation in rock management was almost as legendary as the band. When Jimmy actually came into the office to talk to *Mojo* magazine, he couldn't have been more easy-going. I told him about the ticket I'd kept from seeing the band in 1974 and he joked about promoter Harvey Goldsmith not sticking with the original price of £2.50 this time around.

The shoot was at a studio in Notting Hill that had originally been a showroom for Sunbeam cars and it had retained all the wonderful art deco features. Jimmy was the first to arrive, a distinguished-looking figure, tall and stylish, with silver hair and interesting features. Shortly after, John Paul Jones arrived. He had a quiet and peaceful persona and even brought his own herbal tea.

The first thing I noticed when Robert Plant arrived was the mass of hair – he still had incredible curls. He was tall like Jimmy, although more muscular. Robert put on an obscure CD he had picked up from a radio station in the US called KSAN and throughout the day we listened to original recordings of Bo Diddley, the Sonics and the Byrds. As we were setting up for the shoot, Robert showed us a website selling recordings and T-shirts from Bill Graham's famous Fillmore venues. Someone had bought the rights from Graham's estate and was flogging the stuff, with no royalties going to the artists. Robert was clearly irritated by that.

The demand for the Led Zeppelin tickets was monstrous. The day before, I had sent Harvey a note about Brian Lane, who was a friend of Ahmet Ertegun, the co-founder of Atlantic Records. Harvey responded that he had added Brian's name to the guest list, a list that now included 2,648 'close personal friends'.

Sorrell, the first photographer, a very nice Icelandic gentleman, started the session and the band began the serious business of standing around looking at the camera. They seemed to be genuinely getting on.

There was a brief break for lunch and then fashion photographer Perou started the afternoon shoot. Harvey turned up with his team to meet the band and discuss production issues, so we wound up the photo session. The day finished with Jimmy posing for solo pictures with his guitar – he joked about not being able to enjoy being photographed when you're in your sixties.

Jimmy was back in our offices on Tottenham Court Road the next day and I was reminded that Led Zeppelin was his band. We were looking at the pictures from the shoot and he obviously wasn't overly impressed that Robert hadn't got to bed until 3am the previous night – which, he felt, had left him looking a bit rough in front of the camera.

On Sunday of that week, I dragged my tired bones down

to the O2 for the Led Zeppelin rehearsal. Inside the cavernous venue, there was a palpable energy, excitement and tension. The number of music industry power brokers standing around confirmed that this wasn't just any old concert. People rushed around making last-minute arrangements while we inspected the press facilities. Harvey was a bit upset because he had been chucked out of the Led Zeppelin dressing-room area.

But then Jimmy plugged his guitar in and Robert started to sing. It was obvious straight away that there wasn't going to be any communication breakdown and this reunion was going to work, big time. We started to dust down the superlatives for the press release. It would require our best efforts to come up with awesome enough descriptions to capture the ever so loud – but excellent – blues-rock that Zep were blasting out the way nobody else can.

Some people described the concert itself it as the 'gig of the century'. It felt like Woodstock in north Greenwich. Every manager, agent, promoter and photographer of note in the rock business was there. Coming in on the Jubilee line, many of the accents were American. Mick Jagger was hiding up in Harvey's box and loving it, as was Macca, who was wandering around backstage. At the red carpet VIP entrance, the guests arrived thick and fast. Kate Moss turned up and Julian from our office was practically falling over himself to greet her. Naomi rocked up shortly after, looking both regal and eccentric in equal measure. Dave Grohl of the Foo Fighters and Bob Geldof were there too. The guest list was unprecedented.

The show opened with the rasping blues voice of former Free and Bad Company vocalist, Paul Rogers, which sounded great and just right for the night. Bill Wyman's Rhythm Kings were a bit on the dull side, but they gave people the chance to head off to the O2's bars. And then the moment most rock fans never expected to see: ladies and gentlemen, please welcome Led Zeppelin. The applause was thunderous. It was a simple stage set with one enormous screen. In a way, that just accentuated their greatness. Less is more – and Led Zeppelin don't need props. The volume was high and the band were giving it a hundred per cent. Page was, as always, masterful and Plant was majestic, his vocals soaring to the heavens. Jason Bonham, son of John, was as strong as an ox on drums, and John Paul Jones was the unsung hero, his virtuosic bass work popping up everywhere. The less structured bits of songs, such as when Page uses a violin during 'Dazed and Confused', were incredible. When I saw them at Earls Court in 1974, the acoustics weren't the best and the drum solo seemed too long. This time it was as tight as anything. It dawned on me that, unlike most reunions, they were even better the second time around.

Richard Wallace, editor of the *Mirror*, described the show as being 'an extraordinary display of art and the possibilities of true rock and roll'. After all the running around during the build-up, my back hurt, my feet were tired and I needed to go to the loo, yet I remained fixed to the spot. It was mesmerising. Rock history in the making.

Robert left within minutes of the show ending. This didn't bode well for the much-mooted world tour. However big the cheque – and rumours suggest it was in the hundreds of millions – this was it. The coverage of the show the next day was spectacular, with covers and centre pages everywhere.

What was clear was that, if it had ever existed at all, the early-2000s changing of the guard had changed again. People wanted icons and legends. They wanted authenticity and musical craft. Over the coming years, which saw the acceleration of digital music streaming and the new economics that brought, it became obvious that the public were never going to buy physical albums in the way they had previously. But the hunger for the live experience, to see their favourite artists play their music, was greater than ever before. It turned out that celebrity was no substitute for talent.

Part 3

19

Off the Wall

'Evening Alan. I'm just looking to get a response on the Michael Jackson heart attack story.' It was Gordon from the *Sun*.

What I wanted to say was, 'What Michael Jackson heart attack story, Gordon?' Instead, I said, 'Uh huh' and switched the TV on to Sky News, where a bulletin flashed up from an online tabloid called TMZ. Apparently, Jackson had been taken ill at his home in Los Angeles. I explained that the details were unclear, but I'd let him know as soon as I could. Then I picked up the phone. I had been involved in many crisis stories over the years. I knew the pattern: it starts as a single phone call about a rumour and then you're quickly thrown headfirst into a surreal, intense world where time is suspended and the only thing that matters is the story. The phone started ringing off the hook. I counted 118 texts in less than an hour. I got dressed and headed for the office. My trusted colleagues Celena Aponte and Julian Stockton joined me. We knew that it was going to be a long night.

As ever, when a story broke, I would try to take a quiet minute, even if that meant just going and hiding in the toilet so I could scribble down a strategy. You had to have a plan. However quickly it's constructed, a strategy was vital. A journalist would call and put a story to you. In your mind, you'd be quickly weighing up the possibilities, trying to see how much truth was in it, how it might look, what the ramifications would be. Sometimes you would feign surprise, but you had to know what you were doing.

If you gave too much of a 'steer' to one publication, even if the paper in question deserved it, the rest of the media could become very prickly. If it were a big story, it would be breaking internationally and your phone would be ringing non-stop, sometimes through the night.

After endless phone calls, print-outs, Post-it notes, news developments and cups of tea, we heard that attempts to resuscitate Michael had failed. Then we got the confirmation. It came in the form of an email stating simply that Michael had passed away. It was almost too hard to take in. The calls and messages mounted from celebrities asking if it was true and wanting to pass on their condolences to the family. We swiftly realised it was a 'where were you when you heard' moment.

I had first met Michael three years before, when I got a call from his PR, Jonathan Morrish, asking if I wanted to have dinner with Michael and him at Nobu at 9.30pm. That was in about half an hour and I'd already been to dinner at J Sheekey that evening, but I changed my arrangements on the spot. I was in a black cab and on my way before the call had ended.

When I arrived, it was an insane scene. Hundreds of people were gathered outside. Fans were blocking the entrance and police were trying to keep order. There seemed to be absolutely no way to get into the restaurant. But I didn't need to worry – Jonathan came downstairs and escorted me in. A few minutes later, I was sitting in front of the King of Pop.

Michael seemed relaxed and friendly, and he was looking forward to the World Music Awards, where he was due to pick up the prestigious Diamond Award for selling more than 100 million albums. He was taller than I expected and his voice was deeper than I had imagined. He was especially excited that Topshop on Oxford Street was being opened late for him so he could go shopping after dinner, but there was nothing childlike about him. He had a firm handshake and he looked me directly in the eyes as we spoke. He was a smart guy and seemed in control.

The organisers of the show had asked us to do the publicity for the whole event. The previous year, he had been acquitted of all criminal charges in the Gavin Arvizo trial. Like everyone else, I'd been following the trial and I knew the rumours. But if more than thirty years in the business had taught me anything, it was that whispers were often wrong. At that time, I was told by people I trusted that, while he was undeniably odd, he was not guilty of those accusations. I couldn't imagine how strange his life had been. I fundamentally didn't believe in trying people in the court of public opinion (perhaps because I'd worked in it for so long). Did I factor in my desire to work with a musical legend? Of course, I did.

Michael and Jonathan saw this Diamond Award show as a step back into public life. I thought that if he turned in a solid performance at Earl's Court, where the awards were to be held, it could be a good way of reminding people of his music, rather than other aspects of his life.

The gig itself, on 15 November 2006, was a strange affair. I arrived by tube at Earl's Court where I found hundreds of Michael fans running everywhere and screaming. When I got to the venue, he was already locked away in his dressing room.

Suddenly, I had a problem on my hands. Michael had told MTV that he wouldn't be performing at the awards. The rest of the media were then desperate to know whether he would or wouldn't. Their deadlines were approaching, but the story kept changing. I was rushing around trying to keep the writers happy because the first editions would go to print around 9.30 or 10pm and I didn't want them to run with headlines about Michael pulling out.

Having been given assurances, I told everyone that Michael would be on stage by 9pm. But then it slipped to 9.30pm, then 10pm. When it reached 10.30pm, I was beginning to wonder if he really was going to do a runner. That could have been a complete disaster for his career because in the future he may have struggled to find promoters willing to book him, insurers willing to insure his shows and audiences willing to spend money on tickets. The clock seemed to be going very slowly. We went back to the dressing room once more where a limousine was waiting to drive Michael the hundred yards from his Portacabin to the stage. The message was still 'not to worry'.

At 10.45pm, the media were beginning to drift away. Five minutes later, however, a children's choir took to the stage and, finally, at about five to eleven, Jacko emerged from nowhere. The weird thing was that he looked perfectly fine, like nothing was wrong. There was an 11pm curfew so he managed maybe four minutes of 'We Are the World' before his voice trailed off, as did the performance.

According to reports, Michael thought that the show was a tribute and was unaware that he would be asked to perform. He apparently raged afterwards saying, 'Why would they do this to me?' I never found out the truth. Michael disappeared into thin air once he went offstage and, as I wasn't close to him personally, I never had a debrief. Inevitably, the press had a field day. The *Mirror* ran a picture of Michael with fans, proclaiming, 'He's bad!'

Nearly three years later, I was asked to work on his planned concert residency at London's O2 Arena. Despite having been embarrassed and exasperated by the World Music Awards experience, I was keen to be involved. AEG Live were organising it and they are unbelievably professional promoters who never leave a single thing to chance. Michael would have a world-class team around him and the O2 was the best venue on the planet. Also, I was a huge Michael Jackson fan – I'd loved his music since the Jackson 5 days and considered him the biggest star of our times. I wanted him to be great and it was his final shot at a comeback. As the name of the tour put it: 'This Is It'.

Much of the week ahead of the announcement was spent walking around the O2, making preparations for Michael's visit. Every detail – from how Michael would arrive (perhaps helicopter or boat, depending on the time of day, or car if the weather was bad) to whether or not his kids would be hidden from photographers – was meticulously planned.

There was a lot riding on the shows, not only for Michael's image, but also for AEG, which had probably put up millions of dollars for the concerts.

The night before the press announcement, I had been reading a book by the war photographer Robert Capa. Writing about the eve of D-Day, he eloquently describes his nervousness, faraway thoughts and upset stomach as his date with destiny approached. Obviously, no lives were at stake in our situation, but there was plenty of money on the line. One of the main concerns was that there wouldn't be enough fans. Michael had checked into the Lanesborough on Hyde Park Corner and there wasn't exactly a multitude of them outside the hotel. If there were fewer than five thousand at the event, he may not wish to go through with it. The press conference was being held in the venue's vast foyer, so it risked looking empty if fewer people than expected turned up.

The next day, the stage was set and we were waiting for the arrival of the man himself. Backstage, I was with Rob Hallett and Paul Gongaware from AEG Live, and we were all pacing around in anticipation. Suddenly, we got word that Michael had left his hotel. He was in a car, so now it was all down to how clear the roads were. We listened to reports about traffic 'flowing normally down Lower Thames Street', but Michael's progress seemed incredibly slow. At one point, he entered the black hole that is the Blackwall Tunnel and took such a long time to come out the other end we wondered if the car had turned back. The clock was ticking and our pulses were quickening. Thankfully, no other big stories were breaking, which meant there would be plenty of space for Michael in the papers even if we were a bit late. If our luck held, we could still make the front pages.

At last Michael arrived. He headed almost straight for the stage followed by a lot of men in suits, including myself. After posing for pictures and working the angles, he connected brilliantly with the audience. The crowd went nuts. Afterwards, he appeared whizzing around in a golf buggy, playing practical jokes. I had never seen this side of him before.

The following day, Michael's picture was on about six front pages. Combined with the TV coverage, we'd hit the publicity bullseye. The ticket sales went into a frenzy. In the end, fifty shows were announced and they all sold out. Rumour had it that some tickets were going for as high as £10,000 each on the secondary market. On Thursday 25 June, I had a phone call with Paul Gongaware, who was raving about how well the rehearsals were going. I had heard the same from others; the respected American photographer Kevin Mazur, who had been given access, told me it would be one of the 'greatest shows ever'. Apparently, the dance routines were stunning and Michael's voice was as good as it ever was. I truly couldn't wait.

For those months, Michael was truly once again the King of Pop. And now the king was dead.

Since Jackson's death, further harrowing allegations have been made against him. It has spurred an ongoing debate about whether you can separate the artist from their art. The past tells us that's typically what happens. There are many musical artists who have behaved questionably – or worse – in their private lives and yet whose work is still heard and admired. We quite rightly need to always focus on the rights of victims to speak their truth. But I also think, as we continue to assess the lives and behaviour of our cultural figures by (quite rightly) ever-higher standards, this is going to become an ever-greater issue.

A world in which Jackson's music is consigned to the ash heap of history, never to be played again? I think that's impossible.

Michael's death was shocking and tragic, and acted as a reminder that the entertainment business can be an incredibly lonely place to be.

I was reminded of this almost exactly two years later, when Gordon Smart from the *Sun*'s Bizarre showbiz column and Amy Hitchcock of Sky News phoned me in quick succession to confirm that Amy Winehouse had died at her flat in Camden. I couldn't believe it initially, but it had the ring of truth to it.

Amy's life had been a rollercoaster. Her album *Back to Black* had come out in 2006 to huge critical acclaim. It was a haunting, beautiful record, which harked back to another era but sounded absolutely contemporary. It wasn't like anything else out there. What made it especially compelling was Amy herself: she clearly lived these songs, you could feel it in her voice. This wasn't a record dreamt up by an A&R person. It was authentic. I experienced the magic of that voice in person a year later. We'd been taken on as her publicists, so went to see her at Brixton Academy in November 2007. It was an icy-cold night, but inside the venue was packed and Amy was completely spell-binding. She was small in stature but dominated the room with her energy and extraordinary vocal range – it was obvious she was a bona fide star. It helped that she had a superb band that had mastered most musical styles. When they did reggae, it was like we were listening to the Wailers. When they played jazz, Billie Holiday was in the room. I left tired but buzzing.

Our brief was to try to calm down the out-of-control media coverage. Although the serious music writers saw her as one of the most credible artists going and had enormous respect for her, the news editors and paparazzi saw her as the disaster that never stopped giving. Unlike many celebrities, she was still part of her local community. Everybody knew where she lived in Camden Town, so it was open season. Sometimes the snappers would knock on her door and provoke her – or just take a picture of her looking startled, which implied she was in a state when actually she had simply been interrupted while doing the washing-up. If it was a quiet news day, the papers would just slap a suggestive headline on it and send it to press. There were therefore endless stories about Amy taking drugs, being in bad relationships and drinking too much. It was beginning to distract from the music and the publicists would be the cavalry rushing in to defend her. That was the idea anyway. Nobody was pretending that she didn't have a problem, but stories insinuating that she was doing coke on stage, for instance, were over the top and needed to be stopped.

The next night, Celena, our talented American PR, accompanied me on a second trip to Brixton to explain our strategy to Amy. We had discussed options with her always passionate and committed manager Raye Cosbert and recommended some limited legal action to make an example of one of the papers. It would send a message to the media that it was time to curb their excesses. We went to meet Amy in the green room in the Academy's cavernous upstairs. She was playing pool with the guys in the band, cigarette hanging out of her mouth, and she looked relaxed. Judging by her excellent cue work, the train-wreck headlines were far from the truth. Raye introduced us. Amy was polite, but slightly defensive – I think she saw me as a boring headmaster-type figure. I could see her eyes immediately glaze over once I went into PR-speak, and she began looking for an opportunity to make mischief. That arrived on a plate when Amy revealed that she thought Celena was my wife. Celena was understandably taken aback and made clear that, no, she was a communications professional who worked for me. 'Bet you give him a good blow job though,' Amy replied. Celena was visibly shocked and went bright red. I concluded it wasn't the moment for a big media strategy conversation.

Over the coming weeks, we discussed how we could help

Amy address her personal problems. I had past experience with clients who managed to replace one addiction with another less damaging one. In Alice Cooper's case, it was giving up freebasing in favour of taking up golf. I was pretty sure golf wouldn't do it for Amy, but what motivational carrot could we come up with?

As if by magic, news came through that she had been nominated for six Grammys. We knew she wanted to perform at the awards, but there was no chance of getting into the US if she wasn't clean. Perhaps this would be the spur she needed to kick-start her recovery.

Soon after, I was in my Regent's Park flat preparing for an early night. I checked my phone before going to sleep and I noticed two missed calls. One was from Victoria Newton at the *Sun*, the other from Amy's manager Raye. It could only mean one thing: another big Amy story. One of the people who hung around with her had secretly filmed her taking all kinds of drugs, including – allegedly – crack. The film was up on the *Sun* website and already on the front page of the paper. All hell broke loose.

The next day Lucian Grainge, the chairman of Universal, asked Amy's doctor, her psychiatrist, her father and her manager, as well as myself and my colleague Chris Goodman, to come to his office in Kensington. He called it a 'Chapter 11 meeting'. In the finance world, Chapter 11 bankruptcy is when a struggling company creates a plan with all involved parties that will allow it to get back on track. In other words, this was our moment to sort things out once and for all.

Lucian was so concerned about Amy's well-being that he wanted to cancel her upcoming appearances at the French NRJ

Music Awards, the Grammys and the Brits. Those kinds of appearances tend to translate into plenty of sales, so this would cost Universal a lot of money, but Lucian wanted to do the right thing. The doctors, however, were concerned that if the incentive of appearing at these events was taken away, she'd lose the will to carry on. Mitch, her father, thought that whatever we decided, she'd simply ignore the advice and avoid going into a clinic. I told them that we were in the last-chance saloon as far as the press went. One more mishap and any support she might still have would disappear because the journalists who admired her talent and were rooting for her were swiftly running out of patience. We'd be in Whitney Houston land.

Eventually, it was agreed that Amy would be summoned to Lucian's office at lunchtime the next day. Mitch and Raye both agreed not to divulge to her the real reason for the meeting. But once she arrived, she would be read the riot act: unless she got herself off to rehab, everything would be cancelled, including performances and recordings. Lucian's PA prepared a letter committing her to going for treatment and being available for random drug tests. Everything was ready.

Frustratingly, the news of the meeting leaked the next morning, but by then Amy was already in Lucian's office. The conversation was long, strange and painful. At one point, Amy wandered out of the office. Word got around that she had been spotted with silver paper down by the toilets near the canteen. Eventually, however, she agreed to go to the clinic. We put out a press release and spoke long and hard with various papers. This was now a life-or-death situation, so we implored them to give her a bit of space. They understood and agreed to our request.

A line in the sand had been drawn and nobody could accuse

the label of doing nothing. Universal had done all they could. As Lucian said at the meeting, sometimes there are things that are more important than selling records.

What's more, Amy started making good progress. She went into rehab and the Grammy performance went ahead on 10 February 2008, albeit from London via satellite. It was an incredible success – the crowning moment, arguably, of her short but remarkable career. Watching it, I was reminded of why we were all there. We were witnessing one of the all-time greatest British singers in full flight. It was a true privilege.

Sadly, we quickly came back down to earth. The next few years for Amy were an inexorable cycle of decline punctuated by brief flashes of hope. One such moment came in 2010 when I saw her live at the Fred Perry store in London's Spitalfields Market, where she was promoting her fashion collaboration with the clothing brand. There were only about fifteen or twenty people in attendance and she sang beautifully – no backing band, sound systems or props. Just Amy and that voice. It made me wonder if it might work out after all. But even on days when she wasn't doing anything wrong, the stories kept coming. By that time, the tabloids were locked in a death spiral, frantically trying to outdo each other, and the celebrity media had also firmly established itself online. Amy was an international star, so the coverage was full-on. My colleague Chris dealt with most of it on a day-to-day basis and did a brilliant job in a very tough situation.

Just before her death in 2011, the papers had yet another Amy story. She had allegedly got drunk at an off-licence before beginning treatment at the Priory Hospital in south-west London. This saga had been drawn out for so long that even the most rabid media had lost a bit of interest but, as her PR, the pressure – particularly when combined with all the work I was doing for my other clients – was exhausting. I needed some headspace, so I decided to go away for a couple of days to Marseille, the port city in the South of France. I had a modest house out there and it was always a good place to find some solitude. On the morning of the day I heard about Amy's death, I had climbed the hill to the wonderful, sanctuary-like Notre-Dame de la Garde basilica, with its uniquely haunting atmosphere, looking out to the Mediterranean. The basilica was intended to act as a beacon for shipwrecked sailors lost at sea and in some ways it felt like a fitting place to be at this moment. Amy too had been lost in a storm.

As soon as the Metropolitan Police confirmed Amy's death that afternoon, I immediately switched to work mode. Chris was besieged by calls back in London and I fielded as many as I could from the South of France. There wasn't any time to grieve – it was like being in a war room and feelings wouldn't be dealt with until long after. The sorrow of her death only really hit me when I went to her funeral. It wasn't a media affair; it was intimate and moving. I felt a great deal of sadness for her parents.

It is a tragedy of the entertainment business that so many die young. In fact, so many musicians, artists and actors have passed away at twenty-seven years old that there is a grim name for it: the 27 Club. Amy had sadly become a member, joining, among others, Jimi Hendrix. Jimi was the first rock star whose death touched me. It was September 1970. I had his poster on my wall and his albums on my shelf. My sister and I sat with friends in the Viking Coffee Bar in Worthing and played 'Foxy Lady' and 'Hey Joe' on the jukebox. It didn't seem possible that such a guiding spirit – someone so young and cool – could be gone. Janis Joplin, Jim Morrison, Kurt Cobain . . . they too all joined the club.

Amy will live on in her own iconic way for ever.

Nowadays, drug addiction is treated as an illness, but it has always been entwined with the music business. Often, bands in the '60s were playing two or three gigs in an evening. That meant driving all over the country, rushing from town to town between performances. For many, pills were what kept you running. Even though the live scene was more civilised by the '70s, I'd still find myself in the back of transit vans, zipping up motorways to gigs in northern clubs and then returning home as dawn broke. Having some lines of speed helped to keep you going.

So many performers struggle when they walk offstage after a gig. The adrenaline is flowing so fast that there's no way they're going to sleep. For at least two or three hours, coming down is incredibly hard, so the temptation to have plenty to drink or to smoke a couple of joints – just to calm down and get some sleep, before getting up to go to the airport for the next gig – is almost irresistible. Some performers settle on more advisable strategies. After a Rolling Stones concert, for instance, while most of the band's memorable nights would just be getting started, bassist Bill Wyman would be in his dressing gown having a nice cup of tea and getting ready to turn in. I'd be summoned up there about 11pm to discuss the following day's interviews. He seemed such a sensible chap. Or maybe not. It later transpired that Bill had supposedly bedded hundreds of women. Maybe the early-to-bed routine had been a piece of theatre, an elaborate cover story.

With Amy's saga, everyone wanted to try to find someone to blame. Some pointed the finger at her father Mitch, but I thought that was unfair. He used to come to my office and just sit there distraught, head in hands. He didn't know what the answer was, but was desperate for her to get off the drugs. I empathised with him as a parent. This wasn't the '50s; legally there was a limit to what a father could do and that feeling of helplessness must have been terrible. So what if, in one of the lighter moments, he was able to make a jazz record? I don't see how that changes anything.

Often, record companies simply ask the manager to deal with artist issues, but Lucian Grainge was a notable exception. He really put his neck on the line to try to help Amy.

Then there's the whole issue about whether artists with drug problems should tour. You could ask that question of the Rolling Stones. When Keith Richards was busted for heroin in Toronto in 1979, the judge ordered him to play a free concert. There's a very strong argument that the discipline and routine of being on the road – having to get up at a certain time, be at the soundcheck, be in a reasonable state to perform – is a way of staying clean. If you are busy and doing what you love, you don't need the 'other stuff'. Amy's manager Raye was simply trying to do his best in an impossible situation.

What about the media? It's easy to blame them, but the editors had a job to do: delivering news to the public. The tabloids might have sold extra copies when they had the latest Amy escapade, but a lot of the newspapers dampened stories down or pulled out the worst bits after receiving calls from us. And let's be honest – some celebrities make a kind of Faustian pact with fame. It fills a void in their life. It's a way of feeling loved and it compensates for a lack of self-esteem. I'm sure that was part of the story with Amy.

There's a voyeuristic instinct in all of us, which is why we are inexorably drawn to lurid stories about celebrities. We live vicariously, having others go to the edge and risk their lives on our behalf. We get a buzz when we listen to a song by Lou Reed about scoring smack on the streets of New York, but we wouldn't want our kids doing it. Perhaps as a culture we need to take a look at ourselves.

20

Hanging on the Telephone

'Do you recognise these numbers, Mr Edwards?' the police officer asked, gesturing at the paper he put down in front of me.

There was my home number, my office number, my work and private mobile numbers, along with various PIN codes, some I recognised and some I didn't, which I was told were for getting into my various voicemails. In some ways I felt sorry for the phone hackers. On top of countless messages from various clients telling me they were running late, they would have had to listen to the fifty or so drunken screaming messages that one very high-profile DJ had left on my answerphone objecting to a tabloid interview I'd set up for him. The pages were apparently taken from private investigator Glenn Mulcaire's diary, which illustrated just how strongly he'd been targeting me. I had never met Mulcaire and the thought that he'd been tracking me like this sent a shiver up my spine.

The police then asked me about various celebrity clients who were connected to hacking allegations, about PRs I had previously employed who had been talking to now-disgraced journalists. I learned that, at one stage, I was one of the top ten most hacked people in the UK. The thing that really brought it home to me, though, was a reference to my fourteen-year-old daughter. Her name featured more than once and her number was on the list. Was Mulcaire hacking into her phone for gossip on the Spice Girls? The next day, Ruby came back from New York, where she had been staying, and was astonished to hear she'd been dragged into the phone-hacking scandal. She didn't seem to care, saying she was surprised that anyone wanted to hear her gossiping with her sisters, but it left me with an uneasy feeling. It was very creepy.

When the tabloid era came to an end, it wasn't with a whimper but with a bang.

At first, it was a big laugh. Everyone knew that showbiz reporters were calling people's answering machines and getting their messages. It was mostly innocuous stuff like pop stars saying, 'Meet you for lunch at the Ivy today.' Lots of the celebrities were in on it. Victoria Beckham left a phoney message about buying Canvey Island just to see what would happen, and sure enough it was in one of the papers that Sunday. As the pressure for stories increased and the practice moved to politicians and the royals, it didn't seem so harmless anymore and everyone started to refer to it as 'hacking'. I was, of course, on the side of the celebrities, trying to block these stories ever seeing the light of day.

I remember once having a conversation where I explained that the modern media beast could only be tamed by having a bargaining position and some clout. That meant having a strong hand to sit down and deliver the best for all my clients. However, there was a downside and now I was left standing in the spotlight.

As celebrity-fuelled stories took over the tabloids, PRs became more powerful than ever. I was a gatekeeper for so many big names by the late '90s – musicians, sure, but also models, sports stars and celebrity chefs – that between myself, Matthew Freud (a major PR player, especially in politics) and Max Clifford (the now-deceased publicist who specialised in lurid 'kiss and tell' stories), we had enormous influence with the tabloids. I never had a moment to get smug about it, though, as the work was unrelenting. My roles were multiplicitous. On one level, I did PR, but, depending on the client, I might also be a manager, a fixer or, quite often, a psychotherapist.

The hacking controversy had been rumbling away since 2007 when *News of the World* reporter Clive Goodman and private investigator Mulcaire were sentenced to prison for accessing the voicemails of the royal family. But it wasn't until 2011, when the Metropolitan Police launched a new investigation called Operation Weeting, that it erupted into a full-blown national scandal. Lord Justice Leveson was asked to preside over the investigation and in his courtroom, over the months that followed, Fleet Street's dirty laundry was very publicly aired. As the drama unfolded, so did the effects of Operation Weeting. There were arrests, charges and, later, convictions. For an industry already buffeted by the economics of a rapidly developing digital economy, it was the death knell for a particular era of celebrity-fuelled, big-bucks, high-visibility tabloid journalism.

I seemed to be caught in the middle of it and was at risk of becoming collateral damage. By 2011, while I was still not really part of the media establishment, journalists I had known when they were cub reporters were now in powerful positions at the top of the industry. And at the same time, I represented many of the celebrities who the tabloids were hacking. Our office was like a telephone exchange. It felt like there was nothing happening in showbiz that wasn't going through our building.

I was told that the police were keen to talk to me. They didn't suspect me of any wrongdoing – I had never been involved in phone hacking. Why would I have been? As I say, my brief was to protect the client and prevent their private information ending up in the public domain. However, it was clearly blowing their minds that I was somehow the conduit between Fleet Street and the world of celebrity. They kept asking me if I was getting paid specifically for this and I had to explain that, no, this was just one part of the job.

I think the Met expected me to be more 'shocked' by what had been going on. In retrospect, my attitude possibly came across as a bit glib, but I had grown up in the school of media hard knocks. The journalists I met back then were often tough, hard-bitten, heavy-drinking types who wouldn't care how they got the story, even if it meant bribing someone. Hotels, too, were a danger zone. If you were talking on the landline, the receptionist may have been slipped some cash to listen in while you called the office with 'juicy' bits about whichever pop star you were looking after and who they were sleeping with.

As the competition between the tabloids heated up, and the going rate for celebrity stories and photos started to climb, I found myself on the receiving end of the media's more unsavoury tactics. Print sales were declining, social media was on the horizon and it started to become a fight to the death for the remaining market. Showbiz was a big driver of sales and therefore far more important commercially than I initially realised. Things quickly got out of hand. But it had been going on for years.

One day in the mid-2000s, I got a call out of the blue from a freelancer for a Sunday paper.

'Oi, Al. Meet me in the pub round the corner. I've got something you need to see.'

I duly went along to the Marlborough Arms near Goodge Street and discovered he had photocopies of pages from my diary.

'I was in a pub in east London and they were being hawked around and sold, so I thought I'd snap them up for you as you're a mate. Have them back.'

I was mystified because my diary was always kept locked up in my desk – and to access my office, you had to go through three security doors. I could only conclude that perhaps an office cleaner had made the photocopies and sold them on. The contents of those diary pages were actually quite innocuous. I suspected that the journalist had bought them off the black market hoping to find a story and when they turned out to be anodyne, he thought he'd return them to try to curry favour with me.

'And any tips you can give me for the column at the weekend would be great,' he said. 'No, no, I don't want any money . . .'

Some of the showbiz writers were now doing coke as well as boozing and it was getting edgier all the time. Murky characters on the periphery and small-time crooks were drawn to the money as there was a lot of cash floating around. I was making constant calculations about who to try to distance myself from. Debts of all sorts were being run up, and one way or another, they were going to have to be repaid.

The fact that I had represented the Spice Girls when I did

made me especially vulnerable because they had dominated the front covers, especially at the weekend. Nobody cared about politicians – unless they were caught shagging someone they *really* shouldn't have been.

Perhaps the most eerie incident happened while returning to London from a family holiday in Sardinia. I was at Olbia Airport, waiting for the plane, having a phone conversation with my lawyer Alexis about the Beckhams. I was always fairly careful about eavesdroppers, but there didn't seem to be anybody around. When I landed in London, I had an urgent message from a major media outlet saying that they had a transcription of a call I had made a couple of hours ago and were planning to run a story. My blood ran cold. I had visions of all kinds of scandalous stuff being credited to me.

I asked how they got the recording. They replied that an off-duty pilot had been walking past and thought my conversation was interesting. This extraordinarily quick-thinking would-be tabloid journalist of a pilot decided to tape the call, before flying back to London and giving it to a newspaper. Apparently, he had been so quick off the mark, he had managed to do all this by the time I had landed. It more than stretched the bounds of credulity and I didn't believe a word of it. Had someone been following me and taping me throughout that whole holiday? Certainly, given my client list, I was a known target. The thought made me feel sick; it was such a violation of my family time. I was so shocked I didn't even consider what the legal position was. My main concern was stopping the story. As ever, PRs end up putting clients before themselves.

This sinister surveillance wasn't a one-off. One weekend, I received a call saying that the offices had been broken into. I returned to find that the front door had been forced and the entrance to the sixth floor had been accessed, despite alarms and strong doors. The door to my office had been completely taken off its hinges. This was clearly a professional job and somebody knew exactly what they were looking for. The only thing taken was a laptop. A bulging petty cash tin and other valuables were left untouched. The baddies were clearly stealing information to order. Hilariously, they had stolen the wrong computer. They had lifted a brand-new laptop with only a couple of gas bills on it. The real deal, full of stars' private details and their phone numbers, was in the desk drawer. They were so sure that they'd got what they were looking for that they didn't hang around to check properly.

I called the police and meantime – somewhat foolhardily – searched the six floors by myself. It was quite possible that the interloper was still there and as I opened the door on each floor, I jerked it back suddenly in case anyone was hiding behind it, just like they do in the movies. I was tensed up and ready for someone to jump out at me. I went through the six floors of the building one by one, but they'd long since gone. The police arrived and when they heard that only a computer had been nicked, their interest faded. They didn't think to ask why anybody would have gone to such extraordinary lengths to steal something you could buy down the road for a couple of hundred quid. The potential contents were, of course, worth a lot more than that.

Still, I didn't get freaked out and kept telling myself that you have to take the rough with the smooth. At one point, I called in a professional company to sweep the office for bugs. All day they moved around the building in white coats with contraptions that looked like Geiger counters, taking apart phones and so on. Suddenly a cry went up. Their machines were going mad at one section of the wall, having detected extraordinary levels of electrical activity. They had found a super-bug. Then they looked out of the window and spied the BT Tower, which was only a few hundred yards away. They all looked very disappointed.

Other than taking this precaution, I continued to be reasonably laissez faire about what was going on. But for celebrities, even at the lower level, it caused big problems. Those who didn't realise they had been hacked might falsely accuse close family or their manager of leaking the information. Relationships became irretrievably damaged.

Phone hacking took on a much darker side once it migrated from showbiz reporting to other areas. Politicians suddenly had all sorts of private things popping up in the media and it only got worse when it was reported that missing schoolgirl Milly Dowler's phone had been hacked. The shock was seismic and the public were outraged. The investigations were ramped up.

When I spoke to a lawyer about what was happening, I was rather worried when he told me that in this particular case 'the rulebook had been thrown out the window'. He was a bit too straight-talking for my liking and helpfully suggested that maybe I should go and work in New York for a year. I don't know if he thought he was just being to the point with me, but it was pretty unnerving. I became quite paranoid, thinking someone might be following me and keeping me under surveillance. I avoided the office for about three weeks and had clandestine work meetings with my PA Sarah at a café in Regent's Park instead. I also began using multiple phones. It was a really stressful period and I don't mind saying I was scared.

Was I overthinking and imagining stuff? Maybe, but then again this was very political by now. Something had to be done. I just didn't want that 'something' to be me.

Once the dust had settled, the world of media and fame seemed a very different place. These days, celebrities are much hotter on privacy and don't tend to go out in plain sight the way they used to – the starriest events all happen in private houses. Celebrities aren't front-page fodder in the way they were then, partially because stars are much more careful not to misbehave in public like they used to, but also (whisper it) because the stars aren't as interesting, especially now they've sobered and cleaned up. The media became regulated and chastened and, like in the old Wild West, the cowboys left town permanently. The whole circus of celebrity skirmishes and rivalries played out on the front pages of every newspaper – that era is long gone.

I remember once taking the calculated risk of telling David Bowie something of the heavy pressures I had been under from media scrutiny of our clients. I told him of phone taps and bugs and photocopies of diaries for sale . . . all true and quite sinister. I figured David would be interested in the conspiracy theory. I also knew he was much too intelligent for me to be anything other than totally honest with him.

The experience had changed me. My accidentally acquired national media role, right at the centre of showbiz and celebrity, evaporated while the scandal was unfolding – which was a blessing, really. It was around this time that I met my long-term partner Chandrima, an NHS doctor, who spends her days saving lives – an entirely different universe to mine. She was shocked at how the journalists had been behaving. She helped me gain some perspective on what had been going on, and to think through the various ethical questions it had raised.

When I had left the family home around ten years before, one of the contributing factors in my separation from Valerie had been that, owing to my job, I was never home before 1am. When I started living on my own, my out-every-night lifestyle continued for a while with endless events and boozy dinners with newspaper editors. There were girlfriends over that period, however. There was one delightful woman who was a weather presenter at the time. Once when I was in Rome and lonely, she switched the weather forecast from London to Rome, because she knew I was watching.

All of them were great in different ways, but the way I bounced between relationships is something I look back on now with a degree of shame and regret. I was fundamentally unanchored. I once saw a quote from the war photographer Don McCullin in which he described how he felt like a snake 'shedding a guilty skin'. I knew what he was talking about. Chandrima helped me find stability and stop being an eternal teenager. She gave me a solid foundation on which to work out what truly mattered to me and I reflected a great deal on the importance of family and other aspects of life. She is a passionate music fan and that also rubbed off. I remembered who I was.

After the phone hacking and the scary place I had found myself in, I felt like Bilbo Baggins returning to the Shire after a trip to Mordor. Interesting though it may have been to meet all those monsters and fire-breathing dragons, it was definitely one adventure I could have done without.

21
The Next Day

'Hello Alan. Thank you for coming,' said David. 'I'll get straight to it. I've recorded a new album and I want to release thc first single from it.'

I nodded, starting to make notes. This was big news. The world effectively thought he had retired. We were in his office in Greenwich Village, me and his business manager, Bill Zysblat. David thanked me for his Christmas presents – some Peter Ackroyd books that I thought would interest him – and complimented me on my Paul Smith suit, but I couldn't help thinking that he looked frail. I put it down to the fact that I hadn't seen him for quite a while.

'OK,' I said, scribbling. 'Let's work backwards. When do you want to release it?'

'Tuesday.'

I stopped writing and looked up at him. He wasn't smiling.

'Yes, Tuesday. It's my birthday, and I want to release a track as my birthday gift to the world.'

It was a highly unusual move. Back in the early days of reggae, you might record, press and distribute a song in a matter of days, but now there was a huge, complicated marketing machine. The record company would want to scrutinise and revise the product at length before it was considered finished, and then there were the pressing plants and lorries to be coordinated, shops and radio stations to be serviced, and press strategies to be rolled out. The whole process typically took at least nine months.

David put the record on the hi-fi. The album was first class – I couldn't help but make comments on each song as we went along, but to be honest, it was a struggle finding fresh superlatives. He asked if I could come up with a PR strategy immediately, so, as I always do in these pressurised moments, I took myself off to get some headspace. I walked to a café around the corner and sat there with a pen and napkin and stared at it for twenty minutes. I just couldn't think of anything. Then the penny dropped. The potential consumer was me. What do I listen to? Over recent months, I'd started waking earlier and listening to the *Today* programme on Radio 4. The plan started to write itself.

Given that David had been away for a decade, I realised that there was a good chance we could get the media to treat the announcement as a heavyweight news item rather than just a mere music story about another 'old rocker' making a comeback. It was an opportunity not only to create a huge impact but also to solidify David's status as a true cultural icon.

I laid out the scheme to David, and he questioned the *Today* programme idea. I pointed out that it got more listeners than Radio 1 and that every news editor, TV boss and influential person in the country, right up to the prime minister, would hear it. The fact that *Today* doesn't normally cover music stories would cast David as someone of major national significance.

He looked at me quizzically. 'Well, what about the other

stations?' I explained that Radio 2 would play him anyway, Radio 3 was never going to happen, and Radio 1 – well, David wasn't eighteen. Unlike lesser artists, he didn't need committees of executives and sycophants to make a decision. He said yes to it all and off we went.

A few days later, I was back in London with some serious work to do. David had stressed he was not going to be doing any promotional activity other than appearing in music videos – he would give no interviews and, more importantly, he had been at pains to emphasise that nobody should know anything about the record before it was released. This was a total contradiction for a PR man and a problem I certainly hadn't faced before, but David had correctly assessed that if even a whisper got out, it would diminish the surprise and impact of the story.

We also had to work out a social media strategy. In the pre-Twitter world of centralised, top-down, one-way media, traditional PRs were still the gatekeepers and that made us enormously powerful. But if an artist can communicate with their fans directly over Facebook or Instagram, why on earth would you need the likes of me? Some acts decided what they needed was a social media person rather than a PR person, and a lot of business had flown out of the door to Shoreditch. It was a depressing period and I had started to feel a bit out of sync with the times.

But after two or three years, though, a funny thing happened: people started to come back. One of the big reasons was content creation. They needed someone who knew how to craft a narrative: to listen to an album, come up with snappy messaging full of potential angles and hooks, and articulate it with one-liners that capture the imagination. Being able to do that well is its own kind of art form.

Bands had discovered that although they could send something out to a million people on their social feeds, they had no idea who it was hitting and whether those people were relevant. In a funny way, publishing matters because it chooses *not* to publish some things. More traditional channels – a music magazine, say – have a much more specific audience, and in that respect are easier to target. People were still watching TV, listening to radio and buying magazines and newspapers. In fact, radio listenership was expanding and TV audiences were just fragmenting rather than diminishing. In the end, social media didn't overtake everything else, but was integrated into it. It is now simply one of the many tools in our arsenal.

Nonetheless, we knew that social media would be a vital supporting element of the Bowie campaign. We therefore carefully drew up a list of influential people, including Jonathan Ross and Caitlin Moran. They were all sent an email the night before the launch, simply telling them to wake up at 5am and check their emails. The hope was that they wouldthen tweet the news of David's return to the fray – which they did.

Outside's special projects director Julian Stockton and I also held conversations with senior contacts in broadcast. We had to convince them we had major news warranting top billing but thanks to David's instructions, we couldn't actually say what the news was. That put us in an unprecedentedly bizarre position. When I phoned Sky News presenter Kay Burley, her reply was to the point: 'Stop messing around, love, I'm busy.' I responded that the one thing I could say was that the birthday of the person concerned is 8 January, and it wasn't Elvis. She put the phone down irritably – and then called back in sixty seconds. She had googled it, figured out it was David Bowie and, given that he had been away for so long, knew it was going to be significant. She said I could have the top slot. It was only an hour before they went on air the next day that Sky were given a detailed statement to read. The headline: 'David Bowie is back'. By 7.15am, shortly before the *Today* programme was due to play an entire single for the first time in its history, there was already a critical mass of people talking about 'the return of the Thin White Duke'.

Getting covered on the *Today* programme was essential to establishing the record as something greater than the sum of its parts. We listened with bated breath and sure enough, at 7.20am, they ran the story. The presenters then played the song, 'The Next Day'. Breakfast TV was now running the story with Sky News, BBC *Breakfast* and *Daybreak* all playing the music video. Later, the story was covered in all UK national newspapers, including the *Financial Times*, and on the front page of the *Independent*. There were multi-page pieces in the *Sun* and the *Mirror*. Someone even told me that the second coming of Bowie was mentioned in the House of Commons.

David and Coco dropped off the radar for twenty-four hours. We didn't know why, or where they'd gone, but we assumed that, after semi-retirement, all this fuss was a bit overwhelming for David and he was trying to collect himself. When they resurfaced, they seemed staggered at the hype. One journalist even described it as a 'Diana moment', given how it completely dominated the news cycle in an instant. Suddenly, Bowie wasn't just a musician, he was a national treasure.

There were no promotional trips to undertake, no media junkets, no press conferences, no expensive playbacks. It was hundreds of thousands of pounds' worth of publicity for the price of some phone calls and emails. It was no exaggeration to say our campaign made the entertainment industry re-evaluate its approach to marketing. When we were entered for the prestigious *PR Week* Campaign of the Year award, we were up against British Airways, who had spent half a million on their campaign. The journalist from *PR Week* just couldn't get his head around the fact that our Bowie campaign had cost a few thousand pounds.

The Next Day was the UK's biggest-selling album of the year and this was one of the greatest PR campaigns of my career. In its simplicity and clarity, it distilled everything I'd learned since 1975.

A couple of years ago, I went to see the legendary Shep Gordon at his house in Hawaii. We said hello and he asked me how I was doing. 'Well, I've got to be honest, Shep,' I said, 'I have an admission to make.'

'What do you mean, Alan?'

'Shep, I forgot the money.'

He didn't entirely laugh.

Two years earlier, I had been inducted into the *PR Week* Hall of Fame. I was only the third person they had admitted, the other two being Matthew Freud and Lord Bell. On the night of the ceremony, I was presented with the award by the Who's Roger Daltrey, which was such a special honour, and I couldn't help but think of Keith Moon and the upturned desk all those years ago.

Some people titter at the mention of PR and bracket it with the antics of footballers' wives like Rebekah Vardy. They imply that publicists are helping superficial people sustain non-existent careers, and imagine them to be faceless lackeys leaking stories to tabloid newspapers and mysteriously losing their phones.

However, the truth is infinitely more interesting. At the top of the game, calling yourself a PR rather undersells what you do. In the loftier rungs of the industry, you hold real sway. You become a power broker, working in the shadows, unseen but influential. Of course, I was just doing what I loved – talking about music, hanging out with journalists and musicians. I was quite oblivious to the commercial possibilities, often simply choosing to work with the music I liked, such as reggae. I followed the story, not the money. Perhaps that innocence worked in my favour with musicians who didn't see me as just another suit.

It is an odd thing to realise that you've become the establishment. There's still a part of me that bristles at that. Perhaps because I'll always feel like that long-haired twenty-year-old just back from the hippy trail.

When I started out in music PR, the critics mainly wrote about opera and ballet. Sometimes a more open-minded writer like John Coldstream at the *Daily Telegraph* would be so won over by my sheer enthusiasm that he'd find space for a punk band, but that was an exception to the rule. I have been criticised for fraternising with the enemy, but I never saw the press as the other side. They were professionals, often friends, that I collaborated with for everybody's best interest. It gave me an almost unique influence and ability to make stuff happen. I watched as the celebrity bubble expanded and popped.

One of the essentials of being a PR is to have good contacts. This was a lesson I learned quickly and easily. I'd made a few friends during my time as a music writer and had a knack for keeping in touch with people. When I progressed to being a junior PR, I started filling up notebooks with the names of writers and other people I dealt with. These would be divided into sections like 'national newspapers', 'music journalists', 'record companies' and so on. Soon these books were both tatty from overuse and very full. A lot of my best contacts were scribbled on the back of concert tickets. I always remembered to bring them in with me the next morning and transcribe the details. When the Filofax was invented, I chose a black leather one. At last, I had my proverbial 'black book' and I updated it regularly. Later, it was a eureka moment when the Psion came along. I could input as many names and numbers in there as I liked. When the time came to download the contacts from this device onto the next piece of wizard technology, perhaps the much-missed BlackBerry, I'd somehow amassed 10,000 contacts. Nobody could say I didn't know who to call.

I believe my side of the music industry is now entering a golden age. Not only are all the old forms of media still alive, but we have a whole host of new internet-powered ways to send a story travelling around the world in milliseconds. With that comes licence to be much more creative. Today, new artists don't ask me to call up a load of pop magazines. Instead, they're looking for new ways to paint a picture about themselves. It harks back to the old days of punk when I would create fanzines, high-concept flyers and idea-intensive artwork. During the '80s, '90s and 2000s, music became a much more corporate machine and music PR morphed into a more rigid, checkbox endeavour: do this interview, be on this cover, rinse and repeat. But social media has helped dismantle that machine and allowed PR to regain its imaginative scope.

So much has changed – and yet it hasn't, really. I believe that a lot of being a successful PR is lifting conversations out of the perfunctory and transactional. Anyone can forward a generic press release to an email list. But to find and maintain the human in amongst everything, to somehow frame it as two people talking about something one thinks the other will find interesting, that is the art. It is a fundamental urge to see something remarkable and want to talk about it. And that is what has always powered publicity. Often this involved finding stories to tell around the edges of an event. I was always looking for some intriguing item about the gig venue; maybe someone legendary like Edith Piaf sang there, or perhaps it was said to be haunted by a ghost. There's always something. The ability of the PR to make something out of nothing is irreplaceable. Maybe this is one of the few jobs that won't be threatened by AI. Of course, another aspect of the role is making it seem as if you were never there at all. (This book's title is, in one sense, a reminder to myself.)

I've had a ringside seat as the cultural conversation has shifted on so many issues. I've watched as the different parts of the media have changed size and shape as they've responded to the country's concerns and its confidences, as well as its fears and neuroses.

Thankfully we've moved beyond the times where Jimmy Somerville of Bronski Beat was harassed by police for going into a toilet, or Boy George ridiculed for wearing a dress. When I handled the story about Stephen Gately of Boyzone coming out, it was a major story, a scandal. At the time, there was a possibility that manager Louis Walsh would be dragged into the story, but wonderfully he wasn't nervous because his mother, who lived in a little Irish village, thought that the word 'gay' meant cheerful. Nowadays, a story like that with a comparable pop star would only be a moment of celebration.

While no one could say that racism in music and the media has been solved (as some figures like to claim), it's undeniable that we're having different sorts of conversation with different baseline assumptions and that feels to me undeniably positive.

There's a danger that my life, with its endless flights, exotic locations and stream of superstars, sounds glamorous, but most of the time my biggest concern was hoping a review would be OK, or trying not to get fired so I could still pay the mortgage.

And in the interest of compression and drama, I've left out the thousands of hours spent working with bands who no one has ever heard of. But just because no one remembers One The Juggler, Soho, Gaye Bikers on Acid and Tanz Der Youth doesn't mean we didn't spend hours on them and others like them.

For a PR, most of the time it is decidedly *Upstairs, Downstairs.* My partner Chandrima was crestfallen when she first accompanied me to high-profile events and realised what a publicist's night was really like. She turned to me disappointedly one evening and said that people in publicity are treated as 'staff'. And, of course, she was right. We don't get to sit next to the star at their secret location after dinner, but we do get to see the whole picture and often know a lot more about what's really going on than they do.

As for the travel itself, it ranged from a caravan in a desert to Concorde, from buses roaring through the Midwest American night to a ski lift. I used the opportunity well and got to see the world, unlike the guys in the bar who are probably still there ordering another round, not realising that it's closing time already.

I always recoiled in horror if a client said that they had front-row seats for me to watch the show from and hastily declined, saying that I preferred to stand. I would earnestly explain that I liked to get an idea of how the show sounded in different parts of the hall and to get a feel for what the fans were saying. There was truth in this, but really I just wanted to be able to fade into the shadows or, if necessary, head right out of the door – though you had to be careful not to be spotted by an over-officious manager. It wasn't that I didn't like concerts, but my job wasn't that of a music critic. I might need to make a call, buy a journo a drink in a bar over the road or pop off to catch another show. The idea of having the best seats in the house was anathema to me. If I really wanted to enjoy a concert, I bought my own tickets and went on an off night.

I've worked out of all kinds of places, from my squat in Covent Garden to the swish Sunset Marquis in Los Angeles – and in the back of too many taxis to count. When a story breaks, the thrill of the chase takes over and I couldn't care less where I was as long as I could get a phone line. You become absorbed by the story you need to tell. It's not like you see on television with flashy PRs making heavy calls from their client's private jet – at least it never was in my world, and my world is the real world.

Right now, it feels as if everywhere I look, moments I lived through are being reassessed. Whether it's a Netflix documentary about the Beckhams, or a show about Naomi Campbell at the V&A, figures I was stood just to the side of are taking centre stage again.

As for the future, we're in it already. Holograms are already with us. The U2 shows at the Sphere in Las Vegas feel like a moment when technology has moved the goalposts. It allows music to become an immersive experience like never before. I've seen what's coming down the line and there's no way that this won't become a huge part of the entertainment landscape for a certain level of band. We can't be far away from a show at the O2 where Roger Daltrey will be sharing vocals with Elvis, backed by Prince on guitar and Keith Moon on drums, with Sinatra dropping in to sing lead on a few songs. It's at times like these I especially miss David Bowie, who would see possibilities no one else could.

Backstage, an excited-looking PR will be thinking up a new angle and the show will be thought-beamed to journalists around the world, many of them probably asleep. When it's all over, he's off to the pub for a pint and cheese roll. Or maybe he was never there and he was only a hologram himself.

One thing that has never changed is the difficulty of getting paid properly in PR. Despite the enormous profits, money's always too tight to mention at the corporates. But there are so many more important things than money.

I got to see inside the process of culture being made, in music, in fashion, in politics.

I got to work with artists whose music will be listened to in a hundred years (in whatever form we're experiencing music). There will always be those who write songs that make us think they have seen into our lives and are singing into our ears alone, those people who take those same twelve notes and make us feel love and sadness and joy. It almost certainly won't be in London or New York; perhaps it'll be Mumbai or Seoul. But someone will come up with the new thing. The world will want to know stories about them. And they will need someone to help tell them.

That human impulse to leave an indelible mark on the universe. To say: I was there.

Epilogue

I was at home in Belsize Park watching Arsenal play Leicester when the phone rang. It was an unknown number.

'Hello Alan,' said the voice on the other end. 'It's Mum. It's your mother. It's Mum here.'

For once, I *really* didn't know what to say.

'I thought I would phone,' she said, 'seeing as it's a bit of a grey, dull day.' From my point of view, there were more pressing concerns than the weather.

At sixty-one years old, it was the first time I had ever spoken to my birth mother.

The previous year, my former PA, Sarah, had said to me: 'Do you realise you have a half-sister?' I was applying for an Irish passport in the wake of the Brexit vote, as it seemed a good idea to retain the ability to move freely around the EU. To establish my Irish descent, I had hired a private investigator to untangle my family tree. In addition to discovering that, on my adoptive father's side, I was related to Daniel O'Connell, the nineteenth-century progressive Irish political leader and abolitionist, the PI had just unearthed a living relative. My half-sister's name was Paula. Here was a key to my past – and that was a door I'd long wanted to open. At least I thought I did, but it was bound to be an emotional Pandora's box one way or another.

I wrote to Paula, unsure of how she would receive this news. But she turned out to be a wonderfully warm, kind person. One Saturday morning, she called to tell me about our mother Mary. 'Are you sitting down?' she said. 'You might need a drink.'

She painted a picture of Mary as a slightly eccentric, occasionally difficult woman. She had mood swings and would cut friends off completely if she perceived them to have wronged her. In her younger days, she would lie in bed until lunchtime reading magazines. She would burn old photographs. Apparently, upon hearing from Paula that I had been in touch, all my mother had said was: 'I hope he's well.'

I wanted to find out more and Paula passed on my mother's details. She cautioned that there was no guarantee our mother would want to meet me. Later that week, I took a deep breath and wrote to her. We exchanged a few letters and I enclosed my phone number.

She had grown up in rural Ireland. Her childhood was very tough. She described where she lived as a 'house of horrors' where my religion-obsessed grandmother was always unwell and my lunatic grandfather ruled by fear. She had to get up at the crack of dawn and work in the fields or she'd get beaten. She said she was determined to get out the second she possibly could.

Mary left at seventeen, moved to Dublin and never returned home. Three years later, she went to London where the West End drew her like a magnet – when she first saw the bright lights and clothes shops of Regent Street, she thought she had died and gone to heaven. She used to regularly spend afternoons and evenings at the Astoria, the now-demolished music venue on Charing Cross Road, where she would smuggle in miniature bottles of Tia Maria and eventually got banned for snogging a boy.

I told her about my childhood and my teenage rebel phase. The conversation shifted onto class. I mentioned that one thing I used to hate was public schoolboys talking down to me. She laughed as she identified with that. I had an urge to find more common ground with her, some connective tissue to prove to myself that I wasn't merely speaking to someone who happened to share my genes but that I was, in a more spiritual sense, speaking to my mum.

Mary was a good talker, something I'd obviously inherited. Like me, she enjoyed reading, especially magazines such as *Hello* and *OK!* – some of the content for which would have been provided by yours truly, of course. She was also clearly interested in celebrities. I told her I worked with the Rolling Stones and she was fascinated to hear all about Mick Jagger. Her music taste was straight down the middle of the road, her favourite artist being the King, Elvis Presley. She was glad I'd had such a 'glamorous, interesting life', as she put it, and was 'very proud of me turning out so well'. She said she would love to have a press cutting about me and my company.

I recognised in her a certain emotional survival instinct. It made me wonder: was I cut off from my feelings in some ways? She undoubtedly was. But there were some crucial differences between her and me. She wasn't at one with the modern world and complained about it being 'overcrowded'. She moaned about how many different races there were and how it wasn't like that when she was younger. I didn't exactly get the impression that she was a multiculturalist. When I mentioned that my adopted brother Tony's father was Indian, she didn't seem to take that on board.

Strangely, Mary lived in Willesden, only four tube stops away from me. And, even stranger, we probably crossed paths over the years. Mary told me she had frequented the London scene and the clubs – she even mentioned spending time at the Marquee in Wardour Street. I almost lived there in the '70s. In the '80s, she worked in the theatres on London's Shaftesbury Avenue. I spent so much of my time in Soho that I would have almost certainly been inside some of those theatres. She said she had always thought about me on my birthday. I told her it was a shame I never knew – I would likely have been in the neighbourhood and we could have gone for a drink.

Mary asked me, in her strong Irish accent, whether I had ever been resentful about being adopted. The truth is, I often was resentful. It had certainly been difficult to read the correspondence with the Catholic Children's Adoption Society. My mother had seemed in a hurry to get rid of me and when I first read the letter asking 'how soon' it could happen, I was very upset. I used to begrudge nice, normal families spending time together at the weekends. I had grown to realise that the knowledge that I had been rejected as a baby had affected me in profound ways: I always had a permanent sense of otherness and had spent my life trying to figure out where I fitted in. But I couldn't tell her any of this. Instead, I simply told her I understood. I didn't want to risk her disappearing again and the precious thread being broken. In retrospect, I might as well not have bothered to be so sensitive with what I said.

That two-hour call was the one and only time I ever spoke to my mother.

I hadn't asked her all my questions, as I didn't want to spook her and I hoped it would be the first of many conversations. We exchanged letters, but sadly this exchange ran out of steam. I didn't have her phone number and to my dismay she never called again. I photocopied the letters just in case I mislaid them and treated them as if they were rare manuscripts. I suppose for me they were precious documents that provided traces and clues to the questions I had so often asked myself.

When Covid-19 hit, I wrote offering to help, as I didn't live far away. That only seemed to agitate her. The next thing I heard was that she'd had a fall and the doctors weren't optimistic of her chances of fully recovering. She was admitted to hospital in north-west London. She was in her eighties, her health was already poor and she seemed to have given up the will to live. She died soon after. Like so many, she wasn't allowed visitors. Paula said she had a nice view from her window and seemed quite at one with herself. At least I'd be able to pay my respects at her funeral and maybe glean some more information, I thought. A sort of hello, goodbye. But due to Covid restrictions, even that little glimpse of her life was denied me.

Maybe I'd given Mary a little peace of mind – or perhaps I was more of an irritation. I'll never know. I got some answers but not all of them. Was my father still alive? What was his ethnicity? What did he do in the air force? How did they meet? What were her reflections on her life now?

For so long, I had felt my birth parents as an absence. Something that I needed to fill. I had come to realise that my clients often functioned as a kind of surrogate family for me. There was no length I wouldn't go to for them.

But it meant that I wasn't always there for *my* family, for

Bryony and Lola, Josey and Ruby. It was quite a balancing act, keeping all that going, and living music and running a company and being a partner and dad. We were often living hand to mouth, a bit like musicians themselves. There was never a moment to sit back because there was always another disaster, or mad drama, just around the corner.

Was I selfish? Yes, ultimately, I suppose. But perhaps all my old feelings of being unmoored were also part of this. Why did I find it easier to crisis-manage a client's life than be totally present in my own?

Recently, one of my daughters rang me to say that she was feeling guilty because she liked being on her own and didn't feel comfortable being part of a crowd for too long. She had returned from a work trip and was finding it hard to get some headspace. I told her that I sometimes just had to disappear and that switching off can be the hardest thing. I think she was reassured to find out that it ran in the family, at least on my side. Paula once told me that my birth mother Mary was like that too.

Was I blinkered and obsessive? I think that's a prerequisite if you're going to achieve anything. I've consumed as much music as I possibly could: imports, independent releases, obscure classics and bands that nobody had heard of. I talked about music endlessly until some people just screamed at me to change the subject. My hobby became my job and now my job is my hobby. That endless playing of the same records was all research and would come in handy later. Like David Beckham on the training ground after the other players had left, I found that the more I practised, the better I got.

I was clearly in my own world and I suppose this may have been caused by my lack of belonging. It definitely helped me be an effective operator, if not always a fully paid-up member of the human race.

But it's something I've been working on and I'll keep doing so. Chandrima has helped me work out what I enjoy in life and I've loved getting to know her children Gus and Lola. My four daughters are wonderful, strong, successful women, whom I am grateful to have in my life along with my eleven grandchildren, and I want to be fully present in all their lives. When I think about the future, I want to be able to look back at the key moments in their lives and say: I was there.

Acknowledgements

I'd like to say thank you to: Ian Chapman, whose unerring belief and support made this book a reality. Tony Parsons, who started the whole thing with a battered copy of *The Moon's a Balloon*. Jamie Coleman, who did such a brilliant job shaping and developing the material (thanks, Holly Harris, for setting us up). Alex Eccles, who patiently guided and supported me through the process. Jonny Geller, Viola Hayden and Ciara Finan at Curtis Brown, who believed in the project. Emma Finnigan, because it has been a privilege to have my own independent PR after all these years, and such a good one at that. Sir John Hegarty, who gave me the idea for the title. Dylan Jones, for his support and friendship. Charlie Burton, who helped get things moving!

I'd also like to thank the following people, who did much of the heavy lifting, interpreting my sometimes unintelligible voicemails, making sense of my scribbled notes and transcribing all those words: Sarah Bedford, Graziella Jones, Em Perrone, Meg Jackson, Debi Zornes and Lily Edwards.

I've been privileged to work with so many creative and supportive people over the years: John Reid, John Giddings, Dave Woolf, Roger Daltrey, Pete Townshend, Phil Daniels, Gary

Kemp, Rob Stringer, Kate Bailey, David Joseph, Jon Bon Jovi, Mica Paris, Courtney Love, Joan Armatrading, Jeff Frasco, Akiko Ozawa and Eri, Alex Homfray, Bill Zysblat, Clare Walsh, Dan Chalmers, Danny Rogers, Chris Evans, Geordie Greig, Gary Jones, Pauline Black, Joobin Bekhrad, Ken Sunshine, Max Lousada, Steve Dagger, Steve Dogbe, Sonny Marr, Rudy Reed, Kevin Conroy Scott, Bill Curbishley, Robert Rosenberg, Samantha, Jan Younghusband, Denise Nurse, Rosie Nixon and Thomas Whitaker, Stuart Galbraith, Merck Mercuriadis, Jackie Annesley, David Dinsmore, Rebekah, Amol Rajan, Anita Camarata, Janet and Randy Jackson, Eva Simpson, Justine Simons, Caroline Rush, June, Dave Shack, Rod Smallwood, Paul Cook, Brian James, Steve Diggle, Jon Savage, Nicole Reid, Sarah Jones, Guy Moot, Sonia Ben Maaouia, Dr Christian Kurtzke and Georgia, Caroline Lynch, Fergus and Nancy, Andrew Thompson, Andy Burnham, Annie Lycett, David Miliband, Naomi Campbell, Daiva, Sheila Rock, Kevin Brennan, Dave Benett, Des'ree, Richard Young, Dave Hogan, Carrie Kania at Iconic Images, Rob Hallett, Shep Gordon, Danny Markus, Wasal and Lindsay, Jonathan Shalit, Danni de Niese, Vannessa Amadi, Geoff Marsh and Vicky Broackes, Hala Jaber, Johnny and Angie Marr, Brian and Leigh Message, Gary Farrow, Richard Desmond, Michele and Rob at Arbuthnot.

I'd also like to thank the many people who have worked with me in the office over the years: Chris Goodman, whose role is ever increasing at the company and who will help guide us forward, Suzie Fellows, David Lim, Nick Caley, Jack Kaye, Jack Delaney, Gideon Benaim, Pat Savage, Celena, Mick Garbutt and Tony, Chris Poole, Sunie, Samantha Henfrey, Vicky Hayford, Caroline, Penny McDonald, Anne-Marie Burton, Ronan,

Olga, Debbie, Preeti, Gemma, Ruth, Toby, Rachel, Caitlin, Milo, Ben, Jonathan Morrish, Murray, Julian Stockton and many others.

I'd like to thank in particular two very significant people in my career: Keith Altham and Ian Grant.

Finally, I'd like to thank my extraordinary family. Where to start? Alphabetically makes sense: Alaia, Alaska, Angel, Ben, Bryony, Cassia, Chandrima (for everything), Charles, Chrissie, Cicely, Coco, Danny, Dorcas, Don, Dylan, Edouard, Fifi, Gigi, Gus, Ian, Jake, Jess, Jihan, Josey, Leila, Lola R., Lola H., Mae, Mary, Matt, Michelle, Molly, Neil, Paul, Paula, Peaches, Pippa, Rome, Ruby, Sarah, Sahara, Simon Peter, Tania, Tony, Valerie and Viveka.

Picture Credits

1) Marc Bolan: courtesy of the author; Uriah Heep: courtesy of the author, from the cover of the High and Mighty tour programme
2) Covent Garden office: courtesy of the author; Motörhead: Rick Saunders
3) Both images: Chris Gabrin
4) Mick Jagger on stairs: Associated Press/Alamy Stock Photo; Keith Richards: Denis O'Regan; Jagger and Alan: Dave Hogan
5) Alan on phone: courtesy of the author; Big Country: Terry O'Neill; Alan's hand: Brian Aris
6) Alan with David Bowie: courtesy of the author; Alan, Coco Schwab and David: Denis O'Regan
7) Both images: courtesy of the author
8) Tony Blair: Mark Allan; Usher and Spice Girls: Brian Rassic; Naomi Campbell: courtesy of the author

Index